NEW BLUEPRINTS
FOR GAINS IN STOCKS
AND GRAINS

&

ONE-WAY FORMULA
FOR TRADING IN STOCKS
AND COMMODITIES

William Dunnigan

Introduced and edited by
Donald Mack

HARRIMAN HOUSE LTD
43 Chapel Street
Petersfield
Hampshire
GU32 3DY

Tel: +44 (0) 1730 233870
Fax: +44 (0) 1730 233880
email: enquiries@harriman-house.com
web site: www.harriman-house.com

New Blueprints for Gains in Stocks and Grains
first printed in the United States of America in 1956
One-Way Formula for Trading in Stocks and Commodities
first published in the United States of America in 1957

First published in Great Britain 1997 by Pearson Professional Limited

This edition published by Harriman House Ltd
© Harriman House Ltd 2005

ISBN 1897597576

British Library Cataloguing in Publication Data
A CIP catalogue record for this book can be obtained
from the British Library.

Printed and bound
by Lightning Source

ABOUT THE AUTHOR
William Dunnigan

To our knowledge the greater part of William Dunnigan's life was dedicated to a close association with stock and commodity markets and what makes them tick technically. Technical Analysis was extremely important in his life as it was in this field of endeavor where he eventually decided lay the keys to the exploration of the interacting forces of time and price movements. His prowess as a market researcher and the many papers he produced on his findings, we know, earned him the respect of his peers, a thing he appreciated. His finest writings can be found in the last two books he wrote before passing away in 1957 – *New Blueprints for Gains in Stocks and Grains*, 1956 and *One-Way Formula for Trading in Stocks and Commodities*, 1957.

ABOUT THE SERIES EDITOR
Donald Mack

If any phrase describes the editor of the Traders' Masterclass series, which is dedicated solely to bringing back to traders and investors everywhere many of the great and rare Technical Analysis classics from the past, that phrase would be "a perpetual student of the market." Students in high school or college eventually graduate. Not so students of speculative markets. The study and the work is never finished, especially when there is an enduring interest in Technical Analysis. The editor's interest grew by leaps and bounds when in the late 1970s and the 1980s he established in Los Angeles the only bookstore in the USA that dealt exclusively in stock and commodity books; those that were in print at the time and those that were out of print. Current books were generally unchallenging and of various degrees of quality. Many out-of-print books were also of varying degrees of quality, but so many fascinating rare works from the 1920s to the 1950s, of great creativity and marvelous technical analytics and application came his way, that a life long appreciation of their quality grew.

Almost needless to say, more attention was focused on the old books than on the new, for he found those old books that made up the great classics were superior to the new in so many ways. While operating the bookstore, there was a natural inflow and outflow of many thousands of books and from those thousands of books a personal library and collection numbering a good 5500 plus individual titles was put together. A little of the knowledge contained in these great market classics rubbed off on the editor (actually more than a little) and he trusts that it will also rub off on the many market students of today and tomorrow as they also come in contact with the superb Technical Analysis classics that will come their way through this Series.

CONTENTS

ONE-WAY FORMULA FOR TRADING IN
STOCKS AND COMMODITIES

EDITOR'S INTRODUCTION

Lest the reader hasn't noticed, the book they are holding is not just one book, but two books bound together into one volume. Certainly this would not be so unusual if these were works of fiction, or some other associated field, but in the specialized stock and futures markets field of literature this is something that is not at all usual. For two books like these to be combined into one, obviously there has to be a very good reason, and in this particular case there really is a good reason. It is that these two books by William Dunnigan *New Blueprints for Gains in Stocks and Grains* and *One-Way Formula for Trading in Stocks and Commodities* – fit so well together. To understand the union of these books, we have to know of the author's late-in-life dream, something that was also his ambition to achieve in his personal specialized area of Technical Analysis. He wanted to develop a complete trading system that gave exact buy/sell signals for stocks or commodities, that was 100% mechanical in all its applications, and which didn't require the user to make any mental decisions. Besides the need for the buy/sell signals to be clean-cut, they also had to be preceded by obligatory preliminary signals and confirmations which would act as built-in safeguards.

The first book the reader will meet as they start their journey through this two-books-in-one is *New Blueprints for Gains in Stocks and Grains*, where the author beautifully explores a wide range of technical subjects which he obviously felt deserved to be examined. The second book, *The One-Way Formula for Trading in Stocks and Commodities* was the printed culmination of the author's search for his 100% mechanical system and can be seen as his outstanding masterpiece. That it should take the fair number of years it did to reach his goal is not at all surprising when the magnitude of what was really involved is realized. What he included in his first book, for our later edification, were rare insights into a number of the developmental ideas, concepts, along with the rationale that went into the One-Way Formula. We are all the better off for it as it leaves our appreciation of the merits of the Formula so much richer.

After years of development, the "One-Way Formula" was published in 1957. Mechanical systems like the One-Way Formula were not new then, just as they are not new today. However, there has always been an undeniable demand for an effective mechanical approach to buy/sell decision-making which appeals to investors. Mechanical systems have been evolved by dedicated developers, constantly striving to seek out that all-important factor of extreme (and always elusive) reliability for all situations anyone would find themselves in when they invest/trade in speculative markets. Frankly, based on the yearly performance of most of these systems, they very rarely come close to the claims made for them. In this light, for an evaluation of the One-Way Formula and its efficacy, we turn to the very wise words from he who we consider our spiritual market mentor, William D. Gann, who many times said "Don't take my word for it, prove it to yourself."

To give us a perspective into the performance figures that the One-Way Formula has proven itself capable of, we have to turn to a day back in 1984 when the writer of this Introduction was busy at his devoted-to-the-market bookstore in Los Angeles. That day the store was visited by Charles LeBeau, a regular customer and a successful commodity trader and technician who later became well known as the co-author of the book *Computer Analysis of the Futures Market*.

As we all naturally do in bookstores, he wandered around surveying the thousands of market books that lined the bookshelves and in our chit-chat afterwards the following comments were expressed (which can only be paraphrased after these several years later). Chuck said "You know Don, I was surprised to see that you have in your very rare book section a copy of Dunnigan's *One-Way-Formula*. While thumbing through it I was reminded of some of the very first computer research done on trading systems. Back in the early 1970s I had some clients who had access to multi-million dollar mainframe computers when computers were so large that each one took up an air-conditioned room. Working at night these computer technicians tested every trading method they could get their hands on. After spending months testing dozens of strategies they concluded that the 'One-Way Formula' was the only trading method that really stood out. Their research showed that this simple formula produced results that were astoundingly consistent and highly profitable. It was by far the best of anything they tested. Yet I'll bet hardly anyone has ever heard of it, or knows how good it really is, or has any appreciation of what it represents in market results. It really seems to me that the knowledge in this book is more valuable then anyone can imagine."

In 1957 technology, as we know it today, was still in its infancy. Mr Dunnigan would have relished the chance to apply such technology to his own research efforts. However, the only tool the author had and the only tool today that the user of the One-Way System needs is accurate line and bar charts that display the high, the low, and the close; using weekly charts for stocks, daily charts for commodities. A supply of stock or commodity charts is readily available weekly from the many charting services which advertise regularly in financial papers, or alternatively a comfortable number can be done by hand. For users of candlestick charts, there should (generally speaking) be no problems in using the principles associated with the One-Way Formula.

Returning to *New Blueprints for Gains in Stocks and Grains*, there are several issues worth particular attention. The author makes a strong case for independence of thought and decision-making. That in no way precludes taking in what others have to say. No one has a monopoly in market wisdom, and there are a lot of bright people worth listening to. To add to this point, the reader is bound to be struck by the number of quotes in the text which the author felt particularly reinforced the area under discussion. Even more interesting to this writer are the quotes from correspondence received from other researchers and market students. Definitely fascinating reading.

One major subject that the author draws our attention to is one that in the 1950s had the support and following of large numbers of stock market investors – the very well-known Dow Theory. We also know that Elliott received his initial inspiration for the Wave Principle from the Dow Theory and its observation of the three broad upward price movements and the two downward movements in an overall bull movement. That the Dow Theory inspired Ralph N. Elliott's creation is a tribute to its two creators, Charles Dow, co-founder of the *Wall Street Journal* and William P. Hamilton who succeeded Dow as Editor of the "Journal" in 1903.

Dow in his lifetime never referred to his thoughts on price movements in the market as the "Dow Theory," nor did he ever collect all these thoughts and put them together as a cohesive theory of relationships in the stock market. This was not accomplished until 1922 when Barron's published Hamilton's beautifully written book, *The Stock Market Barometer* wherein the world first witnessed the birth of the "Dow Theory" in its full form. It was based on the only source of material that Hamilton could turn to – Dow's editorials in the *Wall Street Journal* written between 1885 and 1902. It should not go unrealized that there was also a good amount of Hamilton's own thinking in this Theory which he attributed to Dow. For Dunnigan the thirty-plus years that passed since the introduction of the Dow Theory left him well placed in this book to fairly evaluate the Theory with that passage of time. Firstly for those readers who are unfamiliar with the tenets of the Dow Theory, and secondly for others who need their memory refreshed, he lays out the important facets of the Theory, if in brief detail. While he found many good things to have been proven over the years in the Theory, there were also weaknesses that showed up at the same time.

In the marketplace and in the field of market analysis, there always has to be room for future development. One student, Samuel Moment, saw several ways for a better Dow Theory. He formulated a strict set of rules which allowed no room for any errors of human judgment to creep in. The complete Moment rules were first published by Mr Dunnigan after being double-checked by him. The rules are worthy of studying in their entirety and the author fully obliges by laying them out in the book's text leaving it to the student to confirm for him or herself that they are both vital and valid.

Most technical analysts these days are aware of the intriguing value of the Fibonacci Summation Series. For this we can thank Ralph N. Elliott who, in the 1930s, was responsible for awakening our knowledge and interest in the FSS. This writer is a constant user and a strong believer in the Fibonacci numbers. However, as the author points out, there is another group of numbers useful in our analytical work – the "square root approach." In the text he draws our attention to the fact that many times shares, commodities and other instruments have meaningful actions and reactions around the square numbers – 4, 9, 16, 25, 36, 49, 64, 81, 100, etc. Additionally, the same thing applies to the using of their square roots when square numbers turn up in charted action. The reader should find in this novel, approach and possibly very profitable avenue, something to look at and to experiment with if they are so inclined. New ideas (or old, new ideas) are the cornerstone of Technical Analysis which should be seen by its devotees to be a limitless field of study. Here with squares and square roots we find in the Dunnigan writings an almost forgotten approach to analysis.

Of all the Technical Analysis subjects covered in this excellent work, the one that the writer found to be of the greatest interest was the material on "Thrust," a concept that was one of Dunnigan's favorites also. Now, Thrust was not original to the author, nor was it exclusive to his era. It is a technical indication used by many others before him, and we still see references to it in technical books today. Even when it comes to Thrust, the question might arise as to whether there is much that can be gained by following something that is so simplistic, relatively speaking, as it is. For the record, Thrust can be explained as being the price action that takes place any day, or any two successive days, which sees a much longer range of price between the high and low points than the average ranges that have preceded it. The description and the examples that the author gives on this subject should in no way be thought of as all there is to be said on Thrust. What he gives us here is a starting point that could lead on to a whole new area of analytical thinking.

Following "Thrust" is the most important material in the book – the signals vital to the decision-making processes in the buying/selling arena of market combat. The author demonstrates pattern formations that he refers to as "good mechanical barometers." Examples are given for each, with names that give some idea of the pattern itself: the Penetration of Bottom, the Closing Price Reversal, the Test of Top, the Reversal Buy Signal and the Repeat Buy Signal. However, all these patterns and formations were not the author's intended destination. As has been mentioned before, this was just the preamble to the elusive One-Way Formula, that 100 per cent mechanical buy/sell system.

So it was that in 1957 the author published the *One-Way Formula for Trading in Stocks and Commodities* and we are extremely fortunate it was published then. For William Dunnigan passed away just a few months after producing for the stock and commodity world the culmination of what he felt to be the apex of his market life as noted in the Preface to his book – "the One-Way Formula, better than anything I have heretofore seen."

This book, while comparatively short when pages are counted, is monumental in this writer's eyes. The total number of original copies is not known, but owing to limited print processes of the day it can only be estimated that about 1,000 copies were produced. *New Blueprints for Gains in Stocks and Grains* treats us to the creation of a search for a dream, the evolution of the One-Way Formula. You are invited to study it in its entirety, first quickly reading it just to get the flavor of the work, then a second time at a very deliberate speed to pick up the fine detail of the complete system. We trust that whether you come to use the One-Way Formula in its complete form (and we have heard that there are several advisory services that totally rely on the One-Way signals, without revealing this) or just parts of the formula, you will find the journey very worthwhile indeed.

Before turning to these two books written by William Dunnigan, there is one special event that brought this great technical master so vividly and notably back to us, that we have to mention it in this Introduction. One day the writer was working in his backrooms when he heard through the sliding door his assistant talking to someone who had just walked in. What he heard was the starting point of a remarkable market experience that only comes to a fortunate few in their lifetime. For that which he heard was the equivalent of hearing a deity descended from the heights of the Olympian gods (of the stock and futures markets, that is) come down to mix with those earthly mortals whom the gods choose for this to happen to. The words that immediately grab his attention were these. "In the 1940s I use to have the Stock Market Institute in downtown Los Angeles." To the writer this could only have been one person, and pushing the sliding door open, he saw the visitor who noticably, but unimportantly, was along in years (some 85-plus). "Are you Franklin Paul Jackson?" he inquired. And the answer was "Yes, I'm Frank Jackson."

At this point practically everbody reading this will be asking themselves who is Franklin Paul Jackson? Well, stated simply he is one of the all-time great market minds and great market writers that we have seen this century, with his writings published in the *Golden Age of Market Literature*, 1922 to 1957. A few years prior to this meeting the writer issued his personal list of titles and authors who in his opinion ranked in the Top 10 for stock market books and in the Top 10 for Commodities books. Prominent in the Commodities' list was *The Golden Harvest*, 1956 by Franklin Paul Jackson ranking it as one of the great market classics of all time. That his name is almost unknown today is not at all surprising for most all the names on both lists are *also* unknown to practically all market participants everywhere. Time is rarely kind to specialized greatness, and market books can be splendid examples of forgotten authors and forgotten titles. We who have spent years searching out the great market classics have seen our respect for these same books grow and grow as we compare them with technical writings of the present era. For quality of thought, conceptualization, and the depth of technical knowledge, the great works of the past usually come out way ahead.

High on the writer's list of rare market books that he sought were those by Franklin Paul Jackson, and except for the copies he had of his 1944 book *Selecting the Right Stock*, the others were just not to be found. In meeting Mr Jackson, who almost had to be the last of the great classical market masters still with us, this writer found it impossible to call him "Frank Jackson" (the first name shortened as we Americans generally always do). He was to come to the Bookstore many times after that first visit and he always remained to us Mr Jackson or Franklin Paul, certainly a mark of the respect we had for the man, for his market and technical knowledge, and for the flavor he brought us of the great 1930s, 40s, and 50s period in the Technical Analysis field. Authors who were just names to us before, came very much alive after meeting one who knew a number of them personally.

As the material in *New Blueprints for Gains in Stocks and Grains* is covered by the reader, they are going to notice the author's references to Franklin Paul Jackson, something that should be seen in the light that both men were the best of friends. Mr Jackson lived in Los Angeles and Mr Dunnigan in San Francisco and usually they met in LA where Mr Dunnigan stayed with Mr Jackson at his home there. Both men were strong on the Thrust action, Square Roots, the Dow Theory, Pattern Analysis and as Mr Jackson said, they used to have some long and deep discussions on all these subjects as they delved into them. We would have loved to have eavesdropped on these discussions at the time, but we had to settle for first-hand reports from Mr Jackson which was almost as good as being there ourselves. The respect that Mr Jackson had for Dunnigan, or "Old Bill" as he called him, was boundless, the man had such a fertile technical mind that their association was tremendously constructive. Almost needless to say, the writer found his many meetings with Franklin Paul equally as fascinating as we discussed so many facets of Technical Analysis. Now as the reader turns to the text that follows, this writer passes along this word to them – these two authors of the great Golden Age of Market Literature say a lot more than is initially evident from a first reading of their writings. The greater the student's attitude is to having a searching, open mind, the greater knowledge that is there to be gained from these great market minds of the past. Knowledge that is just as valid today as when it was written. For markets don't change, the actions of the people in them don't change, and great analytical thoughts, concepts and methodologies see their greatness remain also.

DONALD MACK
Series Editor

NEW BLUEPRINTS
FOR GAINS IN STOCKS
AND GRAINS

by

William Dunnigan

"Where one man fails in an experiment, another succeeds. What is unknown in one age is clarified in the next. The arts and sciences are not cast from a mould: they are shaped and polished little by little, here a dab and there a pat. What my powers cannot solve I still persist in sounding and trying out. By kneading and working over the new material, turning and warming it, I make it more supple and easier to handle for the man who will take it up after me. And he will do as much for a third."

The Autobiography of Michael de Montaigne, 1533–1592

Part I

LITTLE LESSONS

- Early confession
- Brother economist!
- Call it what you want – you do *speculate*!
- Prophets! – aren't we all?
- Tipsy tipsters
- What's new?
- Heads or tails?
- Trade alone – and like it!

EARLY CONFESSION

Let us get a cheerless matter settled once and for all.

Perhaps you are thinking: "If you are so smart, why aren't you rich? Instead of selling your trading methods, why don't you clean up in the market?"

You have us in an awkward position there, so we had just as well confess that the market deals us bad cards from time to time. We don't always hold the winning hand. Yet, notwithstanding the trials of speculation, the study of trading continues to interest us – in fact, we are so interested in it that rather than to sell peanuts for a livelihood we prefer to sell market research. This gives us the opportunity to study market phenomena as a full-time pursuit, and sometimes it provides us with the necessary funds with which to engage personally in the happy pursuit of fortune.

We might argue that our work is socially important. We did refrain from selling research in speculation during World War 2 when we (and the draft board!) felt that more pressing matters were at hand. But now that democracy is again saved and the right of the individual to speculate for his own private gain or loss is reaffirmed, we might argue that this kind of work is "vital to the public interest."

For instance, it is certain that most persons have no business trying to speculate in stocks and commodities with the methods they now use in their quest for profits. We expect to give in these pages a certain amount of proof that their methods must fail. In doing this, it is conceivable that we might direct a few persons away from common hazards and, if we do, it will make us feel "socially important."

But, all of that is rather high-sounding, so we shall simply say that we are in the business of selling research in market trading because (1) we like the business, and (2) we haven't any hurry-up-get-rich-quick schemes up our sleeves and therefore we are not ready to retire from work.

Now, if that's clear, let's not mention the disagreeable subject again!

BROTHER ECONOMIST!

When we went to school, a long time ago, our teacher said:

> "Economics is the social science which deals with the wealth-getting and wealth-using activities of men."

We were told that we should not think of "wealth" in our usual mercenary manner – visualizing ourselves in the midst of great abundance. It was impressed on us that we were "wealthy" even though our sole earthly possession might be only a loincloth or a sarong.

Economic wealth, we were told, consists of all things, large or small, just so those things possess an exchange value which can be stated in terms of prices.

It is pleasing to reflect that our Alma Mater did not trifle in passing fancies. We were taught what is apparently the undying truth, for in this benevolent era of the 1950s, the new text books still assure us that economics deals with the wealth-getting and wealth-consuming activities of men, and that wealth is still the same old things, large and small, having exchange value in terms of dollars and cents.

Therefore, brother economists and men of wealth, we welcome you to this open forum on market trading!

Yes, you are not only wealthy (at least, in the economic sense) but you are also an economist, whether you like the idea or not. Certainly, a chief engagement of your life has been the getting of "wealth" and the using of same for the satisfaction of your wants – though the getting-and-consuming activities may be interrupted occasionally by such extra-curricular activities as fighting wars, or just plain loafing.

You may not be a very learned economist, but do not despair on that score as there are no very learned economists. Just so you stay with your main job of acquiring and spending wealth, you can, if you so choose, list your occupation on the social register as an economist. If your "getting ways" are socially approved – if you "earn an honest living" – you then immediately find yourself in a competitive world where the satisfying of your wants becomes a life's work of facing economic problems and deciding on their legitimate solutions.

Because of the very nature of competition, those problems are *yours*. The other fellow may give you honest advice which he hopes will help you in your problems, but the understanding, consideration, execution or rejection of his advice rests with you alone. You are the captain of your own ship. Others may explain to you the best-known rules of navigation, but in the high seas of the business world it is up to you to steer your own boat through all kinds of economic weather.

CALL IT WHAT YOU WANT –
YOU DO *SPECULATE!*

As an economist – a wealth-getter and a wealth-spender – you are either a wild, reckless sort of a devil or a careful, conservative type of a fellow, or "something in between."

Webster's Dictionary says you are a *gambler* if you "stake anything on an uncertain event."

You are a *speculator* if you "enter into a transaction which involves unusual risks for a chance of unusually large gain or profit."

Or, you are an *investor* if you "lay out money with the view of obtaining an income or profit."

Perhaps, from those definitions you can figure out just what you are in your economic activities. That is no easy task. There are many types of risks, but it is often impossible to determine the degree of risk you are taking *before you take it.*

The financial chronicles are laden with the records of gilt-edge securities ("investments") which became worthless. On the other hand, wild-cat stocks ("gambles") have sometimes rewarded their owners with fortunes.

In the 1929 stock market debacle, the ultra-conservative "investor," guided by expert counsel, found his wealth badly dissipated, while at the same time the newspapers reported that an escaped lunatic "cleaned up by selling 'em short."

So, the distinction between the gambler, speculator, and investor is hard to define. Perhaps, we are all "gamblers," for when we "stake anything" we certainly are not staking it on a "certain event." But, ordinarily we do not care to think of ourselves as "gamblers." The term smacks fouly on our sense of dignity. Surely though, few of us are deservant of the saintly title "investor."

Shouldn't we strike a happy medium and admit that we are *speculators*?

PROPHETS! – AREN'T WE ALL?

Whatever name you choose to be recognized by – gambler, speculator or investor – the fact remains that every one of your economic activities makes you a "forecaster."

Forecasting is not an undertaking reserved exclusively for professional bankers, investment counsellors, stock market brokers, the captains of industry, or the social planners in Washington. It is a work in which each of us is forever engaged. It is a job we cannot avoid. As Warren Parsons wrote: "You may scorn business forecasters but you cannot help being one. You may forecast badly or well but forecast you must."

The business man – corner-store grocer or tycoon of Big Business Inc. – buys, sells, builds, gives credit, etc., all in accordance with his opinion of future conditions. The doctor, lawyer, accountant, craftsman, clerk, laborer, housewife – all of us – are forever confronted with economic problems involving the uncertainties of the future:

"Should I buy a new car now or postpone it?"
Are prices likely to go up or down?

"Should I buy a home or rent one?"
Are real estate values likely to rise or fall?

"Can I afford to get married now?"
Will I have my job next year?

"Should I start a small business?"
What is the likelihood of a depression?

"As a farmer, what should I produce?"
What commodities are likely to rise in price?

"How should I vote?"
Would I benefit if .... were President?

Chance, risk, gamble, speculation, investment – call it what you will – it is obvious that all of us are dealers in the future. It is *your problem* to make your own plans, decisions, forecasts. The professional adviser may sometimes help you, but often he is a very busy man trying to solve the details of his own personal perplexities. You should be better prepared to understand and cope with your problems, as you are the one who is constantly thinking of them, and, for better or for worse, you are forever solving those problems in the form of forecasts of the future:

> "Let any man examine his thoughts, and he will find them occupied with the past or the future. We scarcely think at all of the present; or if we do, it is only to borrow light which it gives for regulating the future. The present is never our object; the past and present we use as means; the future only is our end." – Pascal

TIPSY TIPSTERS

So far, we have said that you are an economist, a risk-taker, and a forecaster, whether you want to be those things or not. Of these the most important role is that of a forecaster, because you cannot be a successful economist or risk-taker unless you are a successful forecaster.

The question, therefore, immediately arises as to how to go about forecasting. We shall point out briefly the three most popular ways of forecasting.

Many persons turn to the "experts" for economic guidance. This is the logical solution which attracts the novice, and even the old-timer is keeping at least one eye open for the liberator who may free him from work. It is implanted in most of us to follow the path of least effort. Even the most industrious will seek to do a good job in the easiest manner.

Why not seek the services of a professional economic forecaster? When we get sick we call a doctor. If we get into trouble, we see a lawyer. If we build a house, we probably call in an architect and a carpenter. Isn't it sensible to consult a forecasting specialist if we are confused over serious matters embracing future economic events?

Many of these specialists – services, counsellors, etc. – are equipped with statistical and research facilities, the cost of which is prohibitive to the average man or business. Most of them give their full time to forecasting problems. It would seem, too, that they might sometimes have "inside connections" which others might find difficult to acquire. At least, as specialists in forecasting it appears that their concentration in the field should give them a measure of prophetic wisdom not readily obtained by "outsiders."

That's the theory of it. Now let's glance at some of the record. For the most part the record pertains to the stock market, as it is here that many experts specialize. But, since most of these specialists maintain that the broad trends of the stock market usually correspond with the broad trends of general business (a questionable contention), their success as business forecasters can be considered to be related to their records as stock market forecasters. We shall just mention here the results of a few investigations into this subject. Considerable more evidence is available in our files.

> In a paper read before a joint meeting of the *Econometrica Society and the American Statistical Association*, Mr Alfred Cowles 3rd reported that "Professional stockmarket forecasters cannot forecast . . . a review of the various statistical tests applied to the records of these forecasters, indicate that the most successful records are little, or any, better than might be expected from pure chance."

A study which we made of seven services covering a two and one-half year period showed (1) all seven services gave unprofitable advice, and (2) an "investor" following the recommendations of the *best* of the seven services would have lost 40% of his capital.

> **_Professional stock market forecasters cannot forecast_**

From the findings and recommendations of the *Twentieth Century Fund* we are informed:

> "It is safe to say that the majority of advisory services today much more often hurt than help the investor and speculator using them . . . Numerous "sheets" calling themselves advisory services are designed to mislead and make financial victims of subscribers . . . The continuance of the vast number of such services bears depressing witness to the persistence of the popular belief in Santa Claus."

J. A. Livingston reported on "The Flustered Forecasters" in *Commercial and Financial Chronicle*, April 16, 1953:

> "I have kept score on the stock market forecasts of a group of economists since June, 1946. The forecasters were wrong 66⅔% of the time. Sooner or later, financial analysts as a group, are going to be right. Last year the National Federation of Financial Analysts Society forecast a 2% decline in stock prices by the end of 1952. Stocks actually rose 10%. They are mildly bearish for 1953. They're increasingly bearish for 1954."

And so it goes – all the evidence we have seen says that the stock market "experts" cannot forecast. Perhaps their approach to the problem is wrong? Perhaps, Providence doesn't intend that we should be able to see months and years into the future? We do think that many of the experts are doing a good job in furnishing their clients with factual data, but we also believe that most of them abuse the use of their data. We suggest that you try a "new approach."

WHAT'S NEW?

It appears that the idea of letting the other fellow run our financial affairs lacks practical merit. It is logical, therefore, after a few trial subscriptions with the professionals, that the forecaster decides to make his own forecasts. Again he follows the line of least effort and derives his forecasts from his interpretation of the "business situation" as he reads the headlines of today.

The modern-day headline-hunter looks about him and easily finds what he is looking for, or if he happens to be "open-minded," he merely stumbles onto something "significant." If his ulcers have been kicking up, he can find abundant reasons for believing that the country is going, or has gone, to the dogs. Or, if he has been taking his vim and vigor pills regularly, he will find in the day's news sufficient proof for believing that happy days are here again.

At work, on the street, at social lunches, at home – everywhere – the subject is "news," and forecasts from the headlines of today are constantly being formed.

Earnings, dividends, employment, production, sales, the stock market, taxes, inflation, politics, war, etc. etc. – these are the factors which kindle economic forecasts. One man is optimistic because of some "good news" in the building industry; another is pessimistic because of some "bad news" in the labor situation. A decline in railroad carloadings leads to stock market sales, and a rise in scrap iron prices gives confidence to the bulls. Many base their actions on what they believe Washington is doing, others on the foreign situation, and others on the agricultural outlook.

Conceivably, every item of business and political news is used in guiding men in their economic forecasts. But, this is really a simplified consideration of the actual situation. Actually we should try not to think of the barometric meaning of only one or a few factors, but we should try to think at one time of the collective meaning of scores of factors. Wesley C. Mitchell in *"Business Cycles: The Problem and Its Setting"* wrote:

> "... in truth every factor in the situation at every moment is being influenced by, and is influencing other factors – it is not first cause and then effect, but both cause and effect all the time. Further, we cannot follow single chains of causal influences. The interactions among economic processes are so important that we cannot set them aside. Almost every effect with which we deal will appear to be the joint product of numerous causes, and to be one among several causes of numerous effects."

Hence, we should try to think, at one time, not only the effect that higher commodity prices will have on production, sales, foreign trade, interest rates, wages, etc., etc., but also the effect that each of these factors will have upon commodity prices and, moreover, the effect that each of these factors will have upon every other factor. Then, assuming that our notions of causation, which we apply in measuring these effects, are correct, we may come out of the haze with an insight into the future of business conditions – and, maybe, the stock market. Obviously, such a mental procedure is impossible.

Possibly what the country, and world, needs is a huge "correlation machine" which will automatically determine the net meaning of thousands of interrelated, statistical news-items. Then forecasting might become perfected!

Of course, the simpler way, as pointed out already, is to pick up one or a few little news items and let these items serve as the reasons for predicting better, or worse, conditions. Unless you know what to look for, your choice of the "right items" should be right about half of the time.

Properly used, some items of news are useful to the forecaster. In fact, he must, of course, know some of the things which are going on today in order to make a decision which involves the future. What is happening today may be quite important if interpreted in the light of economic history. But, there are not many economic historians. Most of us learn the hard way. For instance, we learn from experience that a company's stock, on which an extra dividend has just been declared, may actually decline in price, not rise as we would logically expect. Labor strikes are sometimes followed by market rallies. Booming business is often accompanied by declining stock prices. Facts often deny logic.

Interpreting the news from a swivel chair usually amounts to wishful thinking – we merely lean on the news which satisfies our hopes and we ignore an investigation into its rightful meaning. It is a plaything of chance and it can be charged with a large measure of forecasting failure.

HEADS OR TAILS?

In the evolutionary process of a forecaster's education, after he has tried the experts and his own hand at forecasting, there often comes the decision to "take a chance" without any "sound or fundamental reasons" for doing so. He figures that he can't get any poorer cards than those dealt to him by the professionals, and he admits to himself that his own judgment of the daily news has not been good. So, when a "strong feeling" possesses him, he decides to follow it.

This method – if it can be called a method – is indulged in at various times by nearly everyone. Now, we are not going to philosophize here on the "magic of believing." If one's feeling is so powerful that it amounts to absolute belief, implicit faith that such and such a thing will occur, without any mental reservations whatsoever, then maybe the thing believed in will come to pass. Our hunches have never been that strong. Always they are accompanied by a feeling of wonderment: "I wonder whether it will really work out that way?"

There is no need to stress here that Lady Luck is a fickle mistress. There is, of course, such a thing as "luck," in the sense that "luck" may be considered as one of the expressions of the natural law of probability. If a *large number* of persons decided to toss pennies to decide economic problems – heads I do, tails I don't – a certain small number of those persons would be extremely successful at the end of a limited period of time. The number who would succeed could be determined beforehand by the mathematics of probability.

The Theory of Probabilities has an indispensable role in the natural sciences and its importance is beginning to be more widely recognized in the social sciences. But, the Theory has no bearing on "black magic," or "luck," inherent in the individual. Life insurance companies determine the death rates of the present population before the separate individuals die. The number of persons who will live beyond 90 years is indeed a small percentage of the total population. But, barring destruction of the entire human race, it is confidently expected that a definite small percentage of the persons now living will survive their 90th birthday.

In much the same manner, it can be said that a certain small percentage of the individuals who play stocks and dabble in business are certain to be extremely lucky in their financial affairs throughout their lives. Unfortunately, the chance that you, or any other separate individual, will be among that lucky group is indeed remote. Some will be very lucky, some will be very unlucky; most of us will run about "average" or a little above or below. It seems that the Creator provided the Law of Probability to sort of "even things out" for the vast number of things involved in the physical and human manisfestations of His plan. At any rate, the Law of Probability is just as real as the Law of Gravity.

If it so happens that you have been very lucky, or very unlucky, it certainly does not mean, from the Theory of Probabilities, that your luck will continue that way. From a scientific viewpoint it is mere superstition to say that some persons are inherently lucky, or unlucky. It is in accord with scientific fact to say that some persons *have been* lucky or unlucky – that individuals *do have* streaks of good luck and or bad luck. It would be a gross violation of the natural Law of Probability if this were not so. But, it is nonsense to assume that a person's luck *will continue* in the future as it has in the past . . . unless there be some astrological or other natural forces which direct the individual's destiny. If these forces exist, they do not appear to be clearly understood at the moment. It seems, therefore, more realistic if we give our practical attention to the forces we are able to understand and demonstrate – and the Law of Probability is the expression of one of these ever-present forces, while pure Luck is nothing but a random, passing experience.

In this brief comment on the subject of Luck, we can add no thought more true than that written in the 1800s by Robert Bulwer:

"Hope nothing from luck, and the probability is that you will be so prepared, forewarned and forearmed that all shallow observers will call you lucky."

TRADE ALONE – AND LIKE IT!

A principal objective of science is to forecast the future.

In many aspects of the physical sciences, failure in forecasting is the exception rather than the rule. We can predict with certainty, under controlled laboratory conditions, that we will get water if we mix oxygen and hydrogen in the right proportions. Those who are well versed in mathematics, physics, and chemistry could anticipate how and why the hydrogen bomb would work before they ever attempted to construct one of the blasted things. Astronomy, the great grandparent of science, is able to foretell eclipses, planetary movements, the coming of comets, etc., centuries in advance.

On the other hand, geologists are not always able to foretell whether there is gold in yonder hills; the weather man is not always correct in his prognostications; the doctor is not always right in predicting a patient's reactions to medicines; and even the astronomer misses on his forecasts of solar radiation with its attending influence on agricultural growth.

The science of economics is particularly susceptible to failure in forecasting. Counsellors, services, political prophets, industrial leaders, systems, plans, barometers – all say their little piece, and the elusive golden key to economic forecasting still remains hidden. Yet, we continue the search for better ways to forecast for the very good reason that *we must forecast* whether we want to or not. Every move, every plan, every decision which we make in our respective ways of obtaining a livelihood, involves forecasting, whether it be good or bad forecasting.

Since we cannot depend on the advices of others, nor rely on the simple methods of reading the headlines or following our hunches, it seems that it would be wise for each of us to make individual, personal forecasts by plans based on careful study of economic history – on the facts as they are known today.

We need not all be doctors, but if we know and practice the facts of hygiene we should have a better chance to live longer. We need not all be forecasting "specialists," but if we know and practice the facts of economic hygiene (taking care of ourselves economically), we should have a better chance to live successfully in a material way. If one is to have a taste of peace of mind in business and financial affairs, he must feel that he knows where he is going and the roads which will take him there. Success in business and the markets usually comes only with organized, tested knowledge.

In brief, our belief is that each individual should do his own forecasting; he should be fortified with a knowledge of facts on forecasting, and he should possess a systematic plan of operation which is *his own*.

It would be presumptuous for this writer to claim that he will give you something which you and he have long sought – a completely satisfactory method of economic forecasting. The "ideal method" will perhaps never be found, or if it is found, its use in time would become so universal that it too would result in failure. In the meanwhile, the quest for perfection goes on, and since the urgency for forecasting is *now*, not later, it seems fitting to evaluate the wide assortment of tools which the forecaster has forged and used in the past as well as those tools which he is building and using at the present time.

You may find in the pages to follow some barometers which seem to give promise that they will fulfill your particular hopes in economic forecasting. If you do find such barometers, *make them your own*. Study them, learn their good points and weaknesses, learn what they can do for you and what they cannot do, improve them if you can, and, finally, use them. If you become well acquainted with the barometers before you use them, you will not become discouraged when they cause you to take losses from time to time. A number of the barometers have accredited themselves with

> *our belief is that each individual should do his own forecasting*

profitable records in actual forecasting over a period of years, yet each of these barometers has been discredited and discarded by someone at some time.

Yes, let us continue to explore for new barometers, but let us not neglect our present store of good (not perfect) barometers.

The writer is indebted to many authors and fellow research workers whose tremendous assistance has made this work possible. His investigations have drawn upon the published works of many large organizations as well as the studies of the individual student.

Of equal importance, the writer is indebted to the business man, the investor, trader, student – the *Subscriber* – who has made it possible for him to make this work a full-time occupation.

To help the subscriber to make his own forecasts – to give him food for thought – is the guiding inspiration of this work.

Part II

BACKGROUND TO TRADING

■ What is "Technical Analysis"?

■ Economic movements reflect natural laws

■ Each market tells its own story

■ Forecasting vs trend-following

WHAT IS "TECHNICAL ANALYSIS"?

The expression "technical analysis" is one which has been adopted by market analysts in order to distinguish this type of analysis from the commonly used approach which may be identified by the term "fundamental analysis."

"Technical analysis" is devoted to "internal" studies of the stock market, of the commodity markets, of specific businesses and industries, and of general business. We rarely hear of "technical analysis" in connection with the movements of business and industry; yet it appears that the tools of technical analysis are nearly as serviceable in the field of business as they are in the security and commodities markets where they have long been employed.

> We are not interested in what a stock should be worth but what people will actually pay for the stock

In technical analysis we are not concerned with the "fundamental" or "outside" forces which influence a specific phase of activity – say, the stock market – but rather we are concerned with the forces *within* that particular phase of activity. These forces may be thought of as dealing particularly with *human* qualities.

We are not interested here, for example, in what a stock should be worth from the viewpoint of "outside fundamentals" such as sales, general business prospects, taxes, war, management, earnings, dividends, etc., but rather we are interested in what people will actually pay for the stock regardless of its intrinsic worth. Our concern here is with the supply-and-demand equation, and we seek to learn which of the two human forces is the more powerful – the force which is demanding the stock or the force which is supplying the stock.

The separate individuals who are demanding and supplying things (stocks, for example) have, for the most part, their own "fundamental reasons" for wanting to buy or wanting to sell. We have no curiosity whatsoever here in what their reasons may be; all we care to know here is which of the two combined forces of these individuals is the stronger. At current prices are the combined buyers more willing to buy than the combined sellers are to sell? The *actions* of the two competing forces, *regardless of their reasons*, are registered in the stock market. We study their actions and ignore their reasons because, in reality, their reasons ("outside," "fundamental" influences) are reflected in their actions. In technical analysis we study the *net result* of all of these outside influences. We work *directly* with the factor we are trying to forecast, not indirectly or in a roundabout fashion.

The nature of the supply-and-demand relationship of the two competing forces is reflected in the markets by:

1. The characteristics of the *price action itself.*
2. The *nature of the activity* (volume, breadth, quality).
3. *When* the action occurred and the *amount of time* spent in it.

A study of these phenomena gives us various "techniques" for detecting strength and weakness in the supply–demand equation at a given time. These techniques are sometimes called 'technical market tools.' They are also called by other names: rules, systems, barometers, methods, gadgets, golden keys, bonanzas, etc., not including the "alluring names" we have attached to some of the techniques we have published (Technometer, Semaphore, Stop–Go Signal System, Barometer X, Barometer ABC, etc.)

The number and variety of these methods seem to be without limit. Our paper, *"115 Barometers for Forecasting Stock Prices,"* explains briefly many of these methods. It would be humanly impossible for one or several persons to investigate the potential merits of all of these methods. One would need a staff of several hundred workers, a payroll which only the Federal government could "afford," to conduct a thorough investigation into the practical worth of the innumerable "forecasting devices" which have been invented.

This is a day of "specialization" in barometers. Our own "specialty" has been in devising ways and means of improving on Dow Theory principles. We suggest that you too do not try to find "all the answers" for all the barometers – that you too "specialize" in one particular phase which has special appeal to you. In any of the many fields of inquiry you will undoubtedly find enough unknowns to provide you with a sideline hobby (if you like to explore) for the balance of your life. And, perhaps – even probably – your explorations will lead to *gains* in dollars and cents.

ECONOMIC MOVEMENTS
REFLECT NATURAL LAWS

More and more economists and statisticians of repute are recognizing that stock market movements in themselves are interesting phenomena capable of yielding significant conclusions in respect to their own future trends. At one time the upper strata of the intelligentsia viewed the "chart reader" as a misguided person, a queer sort of individual, harmless, but a decided bore. Nothing was quite so disconcerting as a chart reader at large with a pet theory, but no capital. To study stock market charts with the hope that they might disclose an insight into the future was something akin to studying a racing form in an effort to pick the winning horses. The theory was that chart readers, along with horse players, always die broke.

Today many distinguished economists endorse unhesitatingly some of the theories of the old school of chart readers. Also, some of today's scholarly publications, such as *Econometrica* and *Journal of the American Statistical Association* have published articles which prove some of the things which the chart "bugs" have been trying to say for decades!

For years Roger Babson* has written of the physical law of action and reaction being reflected in economic movements. We believe he is right. We must confess that it is often difficult to *foresee* the practical application of that law, but if that were not so the problem of economic forecasting would be relatively easy. But, at least we can always see the law of action and reaction at work after the work has been done.

> *More and more economists of repute are recognizing that stock market movements in themselves are interesting phenomena*

We have always had periods of prosperity and periods of depression; we will always have them regardless of New Eras, New Deals, Fair Deals, and other errors of mortal mind. Nature, of which man is a part, has its own "deals," its own laws, which man has never long succeeded in opposing. Emerson called one of these laws the *Law of Compensation*. Physicists term it the "law of action

---

Editor's footnote: Roger Babson remains one of the great names in market analysis in the first four decades of this century. His was probably the loudest voice at the time in 1928 and 1929 warning one and all that the current great Bull Market was soon to end with an equally great crash, but like many ahead of their times, no one, it seems, really believed him.

and reaction." For present purposes we can simply state that economic phenomena *will move up* and *will move down*. They will not go in one direction, without an opposing movement, in obedience to the whims of human wishful thinking.

Another physical law which is reflected in economic movements is the *Law of Growth*, or we can term it "evolution." Statisticians have measured the unfoldment of this law in economic events. They call it the "secular trend." This law accounts for much of our steady progress notwithstanding human errors in dealing with the inevitable ups and downs which are superimposed by nature on this slowly moving trend of growth.

Still another natural law which is expressed in economic movements is the *Law of Probability*. To declare that we can duplicate quite precisely *some* phases of our economic activities merely by tossing a coin – heads, prices go up; tails, they go down – is a startling subject which has been discussed in discourses by this writer and others. It is sufficient to mention here that the *mathematical* law of chance does operate in economic events, and it has an important significance.

There are other natural, physical laws which find expression in economic movements, but for present purposes we shall consider briefly only one law, the *Law of Inertia*. A casual acquaintance with this law is important for an understanding and appreciation as to why many technical market tools *must work*.

The Law of Inertia

If the stock market begins to move in a trend, up or down, as determined by our measures, is there any basic, fundamental reason for believing that the trend will continue at least for a limited period of time? Is there any physical law underlying the structure of stock prices which "compels" (or, at least, "urges") prices to continue in the direction of their present trend, be it up, down, or sideways?

Inertia is defined as "that property of matter by virtue of which it persists in its state of rest or of uniform motion unless some force changes that state." Popularly, inertia is termed "momentum."

Dr. H. T. Davis writes in his text *The Analysis of Economic Time Series*:

> ". . . the positive conclusion is that a profit can be made by this method of making use of the inertia of the series . . . the analysis clearly shows that the time series for the stock market has a structure and that this structure is visable in a predominance of sequences over reversals. Later in the book it will be shown how the Dow Theory of forecasting essentially makes use of this property."

Dr. Davis shows that a theoretical trader averaged an annual profit of 6.66% after deducting 1% brokerage cost by following this simple rule: Buy after the market shows a net gain for a month, then hold that position and sell after the market shows a net loss for a month. Dr. Davis warns

> "a study of the consistency of the data for short periods of time shows that the method is operative only over long intervals and could not be used for obtaining annual profits . . . however, the analysis clearly shows that the time series for the stock market has a structure."

Alfred Cowles, 3rd and H. E. Jones writing in *Econometrica* state:

> "This evidence of structure in stock prices suggests alluring possibilities in the way of forecasting. In fact, many professional speculators, including in particular exponents of the so-called "Dow Theory" widely publicized by popular financial journals, have adopted systems based in the main that it is advantageous to swim with the tide . . . The significant excess of sequences over reversals . . . represents conclusive evidence of structure in stock prices."

Messrs Cowles and Jones say: ". . . the probability appeared to be 0.625 that if the market had risen in any given month, it would rise in the succeeding month, or if it had fallen, that it would continue to decline for another month." Trading on this simple principle "an average net gain of about 7% is indicated . . . but no great consistency is evident" – in fact, "the chance of loss for any one year is about 1 in 3." (We are not trying here to set up any concrete methods for operating in stocks. Rather, we are pointing out scholarly testimony to the fact there is an underlying basic "structure," or law, operating in stock market movements. The concrete methods come later in this text.)

> *There is an underlying basic law, operating in stock market movements*

Mansfield Mills in *Market Trend Analysis Report* writes:

> "It is generally understood that market trends once started are materially more likely to continue than reverse. In studying market advances from 1897 to the present, one of our Research Executives, Mr. Benitz, has found that if you used nothing but amplitude and were trying to estimate the direction of the next 5% move by the averages, you will be right about two times out of three if you simply observe the last 5% move. Suppose you decide to buy at the top of a 5% up-move and sell out as soon as a 5% down-move occurs. In the past 53 years you would achieve gains of 1592% and losses of 495%, a ratio of 3.21 to 1 for success. The ratio is not as great on the downside, but it is still considerable. If you sold short after each 5% decline in the last 53 years and did not cover until the next 5% advance, your gains would amount to 1374%, your losses 553%, a ratio of 2.49 to 1 for success."

In another writing Mr. Mills tells of some of the research by the *Cowles Commission, University of Chicago*:

> "*In the first place,* you want to keep in mind the probabilities of what you might call 'the law of continuation.' That is, once it can be determined either that an old trend has reached an 'exhaustion point,' or that a new trend has been established, the probabilities are about 2 to 1 the new trend will continue rather than it will reverse.
>
> "We believe the following will substantiate that fact:
>
> "*The Cowles Commission, University of Chicago,* made an extensive study of market and stock records. They made long tabulations and studied its record in terms of subsequent hours, days, weeks, months and years; the over-all conclusion was that 62 times to 38 the following period would be in the same direction as the one that preceded.
>
> "What that fundamental principle means to you, of course, is that as soon as your judgment of the evidence of a trend turn apparently has been proved correct, you then want to be twice as eager to stay with your market position as you are to change it. In other words, back your profits by giving them a chance to grow when you are right on the trend."

A few other investigations are mentioned below in order to show that once a movement starts, "the natural thing" is for the movement to continue. We cannot, of course, predict *how far* or *how long* any *single* movement will go (through the Law of Probability we can predict the average rise of *many* movements), but the Law of Inertia assures us that a good majority of those movements will go far enough to give us the *opportunity* for profits. It is up to our "trading techniques" to grasp the opportunities which Inertia provides for us.

Dr. Elmer C. Bratt writes in his *Forecasting Business Cycles*:

> "What has been called 'trading with the trend' appears to be the only important forecasting principle which can be derived. When the market starts moving in one direction, it is likely to continue in that direction for a limited time. The most important scheme which has been developed is embodied in the 'Dow Theory.' The essential proposition involved is that if the market prices reach levels measurably above or below those which have been obtained for a considerable time, the market will continue on upward or downward for an indefinite period. Although this rule has been by no means invariable, it has been correct in the majority of cases."

L.C. Wilcoxen writing in the *Journal of the American Statistical Association* also shows "structure" in stock prices. His study included the prices of *US Steel wheat* and *cotton*. The study included various price amplitudes and time intervals. He observes "the forecasting curves of the several markets are markedly similar. It is quite possible that this is a general characteristic of all free markets . . . This may indicate that fundamentally *all markets* are governed by the same law."

The *Financial News* of London, England, gave evidence of the property of inertia in the stock market when it publicized the "Ten Per Cent System." Under this system "one buys when shares have advanced 10 per cent from a "low" and sells when they have fallen 10 per cent from a "high." The efficacy of this system has been proved and demonstrated by the experience of Mr. Cyrus Q. Hatch, who, from 1883 to 1936, increased his capital from a mere $100,000 to $14,400,000," – says the *Financial News*.

We could add other testimonials on "structure" in stock price movements, but we shall go to no further length at this time. The technical methods discussed later in this text give additional evidence of one or more basic laws operating in the stock market. As long as man in the mass continues to create market trends, we think it is safe to say that stock price movements will continue to reflect the unfoldment of natural laws.

EACH MARKET TELLS ITS OWN STORY

The studies in this volume refer, for the most part, to the stock market and the grain market. But, much of what is written can be applied equally as well to the cotton market, the coffee market, the potato market, the pig-iron market, or to many of the numerous other markets. If the underlying theorems of technical analysis are sound, and we believe they are, then they are sound for all competitive markets and we should be able to use these theorems statistically, and gainfully, in many of the markets.

If the law of inertia ("continuation" or "momentum") is at work in the stock market, then it must be at work in other free markets such as the wheat market or the scrap-iron market. Sometimes, for short intervals, governmental regulations interfere with the freedom of supply and demand in various markets. But, always after such experiments have failed, the markets are given back to the people and the natural laws which govern people – hence, if capitalism and individual freedom are to survive we can generally expect free markets where the natural laws of human behavior find expression without molestation.

If the stock market reflects everything which people know and believe about stocks (which it must), then it follows that the scrap-iron market must reflect everything which the people of the iron and steel industry know and believe about their business. The wheat market must reflect everything that the farmer, the miller, the exporter, the speculator, etc., knows or believes about wheat. And so on for the other free, competitive markets.

Economic forecasting ("planning," if the economists choose to call it such) may become more successful if the endowed institutions studying the problems would give more and more attention to the *internal behavior* of *each* of the factors they are seeking to understand. If the economists are interested in the price of beans, they should, first of all, learn all they can about the *price of beans*. In respect to beans, bananas, or bologna, they should study:

1. The behavior of the *price action itself.*
2. The *character of trading* (quantity and quality) which produced the price action.
3. *When* the price action occurred and *how much time* was consumed in the action.

After getting all the knowledge they can on those three points, it then will be soon enough for the economists to grapple for further enlightenment through the roundabout process: judging the probable production and consumption of beans, the influence of general business conditions and the general price level on the price of beans, the effects which the prices of alternative products have upon the price of beans, the effects of government loans and subsidies on the price of beans, the effects of weather and bugs upon the crop and therefore on the price of beans, etc. Certainly, all these factors do influence the price of beans. Therefore, it is certain that bean *prices will reflect these things*. If the purpose is to "forecast" prices, why become involved in the complications of the fundamental influences? The *net result* of all these influences is faithfully recorded in the bean market; consequently, simply study the bean market.

> *Price movements of the stock market represent the sum of every scrap of knowledge bearing on finance*

The Foundation for the Study of Cycles is on the right track in devoting its main interests to the *very curves it is seeking to understand*, not to the "outside influences" which produce those curves. Others might give more time to similar pursuits. It is hoped that more and more economists of the future will recognize the importance of "internal analysis."

At any rate, let us get back to the stock market. A long time ago William P. Hamilton wrote:

> "The price movements of the stock market represent the sum of every scrap of knowledge bearing on finance. The market reflects all that the jobber knows about the condition of the retail trade; all that the banker knows about the money market; all that the best informed president knows of his own business together with his knowledge of other businesses; it sees the general condition of transportation in a way that the president of no single railroad can ever see; it is better informed on crops than the farmer or even the Department of Agriculture; . . . the market reduces to a 'bloodless verdict' all knowledge bearing on finance, both domestic and foreign.' . . . Therefore, 'there is no need to supplement the price movements, as some statisticians do, with elaborate compilations of commodity price index numbers, blank clearings, fluctuations in exchange, or anything else. The price movements reflect all these things since they represent everything everybody knows, hopes, believes and anticipates."

Jesse Livermore wrote:

> "Remember there is always a reason for a stock acting the way it does. But also remember the chances are you will not become acquainted with the reason until some time in the future, when it is too late to act on it profitably."

W. W. Wakefield expresses this basic argument well:

> "If the President and Chairman of the Board of a giant corporation have in mind to give a large order for goods to another corporation, they might buy a 'few'

shares of the other company's stock before placing the order; then the insiders of the other company, upon receipt of the order might also buy a few shares; probably the news would percolate thru Wall Street via the grapevine telegraph route; and finally it would come over the news ticker in brokers' offices and would reach the public thru the newspapers. By this time the stock is already up several points. So it is that news in business statistics come out when the party is half or all over. Bad news often comes out at the bottom and good news at the top. . . . In the light of all these facts it is little wonder that many investors and traders who rely entirely upon such crude helps as fundamental business statistics, earnings reports, intrinsic values, balance sheets, announcement of dividend changes, etc., come to grief in their market operation."

Dr. N. Molodovsky states the case for the technical approach in these words:

"The study of the general business cycle has to deal with many hundreds of factors, all perplexingly different in their respective movements . . . with the hundreds of factors which constitute a business cycle . . . it is a difficult undertaking to determine by their simultaneous analysis a cyclical turning point. . . . A direct approach to the analysis of stock prices attacks the problem there where it is, instead of arriving at it after much roundabout traveling. . . . The market analyst has his attention focussed on two factors only; stock price and the activity in their transactions in the market. These two factors, moreover, are not extraneous to the general cycle, but are, on the contrary, among its most representative and essential components. The analyst of the movements of stock prices should, therefore, have no undue humility about the nature of his work. . . . This writer is far from suggesting that all other approaches should be discarded or that market analysis suffices unto itself. . . . The investor needs the services of all three basic techniques: value analysis, economic analysis, and market analysis. But market analysis alone can help to solve the all-important problem of timing. For this reason, it is an essential prerequisite of sound investment policy."

There are those who argue that the stock market forecasts worldwide business conditions. Indeed, one Dow theorist wrote that the Dow-Jones averages during 1912–1914 "predicted the Great War if the world had been able to interpret the signs."

We do not put stress on the ability of the averages to forecast events outside of its own sphere. Certainly in several recent years stock market movements have *not* often forecasted business movements. But, we do believe that the stock market will forecast itself, that the wheat market will forecast itself, that the market for scrap iron will forecast the price of scrap iron, etc. We hope to present good evidence to substantiate these beliefs.

FORECASTING vs TREND-FOLLOWING

In the foregoing pages we used the term "forecasting" loosely. "Forecasting the stock market" is usually considered to mean the predetermination of how far a particular movement will go or how long it will last. We do not believe that this sort of prediction is possible with any practical degree of consistent accuracy, notwithstanding that most of the "authorities" are forever trying to see distant trends.

We think that "forecasting" should be thought of in the light of measuring the direction of *today's* trend and then turning to the Law of Inertia (momentum) for assurance that probabilities favor the continuation of that trend for an *unknown* period of time into the future. This is *trend following*, and it does not require us to don the garment of the mystic and look into the crystal balls of the future.

Of course, in our "better moments" most of us admit that we possess no occult powers. But, is it not true that "intuitive forecasts" are forever shaping our market policies? We "feel" that a depression is coming, or we "know" that the market will continue rising for another year or two. We need only look at the current market letters, or this morning's newspaper, or the voice of our friend, or our own voice, to realize how deeply it is ingrained in the human system to want to lift the veil of the future. And, no one has yet done that in the stock or commodity markets with any degree of success other than that which can be explained entirely by the "laws of chance." If you know some "forecaster" who has been reasonably successful in his predictions, you can likely depend that the Law of Probabilities made it so. It would be a gross violation of that law if a small minority of people were not successful *in the past* – whether they be "lucky guessers" or "profound economists" – but do not depend upon their fortune to continue in the future. The Law of Probabilities respects the individual only in so far as he is a single statistic in a multitude of cases – some who are unknown today may be the lucky forecasters of the future.

If we "must" forecast, then let us look ahead a year and say:

"That most of us shall live through it and find many sweet satisfactions in life. That some of us shall see some sorrow.

"That Spring will come. That blossoms will bloom. That the sun will shine and the moon will show itself (on schedule). That young people will fall in love. That many will marry and be given in marriage.

"That many young men will go to far places – and most of them will return to live life fully.

"That we shall have an election (and shall survive it). And that we shall have a harvest.

"That the year will go quickly. That many people will do many fine things and make many mistakes – and that most of the things we worry about won't happen.

" . . . We all wish we knew more about the future. But there is ample evidence that the plan of Providence is best – and that our lives are happier and more effective when we can't see too far into the future."

From *Predictions for 1952*, by Richard L. Evans

So, let us go along with Mr. Evans in his "predictions" of things to come, and let us try to ignore our own thoughts, and those of others, regarding future events in economic trends.

Let us believe that it is possible to profit through economic changes by *following today's trend*, as it is revealed statistically day-by-day, week-by-week, or month-by-month. In doing this we should entertain no preconceived notions as to whether business is going to boom or bust, or whether the Dow-Jones Industrial Average is going to 500 or 50. We will merely chart our course and steer our ship in the direction of the prevailing wind. When the economic weather changes, we will change our course with it and will not try to forecast the future time or place at which the wind will change. Along with Mr. Evans, we will leave that to Providence.

————

We have already pointed out technical analysis falls into three broad classifications: (1) price action, (2) market activity, and (3) time and duration. The specific tools which the technician uses – Dow Theory, moving averages, momentum measures, volume indexes, etc. – each fall logically into one or more of the three broad classifications. Some of the tools are related to *price action only*. Others consider along with the price action, the *activity* of the price movement, sometimes both the quantity of trading and the *quality* of trading. Furthermore, the technician often concerns himself with the *time* element, *when* the movement occurs and *how much time* is consumed in the movement.

In this text we are going to simplify matters considerably by placing our emphasis on *price action only*. We expect to show that an analysis of price action, without consideration to activity or time, is in itself sufficient for purposes of practical, profitable market operations. The pages that follow are in the nature of "an evolution of a market barometer." The popular Dow Theory is the oldest of technical tools and from its basic principles other tools have been forged. Therefore, we will start with an explanation and appraisal of the Dow Theory and work gradually forward to the presentation of recent developments.

Part III

BLUEPRINTS FOR THE STOCKMARKET

- The old Dow Theory
- A checklist of Dow Theory indications
- The record of the old Dow Theory
- The approach to a better Dow Theory
- Samuel Moment's tested improvement of the Dow Theory
- A new Dow barometer
- Trend trading with square root methods
- The use of square roots with the Dow principles
- Quick profits in fast-moving stocks
- Fast-moving stocks
- The thrust method in stocks

THE OLD DOW THEORY

Scores of barometers based on fundamental phenomena such as activity in the iron and steel industry, changes in money rates, vibrations in sensitive commodity prices, shiftings in new and unfilled orders, etc., have been thoughtfully devised, then put to actual tests, and finally abandoned. Through all of these futile efforts to discover the elixir of economic life, the Dow Theory, first publicly expounded in 1902, has survived – and grown in popular acclaim. Its record as a guide to the obtaining of a better-than-average investment return cannot be impeached.

Notwithstanding its record, we do not believe that the Dow Theory of 1902, nor of later exponents, is a fully satisfactory answer to the quest for stock market profits. We believe that the record proves that most of the underlying *principles* of the method are correct. Consequently, we have devoted considerable time in exploring new ways of applying those proven principles.

An understanding of the Dow Theory is, therefore, the first step in the evolutionary climb toward a better method. First, we shall want to know what it is and we shall want to appraise it justly. After that we will be ready to search for new ways of using some of its basic principles.

APPRAISAL

This Review of the Dow Theory follows closely a paper published by the writer in 1932. Since that time the books by Robert Rhea and several others (particularly those published by *Barron's*) have appeared, all of which should be consulted should the reader desire more detailed instruction on this subject. For a concise explanation of the main points in the orthodox Dow Theory, as set forth by W.P. Hamilton, we believe the outline in these few pages will be found accurate.

The Dow Theory is the *only* method which can lay claim to a profitable record of actual forecasts over a *considerable* period of time. Hamilton's editorials, and the writings of his successors, are proof that the method has worked out profitably over a half century. No other method can make that claim in actual forecasting.

Yet, we believe that the orthodox Dow Theory is only a starting point. We should know what it is in order that we work toward making improvements on its imperfections.

Today there are many Dow theories

It seems that Charles H. Dow, back in 1902, intended his "theory" (it was not known as "the Dow Theory" in his days) as a business forecaster, but most disciples of Dow have decided that Dow's ideas are also applicable to stock market operations. Whatever might have been Dow's thoughts on this matter, it is certain that he did not leave a dogmatic set of rules by which traders and investors could be guided. And none of the later writers has handed down a formula which has met with universal accep-

> *Charles H. Dow, intended his "theory" as a business forecaster*

tance. Yet, notwithstanding the diversity of opinion concerning the application of the Theory, the basic principles which Dow recognized remain the same, and in fact, most of them have been fortified with years of test.

Charles Dow first wrote a series of editorials in the *Wall Street Journal* during 1902–1903 on the relationship of stock prices to business conditions. These editorials became the inspiration for William P. Hamilton* to attempt to crystallize Dow's views into a general theory. In this Review we shall become acquainted with Hamilton's "Dow Theory" as it is the forerunner of other "modern Dow Theories."

Underlying premise in Hamilton's Dow Theory

Hamilton introduced his understanding of Dow's idea with this basic premise:

> "It cannot too often be said that the stock market reflects absolutely all everybody knows about the business of the country. . . . There are corporations listed in the Stock Exchange dealing in practically everything the country makes and consumes – the coal, the coke, the iron ore, the pig iron, the steel billet, the manufactured watch spring – and all their knowledge is infallibly reflected in the price of securities."

Therefore, according to Hamilton, the best source of information as to the future of the stock market, and business conditions, is the stock market. (See

---

Editor's footnote: William P. Hamilton certainly was someone to be reckoned with in the first three decades of the Twentieth Century as the man in 1903 who replaced the immortal Charles H. Dow as Editor of *The Wall Street Journal.* As an Englishman educated at Oxford, probably majoring in Literature, his great success in adapting to stock market investment and Wall Street was to represent an outstanding metamorphosis. In 1922 Barron's published his great work *The Stock Market Barometer* where the "Dow Theory" was first comprehensively laid out in probably the finest writings in the English language ever for a stock market book. Mr. Hamilton remained the Editor of the Wall Street Journal until 1929 when he passed away.

preceding Review, *"Principles of Technical Analysis,"* for further comments on this point.)

The three types of movements

Dow recognized that at any given time there would likely be divergent trends in individual stocks, so he reasoned that it would not do to single out one or a few stocks which would serve reliably as a business barometer. Accordingly, in order to find "averages" or "indexes" which would represent "the verdict of the composite market," he did the pioneering work on two market averages which we know today as the *Dow-Jones Industrials* and *Dow-Jones Railroads*. With these two averages constructed and tried, he was reasonably satisfied that their movements represented "the sum of Wall Street's knowledge of the past, immediate and remote, applied to discounting the future."

But even now, the preliminary work was not over, for it was apparent to him that some movements in the averages were significant while others were comparatively meaningless. Logically, therefore, he classified the movements of the averages into three groups:

1. The major movement – the big wave or main tide, popularly known as "bull and bear markets."
2. The secondary movements – lesser waves in opposition to the main tide; sharp declines in bull markets and sharp rallies in bear markets.
3. Day-to-day fluctuations – seemingly random movements.*

The importance of the three movements in forecasting

Having segregated and defined the three types of movements, Dow set to the task of determining which movements were barometrically related to business conditions. It soon appeared evident to him that the major movement, the big wave or underlying trend, was definitely related to the future of business. But, he found no similar correspondence between the secondary movements (intermediate waves) and day-to-day fluctuations (minor ripples) and subsequent business conditions. If the main tide of the stock market pointed up, it foreshadowed rising business conditions regardless of whether the stock market

---

* It has been demonstrated that these day-to-day fluctuations appear to move *mathematically* in conformance with the Law of Probabilities. Therefore, they may not be random, or haphazard, movements, as Dow apparently conceived them.

was in a decline because of the force of a temporary secondary or minor wave. Market students pondering over Dow's ideas began to ask: "If Dow's principles of interpreting market action can be used to forecast business, cannot the same principles be used to forecast the stock market itself?" As a result, today we do not often hear of the Dow Theory specifically mentioned in connection with business forecasts.

The three types of movements combine to make the price level at a designated time. In applying Hamilton's Dow Theory to the stock market, one gives attention to all three types of movements, although the attempt is made to predict no movements other than the major trends. That is, one observes even the day-to-day fluctuations for their possible bearing on the major trend, although the attempt is never made to forecast these minor fluctuations. The secondary swings are always under scrutiny, again in connection with the major movements; and while at times the Dow method will give light on forthcoming secondary swings, no great importance is attached to this occasional feat. Hence, the Dow Theory, as Hamilton conceived it, is concerned with forecasting the major trends. The way this is done is found in the methods of interpreting the movements in the averages.

THE METHODS OF INTERPRETING THE AVERAGES

There are four essential ways in which Hamilton interpreted the averages under his conception of the Dow Theory:

Double tops and bottoms

The first manner in which the averages are interpreted is that of detecting "double tops and bottoms." It is explained that when prices reach a top, they will often have a moderate decline and then go back again near the former top. If after such a move prices again recede, there is strong presumption that the trend is changing and that a decline of considerable proportion is in store. The theory is also applicable to bear movements, where a double bottom often signals a change for the better in the main trend. The idea of double tops and bottoms is "by no means infallible, but it is often useful; and experience has shown that when the market makes a double top or a double bottom in the averages, there is strong reason for suspecting that the rise or decline is over."

Lines

An average is said to be making a "line" when it moves horizontally, that is, when it moves neither up or down more than a few points over a period of at least several days. After such a line is made, should the average break through the upper limit of the line, it is contended that the period of the line was one of accumulation, and that the main trend is therefore probably pointing up. Should the average break below the lower limit of the line, the period of the line is construed to be one of distribution, indicating at least tentatively that the main wave flows toward lower levels.

Resistance levels

Reactions (reversals) take place in every main trend movement. These reactions set up what are known as "resistance points or levels" – the points at which the reactions begin and terminate. Once a lower resistance point is established, then subsequently broken, a sign of weakness is shown. It reveals the absence of "good buying" at a previous support level. Conversely, when an upper resistance point is broken, it shows strength because the market is now able to forge above a previous offering level. The Dow Theory uses this principle in this manner:

An average is said to indicate a reversal from a bear to bull trend (or a continuation of a bull trend if already established) when it declines toward a previous low point but does not penetrate below that low point, and then subsequently it rallies above the peak of a previous high point.

An average is said to indicate a reversal from a bull to a bear trend (or a continuation of the bear trend if already established) when it rallies toward a previous high point but does not go above that high point, and then subsequently it declines below the bottom of a previous low point.

Confirmation

A signal from one average alone is without importance according to the Dow Theory. Both averages must confirm a bullish, or bearish, trend before an investor is justified in buying, or selling, stocks, as the case may be. The theory is that we cannot have industrial prosperity, or depression, without such prosperity, or depression, being reflected in the railroads, and that both industrial and railroad stocks will testify to the prosperous, or depressed, outlook for general business. The conformation, however, need not be simultaneous. One average may delay giving its approval of the action of the other average for days, months, or even years, but a valid signal is never given before confirmation is obtained. The absence of confirmation may give the investor an early clue as to subsequent trends, but the orthodox Dow Theory insists on ultimate confirmation before action is taken.

A CHECKLIST OF DOW THEORY INDICATIONS

The foregoing methods of interpreting the averages may now be summarized. This summary may assist orthodox Dow theorists as a convenient check list in interpreting current movements of the averages.

A. Reversal from bear to bull market

The *Preliminary indication* of the completion of a major bear market is given when:

1. Both averages make double bottoms, or when

2. Both averages "refuse" to make new lows, or when

3. One average makes a new low and the other average "refuses" to make a new low, and subsequently the weaker average confirms the indication of the stronger average by also turning strong, or when

4. Both averages make a line, at either a low level or after a secondary rally, and both break through the line on the up side, or when,

5. One average makes a line and breaks through the upper limits of the line, and the other average confirms the bullish indication by either failing to make a new low or by breaking above the high point of its preceding secondary rally.

The *Final confirmation* of the inauguration of a major bull market is given when:

> Both averages rise above the high points established in the preceding secondary rally.

B. Continuation of bull market

It is a bull market as long as:

1. The recent highs in both averages exceed the previous highs and the recent lows in the secondary declines of both averages have not penetrated the low points of the preceding secondary decline, or

2. Both averages make a line, either at a high level or after a secondary decline, and both averages break through the line on the upside, or

3. One average makes a line and breaks through the line on the upside, and the other average fails to go below the previous low or makes a new high.

C. Reversal from bull to bear market

The *Preliminary indications* of the completion of a major bull market is given when:

1. Both averages make double tops, or when

2. Both averages "refuse" to make new highs, or when

3. One average makes a new high and the other average "refuses" to make a new high, and subsequently the stronger average confirms the indication of the weaker average by also turning weak, or when

4. Both averages make a line, at either a high level or after a secondary reaction, and both break through the line on the downside, or when

5. One average makes a line and breaks through the lower limits of the line, and the other average confirms the bearish indication by either failing to make a new high or by breaking below the low point of the preceding secondary reaction.

The *Final confirmation* of the completion of a major bull market is given when:

Both averages drop below the low points established in their preceding secondary declines.

D. Continuation of bear market

It is a bear market as long as:

1. The recent lows in both averages are below the previous lows and the recent highs in the secondary rallies of both averages have not exceeded the high points of the preceding secondary rally, or

2. Both averages make a line, at either a low level or after a secondary rally, and both averages break the line on the downside, or

3. One average makes a line and breaks through the line on the downside, and the other average fails to go above the previous high or makes a new low.

The property of inertia in the Dow Theory

We see that the Dow Theory relies on human action to continue moving in one direction for an unknown period of time. Once the main tide is flowing in a given direction, it continues to move in that direction to an extent which more often than not provides the opportunity for profits for those willing to ride with the tide. Sooner or later "new forces" change the direction of motion. But, while a tide is moving in a designated direction, the proper thing to do is to swim with it.

Other Dow theories

The foregoing observations represent our understanding of the Dow Theory which was formulated by William P. Hamilton. Inconsistencies appear in the writings of Hamilton, but the points observed here probably portray the principles Hamilton particularly stressed. Later we shall note some of the inconsistencies in Hamilton's writings and we shall take notice of other investigators' views on some of the debatable points. Also we shall observe that other writers have included other tools in their interpretations of the Dow Theory – for example, volume of trading and extent and duration of movements. To Hamilton we owe particularly a debt of gratitude for formulating some of the basic principles about which most Dow theorists agree.

THE RECORD OF THE OLD DOW THEORY

In view of the popularity of the Dow Theory the question arises, *"Just how good is the Dow Theory?"*

Alfred Cowles, 3rd gave the first answer to this question when he published the results of a careful investigation into the efficiency of William P. Hamilton's editorials in the *Wall Street Journal* over the years 1903 to 1929.

"His editorials are adequate in number, 255 in all, they extend over a 26 year period, and are sufficiently definite to allow scoring as bullish, bearish or doubtful. These materials were derived from the files of the *Wall Street Journal* by Dr. Henry B. Kline of the University of Tennessee, in compliance with a request from Robert Rhea, of Colorado Springs, to assemble all editorials that dealt with stock market action. Dr. Kline was selected as a highly intelligent man who knew nothing of Hamilton, speculation, or the Dow Jones averages, to avoid any possible bias in selection."

Mr. Cowles further states:

"Each of Hamilton's 255 editorials has been scored by majority vote of five readers as bullish, bearish, or doubtful. When doubtful it is assumed that he abstained from trading. When bullish it is assumed that he bought equal dollar amounts of the stocks in the Dow Jones railroad and industrial groups, and sold them when he became bearish or doubtful. When bearish it is assumed that he sold short equal dollar amounts of these stocks, and covered only when he became doubtful or bullish. The percentage gain or loss on each such transaction is calculated, and the results accumulated through the 26 years.

"Since the Dow Jones averages have only recently been corrected for the effect of stock rights, stock dividends, and stock splits, it has been necessary to effect such adjustments through all the previous years. This has been done on the basis of tables in *Investment Management* by Dwight C. Rose. After this, the final step is to correct for the effect of brokerage charges, cash dividends, and the interest presumably earned by Hamilton when his funds were not in the market. The fully adjusted figures resulting are then reduced to an average annual figure which is the measure of the efficiency of the Dow method.

"Our final conclusion is that from December 1903 to December 1929, the Dow method as interpreted by Hamilton earned a total return of exactly 12 per cent per annum compounded (industrial average) . . . Hamilton announced buy signals 27 times. In the industrial group 16 of these profitable, 11 unprofitable. He gave sell signals 21 times, 10 were profitable, 11 unprofitable. He gave signals for retirement from the market 38 times, gaining money on 16, losing money on 22. In all, 44 of his forecasts were unsuccessful, 42 successful. The application of his test to the railroad group verifies these conclusions except that of the buying signals 14 were correct, 13 incorrect . . . and an average annual gain of 5.7 per cent compounded was recorded."

Mr. Cowles further points out that in the same period, December 1903 to December 1929, an investor who has made an outright continuous investment in the industrial average would have earned 15.5 per cent per annum compounded as compared with Hamilton's 12 per cent. However, were the results carried through to 1932, Hamilton's results would likely have shown superiority. (Hamilton was short the market when he died in 1929.)

A considerable number of stock market theories are based mostly on wishful thinking

Mr. Cowles concludes:

"Our analysis of the Dow method as interpreted by Hamilton, reveals a distinctly satisfactory record. It is true that in markets where the secular trend for a matter of decades is upward, despite the periodic interruption of major bear markets, Hamilton fails to score gains equal to those made by an outright continuous investment. In declining markets, however, though he registers only negligible profits, he conserves his principal intact, while the long-term investor's funds undergo steady and dismal attrition. In horizontal markets running for years and even decade, Hamilton slightly more than holds his own."

Mr. Cowles' investigation has been quoted at length because it exemplifies the type of research so badly needed in stock market inquiries. A considerable number of stock market theories and methods are based mostly on hearsay and wishful thinking. There has not been nearly enough of the pick-and-shovel work of actually digging in and testing the theories and methods some persons would have us believe.

We are in accord too with Mr. Cowles' conclusion. 12 per cent per annum compounded is a "distinctly satisfactory record." We should remember that Mr. Hamilton's forecasts were *forecasts*, actually published at the time they were being made. They were not *backcasts*, after the market had acted in such-and-such a way. We know of no market advisory service who can prove a record equal to that of Mr. Hamilton's.

Samuel Moment carried on the exacting work of Mr. Cowles (we had the privilege of publishing both of their investigations on the Dow Theory in our research reports several years ago). Mr. Moment accepted the fact that Hamilton showed a satisfactory profit record over a period of years, but he was particularly concerned in knowing whether the average man, perhaps not with a mastery equal to Hamilton's, might do as well. In answering this question, Mr. Moment formulated a set of rules*, and applied these rules strictly to a reading of the averages. In setting up concrete rules, the element of personal judgment in deciding when to buy and sell was automatically eliminated. Consequently, in Mr. Moment's test of the Dow Theory, there is no place for exceptional or poor judgment – the test is purely mechanical and everyone should obtain identical results. His test showed that a $1000 fund invested in the Dow Jones industrial stocks in 1897 would have grown to approximately $29,370 in 1933. This return is equal to about 10 per cent per annum compounded. From 1933 to date of this writing, the fund has continued to grow.

Robert Rhea computed that $100 placed in the Industrial average in June 1897 would have grown to $3602.88 on September 7, 1937, investing on the long side of the market only under the guidance of the Dow Theory. "Under this plan stocks would have been purchased only ten times in forty years." A fund of $100 in the Rails during the same period would have grown to $533.24 (dividends not credited). On both long and short sides, $100 in the Industrial average would have increased to $14,087.89 and the Rail average to $1370.42.

There have been other tests of the Dow Theory, the results of each depending upon the particular methods employed by the person doing the testing. For example, Richard Durant has published a test which shows a $100 fund in 1897 increasing to $5661.47 in 1946, investing in the long side only. His backtest showed 13 long commitments, one of which resulted in loss, two in reinvestments at higher prices than previously sold at, and the remaining gains.

It seems to us that the man accustomed to losing money in Wall Street might well give serious consideration to the Dow Theory. Those who denounce it often find that their own theories do not do nearly as well in actual practice.

Notwithstanding this, we do not believe that the theory of Hamilton, nor of later expounders, gives about all we should expect from market operations. Consequently, while we have accepted most of the *principles* of the theory, we have devoted considerable time in trying to improve on the application of those principles.

Hamilton's editorials had the annoying habit of being wrong about half of the time. Moment's mechanization of the Theory shows a loss for every two gains. It has long occurred to us that there must be ways of cutting down on the number of losses.

---

*These rules are explained later.

THE APPROACH TO
A BETTER DOW THEORY

We have learned that Hamilton's Dow Theory emphasizes these factors:

1. Prices.
2. Double Tops and Double Bottoms.
3. Lines or Trading Areas.
4. Resistance Levels.
5. Confirmation.

Later theorists have added other tools to Hamilton's preferred list, particularly:

1. Volume of Trading.
2. Amplitude of Movements.
3. Duration of Movements.

Our purpose here is to point out some of the stimulating thought on the use of each of these factors. In doing this we will gain a broad idea of some of the problems before us in using Dow Theory principles. In this Review we will not be particularly concerned with "solving" anything; rather we shall merely try to gain a sweeping view of some of the landscape before us.

PRICES

The averages discount all things?

Hamilton was usually consistent in maintaining:

> "The average price of average stocks is a result of all influences. We prefer to ignore the volume of general business, the state of trade, the condition of crops, the political outlook. The averages discount all these things. It is the impartial summing up of every possible market influence." (Hamilton excluded "events beyond human foresight" – such as earthquakes.)

Yet, Hamilton wavered occasionally in his faith in the basic premise of the Dow Theory. For instance, he once wrote:

> "This analysis is based solely on the movements of prices and does not profess to take account of general conditions. . . . The averages are not to be regarded by themselves as conclusively presaging future markets. They are only one of many indices of the financial position and should not be overweighted."

However, since Hamilton usually maintained that "the averages are to be regarded by themselves as conclusively presaging future markets" we are obliged to ignore his occasional expressions of doubt in his own teachings.

It will be noted that Hamilton placed his primary emphasis on the barometric nature of the *averages*; he neglected to see, or at least to emphasize, that *individual stocks* often do not conform with the movements of the averages.

In 1936, when the Dow Theory was enjoying a peak of popularity, Homer Fahrner came out with an analysis of "cycles in individual stocks." He stated:

> "It takes money to buy the Industrial average. It is a feat which only the very wealthy or the investment institution can well afford, and that person or institution *should most certainly not care to buy the Industrial average* even though they can afford the undertaking. . . . A study of the table will reveal many conflicting trends. . . . Each security has its individual cycle and this cycle may be contrary to general trends as often as it conforms with the market as a whole."

In recent years the divergence in trends among individual stock issues and groups of issues have become even more conspicuous. That is why Franklin Paul Jackson* stresses the importance of individual and group price-charts in his studies. He warns:

> *"They don't move together.* So much has been written about the Dow Theory in recent years that there is some excuse for the thought that stocks all move together and that if one can interpret 'the Averages' he need not bother about trying to select the right stock. It is true that there are many periods of time in which nearly all stocks appear to join together in a broad upswing or downswing. But, particularly in the upswings, the movements of the Average does not truly reflect the movements and the *timing* of the individual issues. . . . Possibly half the time the market is engaged in consolidation or horizontal movements . . . and it has been observed that many individual stocks will for a time often pursue a trend not conforming to that of the majority."

All of which brings us back to the preceding Review in which we state "each market forecasts its own movements," and to which we might now add

---

*Editor's footnote: In the 1930s, the 1940s, and the 1950s Mr. Jackson established himself as one of the best market minds on the West Coast and his several works on stock and commodity markets, long out of print now, are among the finest of writings generally unknown today. The author of the two combined books published here lived in San Francisco during the same period and the two got together many, many times holding what certainly was memorable discussions about the intricacies of market price action (we can only wish that we were party to these same discussions). See Introduction for more details on the Dunnigan/Jackson collaborations.

"each stock forecasts its own movements." (Parenthetically it can be noted here that we have prepared and published a list of "Fast-Moving Stocks" which have usually conformed well with the Averages. Quite possibly this list will serve the trader more profitably if he will analyze *individually* the movements of each of several of those stocks rather than to select one or a few stocks blindly from the list.)

High, low or closing prices?

At any rate, all market technician agree that price movements possess barometric significance The question is what prices should we give particular attention to – high, low or closing prices? Daily, weekly or monthly? Most studies use daily prices, although there is some growing evidence that we might be able to lighten the load and deal with weekly data. As for high, low or closing prices, the weight of authoritative evidence seems to favor closing prices:

> "It is well not to attach too much importance to fractional crossing of an apparent resistance level during a single day or two. . . . It is usually best to base conclusions on the daily closing prices rather than on daily 'highs' and 'lows'."
> – Lewis H. Haney

> "Recording the closing price is important because it is often a clue to manipulation. It must be remembered that the closing price is the only price that is considered by many speculators who watch the market only through the closing prices in the daily newspapers." – Owen Taylor

> "The closing point is more important than the extreme point in calculating resistance levels and forecasting trends." – W. F. Hickernell

> "In attempting more accurately to forecast the movement of a stock it has been found that the closing price is an index of value."– Leland Ross

> "The closing price is important. It represents the final evaluation of the stock made by the market during the day. – Robert Edwards and John Magee, Jr.

VOLUME OF TRADING

Market analysts today ordinarily attach considerable importance to the volume of trading. For instance, Dr. N.J. Silberling wrote:

> "It is well to emphasize that correct interpretations of changes in volume of turnover are probably more important than price changes and should not be ignored. . . . The technical position of the market (i.e., whether stocks are in strong

hands or weak hands) is capable of tolerably accurate appraisal if the volume of trading and the price movements are correlated in the proper fashion."

But, Hamilton was far from consistent in his views on the significance of volume of trading:

"It would perhaps be occasion for suspicion rather than congratulations were we to find entire consistency in writings extending over almost three decades. A notably inconsistent element in Hamilton's system is his treatment of volume. In its purest orthodoxy the Dow Theory holds that whatever significance volume of trading may have, is comprehended, as is everything else from production to politics, in the averages themselves. But Hamilton permits himself frequent hearsies. Activity on the declines, dullness on the rallies, he says is a bearish fact. Strength on volume is bullish. In a bear swing the rallies are dull, the reactions active. . . ." – Alfred Cowles, 3rd

"62 out of 252 of Hamilton's editorials discuss volume in some connection. 16 of the 62, or 26%, tie volume closely to the reasoning behind the forecast. 29, or 47%, specifically state that volume is excluded, having already been discounted by the averages. Finally, out of 94 editorials that mention the line, only five connect volume to the line. 89, or 94%, ignore volume relative to the line."
– Samuel Moment

DURATION OF MOVEMENTS

"It is recognized as fundamental that TIME is essential in all economic changes. TIME may be but a concept in the mind of the philosopher, but with ruled lines on paper the statistician can give form to this concept, can map its passing, and give it a mathematical value in the equation of Change and Time. Thus, like other mathematical equations a given rate of price or value change in a given period of time will have its individual pattern." – Franklin Paul Jackson

"The price formations from which extensive new trends proceed take *time* to build. One does not bring instantly to a stop a heavy car moving at seventy miles per hour all within the same split second, turn it around and get it moving back down the road in the opposite direction at seventy miles per hour. Speaking in broad generalities, the greater the reversal area – the wider the price fluctuations within it, the longer it takes to build, the more shares transferred during its construction, the more important its implications. Thus, roughly speaking, a big reversal pattern suggests a big move to follow and a small pattern a small move." – Robert D. Edwards and John Magee, Jr

"While we can calculate that the average of business cycles is some forty months, individual cycles vary from 18 to 60 months." – Alfred Cowles, 3rd

"The bull markets from 1897 have varied in duration from approximately 15 to approximately 73 months. The median, or central case, was 26 months,. . . . The bear markets from 1899 to 1932 have varied in duration from approximately 11 to 34 months. The median was 15 months."– Harold Gartley

"Because 9 primary bear markets averaged 552 days' duration for the Industrial composition, I hope no one will go long in the next bear market on the 553rd day without recalling that one bear market was 1039 days long." – Robert Rhea

"Intermediate movements are minor ups or downs of uncertain duration, but frequently occupying from one to six months. During a cyclical upswing such movements are thought of as reactions in a bull market; during a bear market they are called rallies." – Lewis H. Haney

"The Time Factor is the most important. Keep a record of the days that the market reacts, that is, actual trading days. When a reversal comes that exceeds the previous Time movement, consider that the trend has changed, at least temporarily. . . . Your rule is to watch for an overbalancing of a previous Time period before deciding that the trend has changed. The 'overbalancing' of Time is the most important indication of a change in trend." – W. D. Gann

"The market as a whole, almost never moves up for more than five days without a reaction. Except toward the end of a bear market it seldom declines more than five days without a rally." – Charles Ringwalt

"The market rarely proceeds in one direction more than five consecutive days without encountering some degree of reaction, however trifling." – Glen Munn

"A stock which shows strong up trend will never close 3 consecutive days with losses. . . ." – W. D. Gann

"A good rule for setting stop levels is to consider that a bottom has been made when the stock has moved 'three days away' from the day marking the suspected low. If a stock reacts for some days and finally makes a low at 24, with the high for the day at 25, then we will have not have an established bottom until we have had three days in which the stocks sells at no lower than 25⅛. The entire range for three full days must be entirely above the top price for the day marking the low." – Robert D. Edwards and John Magee, Jr

AMPLITUDE OF MOVEMENTS

From the researches of Robert Rhea, Harold Gartley and Charles Collins we have gathered that bull markets show an average rise of about 87 per cent measured from the start of the rise, while the bear movements show an average decline of about 37 per cent measured from the peak of the decline. But, bull markets have accounted for advances ranging from 26 to 339 per cent, and bear markets have accounted for declines ranging from 15 to 89 per cent. These wide variations give the investor no assurance that any given bull or bear movement will terminate after it has progressed "some certain distance."

"Usually, after a reaction in the industrial averages has run to between 40 and 50 per cent in the severe major declines that follow great inflation (or between 15 to 25 per cent in the less violent cycles), a smart recovery occurs, which regains from 30 to 50 per cent of the ground lost. About 15 per cent is usually recovered in the first month. . . . There then follows, in most cases, a period of several months – often four or five – in which a relatively dull and irregular market swings narrowly in a virtually sidewise direction. This period often terminates in a "secondary" reaction running from 10 to 20 per cent. The sidewise period, however, may last for a year or more, as in 1893–1894, 1910–1911, and 1923–1924. . . . When the market has been severely tested by a secondary decline a few months after a prolonged major recession, and new lows fail to develop, one can be fairly sure that the next broad swing will be upward." – Lewis H. Haney

"Bear markets bear no particular relationship to the preceding bull period so far as per cent of retracement is concerned. One period retraced only 41.79 per cent of the preceding advance, while four others ran to more than 100 per cent, and two of them retraced more than 180 per cent. The average was 98.17. It is interesting to notice how the average figure seems to reflect that over a long period of time, the price movement, as is true of other things, obeys the law that action and reaction must be equal." – Robert Rhea

" . . . recording the experience of more than 49 years, the above chart, in a way, represents a mortality table of the probable size of the primary upswings which may be expected in any bull market. Although certainty necessarily is lacking as to the height which any particular bull market leg will attain, the evidence presented in this chart does seem to justify the conclusion that whenever either average has moved by more than 30 points without encountering a secondary reaction, an increasingly alert attitude is warranted. . . . For those who attempt to to trade on secondary movements, one other deduction seems justified – that is, when uncorrected 30-point rallies have occurred, one should, as prices work upward, keep revising his plans to protect commitments on any indication of impending weakness or reversal." – Perry Greiner

"The intermediate swings may be very violent at times, but rarely exceed 20 per cent in the averages, and usually not 10 per cent. They are apt to be numerous and sharp when the peak of a cyclical swing is nearly reached. . . . Monthly averages of the market often show but faint traces of them." – Lewis Haney

"When there is a downward correction, it is likely to come down to or near the top of the last previous Minor high. . . . If the move is upward, the reaction after each advance tends to stop at the level of the preceding peak. If the move is downward, the rally after each decline tends to stop at the level of the preceding bottom. – Robert D. Edwards and John Magee, Jr

RESISTANCE LEVELS AND DOUBLE TOPS AND BOTTOMS

"Resistance levels are the price levels at which stockmarket movements, whether up or down, meet resistance. . . . So-called double tops and double bottoms should be considered as being merely indications of upper or lower resistance levels. They mark the price levels at which either selling or buying becomes the predominate factor. . . . Although the importance attached to the matter may be exaggerated, there can be no question that logical conclusions are to be drawn. The decisive breaking of upper resistance levels is a good indication of a further rise, and vice versa. . . . When market reactions are checked at levels above the low points of preceding reactions and successive peaks are higher, one may conclude that the effective resistance levels are rising and the broad underlying trend is upward. When the opposite is true, the broad trend is downward." – Lewis H. Haney

"In his later editorials, Hamilton referred increasingly to double tops. A double top is formed when a high point is reached by both averages, a reaction of some 4 to 8 per cent follows, and prices from 3 to 15 weeks later rise again to, or near, the previous high, but fail to break through it. The implication is bearish. Double bottoms are similar actions inverted. On the strength of this characteristic of the double top, Hamilton in his later years made forecasts. Even when he did not admit it to be a conclusive danger signal, he spoke of it as an occasion for caution. Double tops do not occupy nearly so much space in Hamilton's system as the line, but in the latest years they increase in prominence. It must be taken as part of his system that double tops give a definitely bearish, double bottoms a definitely bullish, inference." – Alfred Cowles, 3rd

Double tops and double bottoms should be considered as indications of upper or lower resistance levels

"Congestion levels, where stocks have remained for periods of time, usually resist the move when the stock again approaches them. During the bear market, there were numerous of these congestion levels which acted as temporary stopping places in the downward decline. These become resistance to the advance when the trend is reversed. However . . . resistance levels lose their power of resistance in proportion to the time which separates them." – H. B. Neill

"When the market fails to move for a week or more, marking time in a narrow range, this trading zone may be called a 'congestion area.' A congestion area in a bull market represents accumulation of stock by bull interests. Experienced traders have observed that, after prices rise above this area, the next reaction is likely to stop at or slightly above this congestion area . . . if economic conditions are at all favorable. . . . The influence of a congestion area . . . is short lived. It offers resistance to the first reaction, but not to the second or third." – W. F. Hickernell.

"After a bull market advance has continued for a number of months and prices have risen appreciably, it is essential to realize that each succeeding topside penetration of an earlier peak may be the last one in the series, and that the signal extension of the upswing need not continue very far before an important reaction sets in. In other words, the amount of bullish authority to which any signal is entitled varies in almost direct proportion to the duration and extent of the uncorrected advance which preceded it. The principle here involved has to do with 'the diminishing validity of forecasts' in a succession of similar and repeated signals." – Perry Greiner.

"Here is an interesting and important fact which, curiously enough, many casual chart observers appear never to grasp: these critical price levels constantly switch their roles from support to resistance, and from resistance to support. A former top, once it has been surpassed, becomes a bottom zone in a subsequent down trend, and an old bottom, once it has been penetrated, becomes a top zone in a later advancing phase." – Robert D. Edwards and John Magee, Jr.

WIDTH AND DURATION OF TRADING AREAS

"The market, or individual stocks, seldom advance or decline without first forming accumulation or distributional areas. This usually consists of a trading range in a relatively restricted price area. If it is accumulation, the area is called a base. If it is distribution, the area is called a top. Technically, the length of time and width of these base or top areas gives a fairly accurate idea of how high or how low the stock may move if the trading range is broken. Thus, the stock has an upside objective or a downside objective." – Edmund Tabell.

"Hamilton does not use percentages to indicate width. Nevertheless, his editorials show a tendency to recognize that width of line depends on the price level. However, many contradictions argue against using any one width as included in Hamilton's definition of a line. . . . Hamilton refers to the length of lines as 'a sufficient number of days for a fair volume of trading,' 'a long series of fluctuations,' 'a fluctuation for a measurable period.' Hamilton has used 9 days as the length of a line and on one occasion regarded 23 days of narrow fluctuation as not involving a line. The conclusion, of course, must be that since the line plays so important a part in forecasting movements, this phase cannot be accepted as satisfactorily defined by Hamilton." – Samuel Moment.

"Hamilton wrote: 'In all the applications of Dow's theory the best is the line of accumulation or distribution. A line means length with very little breadth. The period should be long enough to afford a real test, say a month or more, and fluctuations should be confined to a range of at the most four points.' Definition is made clearer by examination of all Hamilton's lines. What is the smallest possible period, and the longest possible fluctuation, he allows for a line? Nine trading days are too short, 22 trading days are sufficient. Hamilton's use of points instead of percentages is naive and confusing when averages range from 40 to 380. The largest fluctuation allowed is 6 per cent, with one glaring and inexplicable exception of 12 per cent. The normal is about three per cent. A line, then, exists when both averages for 22 or more trading days fluctuate within a range of about 3, and at the most 6, per cent. It represents accumulation or distribution of stocks. When both averages break out of this line in the same direction, the course of stock prices will for some time be in that direction. The formation of a line indicates doubt. Emergence from a line indicates direction." – Alfred Cowles, 3rd

"A trading area offers one type of market situation in which the trader may have his decision made for him with a minimum of risk. Since a trading area is an interruption of the trend, the market will show by its own action, what the direction will be when the trading market has terminated. Just as soon as the averages break out of their trading range in one direction or the other, the action can be followed almost blindly. Almost invariably, it is a signal for a continuation of that directional change.

"Referring solely to the movement of the averages, a trading area on a high plateau in a bull market almost invariably is an interlude to what later proves to be a resumption of the rise, else the energy required to hold prices within the area would not have been expended. The technical rule is that the line of least resistance is motion, and stocks having risen to a temporary apex, would be more apt to round off and with little hesitation to start downward. Similarly, a trading area at the bottom of a sharp decline is a breathing space to take account of fundamentals. If the decline has gone too far, recovery, if there is to be one, will lose no time in asserting itself. Consequently, a trading area following a declining movement is usually the precursor of a resumption of the fall." – Glen G. Munn

"It is interesting to note that the longer accumulation continues in a stock the longer the upward movement is likely to be in order that the complete line of stock acquired may be sold." – Leland S. Ross

"Stocks usually form a line at the bottom of a bear market. In bear markets from 1897 to 1921, the duration of the line at the bottom was from 8 weeks to 23 weeks . . . 12½ weeks average." – Kenneth Van Strum

"During the final six months of each bear market there was an interval of from two to four months when price fluctuations were within 5% of a mean price." – Robert Rhea

CONFIRMATION

"There is sense in this sort of reasoning . . . it seems that the logic of the confirming process lies in part merely in the action of two different groups, and in part in the semi-investment character of the rails. Like bonds, rail stocks are more directly influenced by interest rates and other investment considerations. Their moves are apt to be more sustained than those of industrials, and a rally in the more speculative industrials which does not extend to the rails is not likely to be sustained." – Lewis H. Haney

"It is not required that both Industrials and Rails penetrate on the same day, nor in the same week or month. . . . It is not until the lagging average has confirmed the earlier signals of its companion indicator that a change of primary trend can be definitely said to have occurred." – Robert Rhea

"The most memorable instance of long-delayed confirmation occurred in the 1932–1937 bull market when, between October 1933 and September 1936, actual technical confirmation on the part of the rail index was postponed nearly three years, much to the annoyance of those who expect exact mathematical precision from the averages." – Perry Greiner

"The fluctuations of the Dow-Jones industrial average follows very closely those of the highest-priced stocks, indicating that it really depicts the behavior of the expensive 'blue chips' rather than of the general market. . . . Railroad stocks have lost much of their former, and once almost exclusive, importance. At recent bull market highs, the market value of chemical shares listed on the New York Stock Exchange exceeded the value of the listed railroad shares by more than 50%; listed oil shares had a total value almost 50% larger than listed rail stocks whose value exceeded listed automobiles by a trifling margin." – N. Molodovsky

"The requirement of confirmation by the rails is not necessary. Hamilton never justified the requirement on grounds other than it worked. The claim seems equally valid that the method without confirmation works just as well." – Samuel Moment

"One of Dow's prime canons is that the averages must confirm each other before conclusive inferences can be drawn. The action of one average breaking out of a line or making a fresh high is, according to Hamilton's mood, 'sometimes misleading,' 'frequently misleading,' 'constantly misleading'. . . . Whether confirmation need, or need not, be simultaneous, Hamilton uses the expressions 'about the same time,' 'simultaneously,' 'practically simultaneously,' 'a simultaneous movement would be necessary,' 'unless made simultaneously more apt to be deceptive than not,' 'not necessarily in the same day, or even in the same week, provided only that they confirm,' 'a low or high point in the same day or even week is merely a coincidence when it happens to occur,' 'by no means involves simultaneous action.' Hamilton invariably demands confirmation. He evidently craves, but frequently waives, simultaneity." – Alfred Cowles, 3rd

CONCLUSION

The purpose of this Review has been primarily to point out that there are alluring fields in technical analysis which were not approached by Hamilton's Dow Theory. Hamilton blazed a trail and left a trend of thought. But, he did not leave a one-two-three explanation which would serve all of us uniformly. Others have tried to make Hamilton's trail a smoother road.

Hamilton's record is proof that the broad principles of the Dow Theory are fundamentally sound

We shall often see offshoots of Hamilton's ideas interwoven in the methods discussed in these Reviews. We shall try to weed out some of his inconsistencies; we shall try to be more specific in our definitions. We shall try to improve on the application of some of the principles of his theory so that we may buy lower and sell higher than is possible with the orthodox Dow Theory. Notwithstanding Hamilton's lapses in the details of his theory, his record is proof that most of the broad principles of the Dow Theory are fundamentally sound. We might well give more attention to these principles.

SAMUEL MOMENT'S TESTED IMPROVEMENT OF THE DOW THEORY

59-YEAR PROFITABLE RECORD WITH 23 YEARS ACTUAL TEST

On June 29, 1951, the Dow-Jones industrial average plunged, for a day, through a supposed barrier to close on that day at 242.64, and as a result many Dow theorists announced that a bear market signal had been given. Other Dow theorists refused to concede to that belief, and held that the situation was still bullish, or at least indefinite.

That occasion was not unique in Dow theory history; the theorists have often squabbled among themselves. With various schools divided so that bullish forecasts are, at times, coming from some camps, and bearish forecasts from others, the average man who seeks understanding is quite willing to consider a non-opinionative interpretation of the averages.

In 1933 Samuel Moment gave just that. He formulated a set of rules and applied those rules to a strict reading of the averages. Under his procedure the errors of human judgment, fancies, and emotions, are outlawed; no two persons should obtain radically different results at any given time. His rules have stood up well in practice; since 1933 they have done a consistently better job than the orthodox Dow theorists. These simple rules are repeated herein. First, though, let us review briefly some history of the method.

On May 12, 1933, we published a paper, *The Dow Theory: A Test of its Value and a Suggested Improvement*, by Samuel Moment. At that time Moment was doing graduate work at Stanford University where he received a PhD degree in economics. The study on the Dow Theory was not part of Moment's work for a doctor's degree, but was completed, under our sponsorship, as an outside, "extra-curricular activity."

APPRAISAL

It is likely that Samuel Moment's improvement on the Dow Theory will continue to show a profitable record over the next 5, 10 or 50 years. It is only "natural" that it should work in the long run – if we continue to have a stock market in which supply and demand are not greatly hampered by regulations.

This barometer, published first in 1933, has stood up well under "the test of time." Investors may well give consideration to its major bull and bear market signals.

We anticipated that the paper would not be received enthusiastically by orthodox Dow theorists. In the first place, it infringed on human vanity when it eliminated the individual's right to argue whether an interpretation should be bullish or bearish; and, in the second place, it set fire to a central idea of the Dow Theory – namely, that confirmation of the industrial and rail averages is necessary. We stated in our Foreword to Moment's study:

> "In Mr. Moment's test of the Dow Theory, there is no place for either exceptional or poor judgment – the test is purely mechanical; anyone should attain almost identical results. Moreover, Moment's 'Modified Dow Theory' seems to explode the central idea of the Dow Theory – namely, that confirmation of the averages is necessary. Apparently, it is not at all necessary; and, in fact, from a standpoint of potential maximum profit, undesirable. We feel that Mr. Moment's study is a contribution to financial literature, and we are pleased to present it to you at this time." – *Dunnigan's Forecast Reports May 12, 1933.*

Moment expressed his views on "rules" and "confirmation" in these words:

> "The rules are adaptations to recurrent peculiarities of the stock market, and, for the present, represent effective conclusions. . . . No claim is made that Hamilton would have applied these rules. What is claimed is that this test covers the minimum points that students should agree are included in the theory when it is applied to forecasting the major trends. Beyond these points, there is room for disagreement over what additional rules should be followed. . . . Anyone duplicating the test of these rules should arrive at the same results, or very similar results, if we allow for a possibly different treatment of one transaction. . . . In addition to a test of the Dow Theory, this study offers a modified theory based on forecasts of the industrial average without the requirement that the railroad average confirm the industrial. . . . The use of the industrials alone should continue to be profitable. The requirement of confirmation by the rails is not necessary. Hamilton never justified the requirement on grounds other than it worked. The claim seems equally valid that the method without confirmation works just as well."

Moment's study received a favorable reception by some market students. For instance, H. M. Gartley reprinted the study and said:

> "Only one important critic has assailed the principle of confirmation. He is Samuel Moment."

But, as we anticipated, the study brought forth a bombardment of adverse criticism. One well-known Dow theorist, for example, voiced his disapproval under the headlines, "WHY BREED A MONGREL?," this writer's contention being that the pure-bred gospel-truth of Hamilton's teachings should not be tampered with. Moment answered his critics patiently and wisely.

As the instigator of the controversial publication, it gives us today a contented feeling to know that Father Time, over the past 23 years, has given his approval to Moment's "suggested improvement."

23 years may be too short a period from which to draw an everlasting conclusion, but we are inclined to feel that the "suggested improvement" can now be rated as a "tested improvement."

In the 1948 edition of his book Garfield Drew rates Moment's method highly, Mr. Drew writes:

> "For dealing with the major trends Moment's rules have been consistently successful for fifty years. The best-known exponents of the Dow Theory have never approved of reducing it to such a formula, but the rules do have the virtue of eliminating the indecision or difference of opinion which so often mark the orthodox interpretation of the Theory. Moreover, the results covering all types of markets do seem to demonstrate conclusively that over a period of time, profits will be greater than under the accepted principles of Dow theory interpretation. . . . In the class of methods determining and acting upon the major trend, they deserve a high rating, despite the fact that they lack publicity."

Mr. Drew's views in 1948 coincides very well with our views today. During the test period, 1897–1932, Moment built up a theoretical fund of $100,000 to $3,679,800. According to Mr. Drew's calculations, this fund had grown to $7,617,700 at prices near the low of October, 1946. The fund will exceed the latter figure when the next sell signal comes.

Moment's original paper, now out of print, gave considerable detail including a tabulation showing every forecast by the method from 1897 through 1932. We need not repeat the paper here, but shall simply quote some paragraphs which give the essential ingredients of the method.

For dealing with the major trends Moment's rules have been consistently successful for fifty years

In 1933 Moment wrote:

> "A secondary reaction is a movement in a bull or bear market that retraces 33D% or more of the primary price change since the end of the last preceding secondary reaction. When the low or high point of the last secondary reaction is penetrated by the following amounts, the signal is to reverse one's position: cover and go long if short; sell and sell short if long–

1 point if the average is under 100.
1% if the average is between 100 and 150.
1.5% if the average is between 151 and 200.
2% if the average is over 201.

"These points are selected because they work best. They avoid most misleading signals when a secondary point is slightly penetrated. Such slight penetrations are apt to be greater as the average moves higher. This is allowed for by the gradual increase in the percentage required before a definite signal is given. Hamilton gave no precise measure of penetration and was occasionally misled by a slight penetration that was never continued.

"It must be noted that when a movement approaches the last secondary movement, penetrates it by less than the required amount, and then hesitates for a few days, the point to be penetrated before a new signal is given is not the old point of the secondary movement, but the very last point which partly penetrated the secondary movement. This is conservative recognition that the very hesitation of the average around the last secondary movement should require a decisive signal, and that is given when the farthest point is penetrated.

"A signal remains in force until reversed.

"The results are highly satisfactory viewed from a speculative and investment angle. Profit is made during both depression and prosperity at a rate far above the standard of normal. . . . Unless profound changes occur in security markets and our economic system to narrow the amplitudes of the business cycle and the cycles of stock prices, the method should continue to work in the future."

Current data

For practical purposes in today's market, the investor interested in Moment's method can simplify matters by watching the signals by *Rule #2* in the section which follows, "A New Dow Barometer." Rule #2 will not give results identical to Moment's method in all cases, but we are inclined to believe that Moment's procedure is somewhat improved in the New Dow Barometer.

A NEW DOW BAROMETER

The "New Dow Barometer" has worked out profitably since first published in 1951.
   This barometer is based on three principles derived from the Dow Theory:

1. William Hamilton occasionally mentioned Double Tops and Double Bottoms as having forecasting implications. Apparently, Hamilton never used a Double Top or Double Bottom as the sole criterion for a signal; nevertheless the double top and bottom formations often give valuable indications in individual stocks and commodities as well as in the "averages."

2. Robert Rhea, and others, stressed the necessity for a former top, or bottom, to be tested, but not exceeded, before a valid signal is given. Mr. Rhea wrote:

> "If, after a severe secondary reaction in a primary bull market, *the ensuing rallies fail to go to new highs* within a reasonable time and a further drastic decline occurs extending below the low points of the previous reaction, it is generally safe to assume the primary trend has changed from bullish to bearish. Conversely, when, after a decline has carried both averages to new low ground in a bear market, an important secondary reaction has taken place and *the next decline fails to carry either average to a new low*, one may infer that the primary trend has changed from bear to bull if the next rally carries both averages above the high points of the last important rally."

APPRAISAL

The Dow theorists are often divided – some believing that price action indicates a bear market and others maintaining that the same action denotes a major bull market.

   If one will turn to Moment's "Tested Improvement of the Dow Theory," or to the present paper, "New Dow Barometer," he will find no place for arguments. The rules are definite, precise. Right or wrong, everyone arrives at the same answers. These "answers" would have provided large net gains in past years, measured by the Dow-Jones industrial average.

   The New Dow Barometer includes a modification of Moment's method and it also provides a means of buying lower and selling higher than is possible by either Moment's method or the orthodox Dow Theory. Checked back to 1921, the New Dow Barometer merits your consideration. The principles underlying this Barometer are applicable to individual stocks.

The words "fails to go to new highs . . . or lows" again implies the double top and bottom formations*, but particularly from this we gain the idea of the importance of *Descending Tops* and *Ascending Bottoms*. The market approaches a preceding top, or bottom, but fails to reach it, thereby resulting in a Descending Top, or Ascending Bottom.

3. The most important and deciding requirement of the Dow Theory, in changing from a bull to a bear position, is the penetration downward of the last secondary low point. And, in changing from a bear to bull position, the deciding factor is the penetration upward of the last secondary high point.

> *In changing from a bear to bull position, the deciding factor is the penetration upward of the last secondary high point*

We use the three foregoing principles in this new barometer. Especially, in this attempt to improve on the Dow Theory, we are interested in the first two principles, although we use the third principle when the first two fail to work. We desire, whenever possible, to sell shortly after an important Double Top or Descending Top, and to buy shortly after an important Double Bottom or Ascending Bottom. When we are successful in doing this, we will buy and sell earlier, and at better prices, than the Dow Theory. When we are unsuccessful, we can still resort to the third principle and be as well off as the Dow theorist.

In accord with Samuel Moment's findings we discard the notion that confirmation of the rail and industrial averages is necessary. The underlying principles of the method are applicable to individual stocks and commodities. If one is to derive a "universal formula" applicable to all, or nearly all, stocks, he should make his calculations on a square root basis, not a percentage basis as is done herein.

We have applied the method to the Dow-Jones industrial average back to 1921. Inspection of charts for years prior indicates that the method will also work well if carried back to the inception of the industrial average in 1897. The record permits comparison of results obtained through use of the conventional method (Rule 2) and the New Dow Barometer (Rule 1 and 2) . . . trading in both the long and short sides of the market. The evidence favors the New Dow

---

*In our adaptation (see Rules) we consider it a Double Top even if the market rises as much as 1G% *above* a former Top. And, we consider it a Double Bottom even though the market declines *below* a former Bottom by $1\frac{1}{2}$% or less. In other words, we have found that better results are obtained by disregarding Mr. Rhea's requirement that the averages *fails to go into new high – or new low – grounds*.

Barometer by a large margin. Profitable long positions are usually held longer than six months – a tax advantage.

The signals are based on closing prices. A trade would be made on the morning following the day of the signal. Actual executions would usually be made at slightly poorer prices than the signal prices used in this study. The assumption has been made that a trade would be held until a reversal signal is given. In other words, no stops have been used to limit losses or protect profits. In actual practice, trading in specific stocks, the trader should use some "Operating Plan" other than dependence solely upon reversal signals.

NEW DOW BAROMETER

A *downswing* is a decline of 4% or more. The low price in a Downswing is a *bottom*. An *upswing* is a rally of 4% or more. The high price in an Upswing is a *top*. (Using closing prices, we chart each movement amounting to 4% or more.)

How to buy

Rule 1: *If the current low price in a Downswing is within the range "2½% above to 1½% below" either of the last two Bottoms, buy on a 5% rise above said low price.*

The principle here is buying on a rally after the market has tested a former Bottom. We consider it a "test" if current prices decline to a point where they are 2½% or less above either of the two preceding Bottoms. Also, we consider a test if the current decline stops at a point 1½% or less below either of the two preceding Bottoms. If such a test has been made, and prices then rally 5% above their low price (using closing prices), we are then willing to buy.

or

Rule 2: *If the above rule does not give a buy signal, buy if closing prices rise 2% above the last Top.*

How to sell

Rule 1: *If the current high price in an Upswing is within the range "2½% below to 1½% above" either of the last two Tops, sell on a 5% decline below said high price.*

The principle here is selling on a decline after the market has tested a former Top. We consider it a "test" if current prices rally to a point where they are 2½% or less *below* either of the two preceding Tops. Also, it is a test if the current rally stops at a point 1½% or less *above* either of the two preceding Tops. If such a test has been made, and prices then decline 5% below their high price, we are willing to sell.

or

Rule 2: *If the above rule does not give a sell signal, sell if closing prices decline 2% below the last Bottom.*

That is all there is to the New Dow Barometer – simple but much more effective than orthodox, controversial Dow theorists.

TREND TRADING WITH SQUARE ROOT METHODS

It would be a pleasant situation if the technician could place all stocks on a common-denominator basis – to possess a single formula which would apply to all stocks regardless of price level or relative price activity. For purposes of many studies, the Square Root Theory offers the best tool, so far devised, for approximating a common denominator, or single formula, for stocks in respect to their price levels and movements. (Other means must be employed to equalize their volume activities.)

For instance, if we are to find the individual stocks which are relatively weak and strong, it appears appropriate that the comparisons be made on a square-root basis rather than on a percentage scale as is done in most studies. Another example of the appropriate use of the Square Root Theory is in setting up "significant movements" for point-and-figure charts or swing charts in individual stocks. If we assume that it is suitable to show $2 swings for a $50 stock, then what price swings shall we show for a stock selling at $25, $10, $1, or $100? If experience should show that a $2 scalping profit is ample in a stock selling at $50, then what is corresponding "ample profit" during the same movement in a stock selling at $25, $10, $1, or $100?

> *The Square Root Theory offers the best single formula in respect to price levels and movements*

APPRAISAL

In turning from the general market, or "averages," to individual stocks, the "square-root approach" is to be recommended.

Here we can begin to get all stocks on a "common-denominator basis," with the result that, among other things, we may discover a "universal formula" applicable to many stocks regardless of their individual price levels.

Acknowledgment is made to Mr. Homer Fahrner for his assistance on the square-root theory and other matters pertaining to this study. Mr. Fahrner has been of considerable help in offering me criticism, suggestions, etc., in a number of my studies. (Of course, I alone am responsible for the "rules" of my methods and for their performance in actual tests.)

The "proper" distance to place stop orders is another problem which may well require a square-root solution, since stops should not be set at a fixed arithmetic or percentage figure regardless of price level. Also, in the construction of a market average, the use of the square-root method seems appropriate as it tends to give proper importance to the movements of both the high and low priced stocks which may be used in the average.

There is nothing basically complicated about square roots. Many of us have forgotten how to extract the square root of a number, but convenient tables and charts are available for those who may be inclined to deal with square roots without reviewing their grammar-school arithmetic. The square root of a given number is simply a number which when multiplied by itself equals the given number. Thus, the square root of 4 is 2 because 2 times 2 equals 4. The square root of 49 is 7 because 7 times 7 equals 49. What this has to do with the stock market can be introduced by quoting from a column written several years ago:

John D. Van Becker, *San Francisco Call-Bulletin*, September 26, 1932.

> "The chartist has his troubles. If he uses the arithmetic scale to plot price changes he finds that he has to give the same space on his chart for a rise from 1 to 2 as from 100 to 101. Yet the former is an increase of 100 per cent and the latter only 1 per cent. At extremely high prices the whole side of a wall might be necessary to show the stock movement. The arithmetic scale gave a great deal of room to stocks in 1929, while now (Sept. 32) it devotes very little space to stocks at low points, although price movements from a percentage standpoint, might now be greater.
>
> "So, some of the chartists have turned to the logarithmic or 'log' scale in which market fluctuations are shown in percentages. In this scale, if the stock moves from 2 to 4, or from 40 to 80, (in each case 100%), the line for each would occupy the same space. Consequently, the upper part of the log scale is very crampled and prices are not given their proportionate due. On the other hand, the log scale lays great emphasis on stocks selling at the lower levels.
>
> "A compromise scale has been worked out. Frederick R. Macaulay several years ago observed that stocks tend to fluctuate in equal increments on their square roots. Macaulay said that when plotted on square root paper, the fluctuations of all stocks for any particular period tend to be equal. In other words, if one stock selling at 49 moves to 64 (the difference of their square roots being 1) another stock selling at 4 should move to 9 (the difference of their square roots also is 1)."

So, apparently Dr. Macaulay originated the proposition that the square roots of prices have something to do with the relative movements of stocks at various price levels (his original statement appeared in the *Annalist*, March 13, 1931). Homer Fahrner expanded on Macaulay's theorem by producing some square root chart paper and by experimenting with specific methods in using the theory. We did some publishing on square-root methods in the 1930s, and many others undoubtedly took up with Macaulay's idea and worked with it. Among our notes we find these comments:

Victor S. von Szeliski, *Econometrica*, October, 1935:

"Newspapers furnish the raw statistical material: volume of trading during the day or other interval, and the price movement, high, low and close. This raw material is obviously not usable as given, it must be worked into coefficients or indexes of some sort. . . . Prices and price changes as quoted daily in newspapers in points are not technically comparable. Not only are price changes as measured in points not comparable for the same stock at different price levels – a point move in Anaconda selling at 7 is technically more significant and statistically less probable than a point move when it is selling at 160 – but the prices of different stocks at any one time are not comparable. The point moves of Anaconda cannot be compared with the point moves of American Telephone. Unless we invent some way of remeasuring these prices in terms of some common denominator, we forego the possibility of getting large numbers of essentially repeated observations.

"The first answer to this problem was furnished by the ratio chart . . . This was fairly satisfactory as long as stocks sold above 40. But as soon as lower price ranges had been experienced, it was seen that the percentage measure overestimated the moves of the low price stocks, as the arithmetic point measure had overestimated the moves of high price stocks. . . .

"Obviously, something between points and percents is required. A recent suggestion is the square root law . . . the technical significance of price movements is proportional to the square root of the price. . . . Thus a move in a low-priced stock from 4 to 9 is technically equivalent to a move in a high-priced stock from 144 to 169." (The square root of 9 minus the square root of 4 is equal to the square root of 169 minus the square root of 144.)

Harry D. Comer, *Barron's*, March 13 & 20, 1944, and *The Analysts Journal*, April, 1945:

"While most investors know that it is much more accurate . . . to measure movements of stock prices by percentages than by points, few realize that an even more accurate way is to add or subtract the square roots of prices. This method 'equalizes' percentage movements which are usually much wider in low priced stocks than in the higher priced ones. For instance, a rise of 69% from $100 to $169 a share is thus 'equalized' with an advance of 300% from $9 to $36 a share. This calculation is:

"Square root of 169 (or 13) minus square root of 100 (or 10) equals 3.
"Square root of 36 (or 6) minus square root of 9 (or 3) equals 3.

> *To measure movements of stock prices an even more accurate way is to add or subtract the square roots of prices*

"This principle, first propounded by Frederick R. Macaulay in the 1920s, works with surprising accuracy. It has been tested and rather widely used in research circles. Coming back to the foregoing example, the system can be adopted to the following purpose:

"If a market average goes up from 100 to 169 in a bull market, where should a stock go if it started at 9? As shown above, the difference between the square roots of 100 and 169 is 3. Add that number to the square root of 9, square the total, which is 6, and the answer is 36.

"The phenomenon of big profits from little stocks is common to all bull markets. What the square root rule does is to express this phenomenon in a formula that can be applied by anyone, in the market, at anytime. . . . Even over a short period of time the market is shown to have bowed to the all-powerful forces summarized in the square root rule. Whether the stock was an industrial, a rail, or a utility, the reaction hit all price groups with equal 'square root' force. Such is the mechanistic nature of stock price movements. . . . The fidelity with which the square root rule conformed to the average bull market experience through all the years is unquestionable proof of a definite mathematical law operating in the stock market."

Zenon Szatroski, *Journal of the American Statistical Association*. December, 1945:

"The fact that price changes do depend on price level should be taken into account by averaging that function of price which tends to have constant change with respect to level. An index . . . which is based on the average of square root of prices, should give a better approximation of the general changes in price that were taking place because it would tend to reflect the kinds of changes which were independent of the level of the variable. . . . Also the use of such indices might increase the effectiveness of the Dow Theory in indicating changes in trend . . . the use of square roots reveals a remarkable tendency for the changes in the variable (variations in price changes) to be constant regardless of price level. . . ."

We have been informed of a later study which confirms the above observations on the validity of "the square root law". This study was completed in 1951 by Robert Cole under the direction of Jacob O. Kann, Director of School of Commerce, Baldwin Wallace College, Berea, Ohio.

The word "tends" stands out in the foregoing quotations. The square-root law expresses the mathematical *tendency* of price changes in respect to price levels; it does not express mechanically the behavior pattern of all stocks. Some stocks are "naturally" more sensitive or volatile than other stocks, and this fact is best brought to light by comparing movements of individual stocks, or groups of stocks, on a square-root scale rather than on an arithmetic or percentage scale. The square-root scale automatically makes appropriate allowance for the difference in price movements which are due to differences in price levels. If an individual stock moves consistently farther than should be expected on a "normal" or square-root basis, we might conclude that this consistent deviation from normal is due to the "natural volatility" of the stock.

Hence, the fact that various stocks do not conform closely with the square-root law, can be turned into an advantage – we may be able to discover those stocks which are *habitually* fast or slow movers, and we may find better rules for moving into, placing stop orders, and taking profits in these fast and slow stocks.

In single movements we may find, through the square-root law, those stocks which are ahead or behind the market. And, as also pointed out before, it is appropriate to use square roots in the construction of a market average. But, let us turn now to the possibility of deriving a "universal formula" for use in many stocks.

THE USE OF SQUARE ROOTS WITH THE DOW PRINCIPLES

Some of the essential ingredients in the Dow Theory deal with the penetration of resistance points and lines. The orthodox Dow Theory leaves the identification of resistance points, lines and penetrations more or less up to the individual. As a result, Dow theorists do not always agree on the meaning of current market trends, and back-testing the Theory becomes a matter of personal judgment.

Samuel Moment in his studies of the Dow Theory obtained consistency and greater accuracy by assigning definite percentage calculations to the determination of lines, resistance points and penetrations in the Dow Jones industrial average.

Going another step forward, it appears that we can equalize (or at least TEND to equalize) the diverse price levels and fluctuations of various stocks through the use of the Square Root Theory. If the Square Root Theory states a definite tendency, as many authorities maintain, then we can apply some of Dow's principles in order to place many stocks on a common plane regardless of their price levels.

Casual research has indicated that we may define "significant minor movements" as those movements which amount to 0.15 or more on a square root scale. That is, we plot all price movements in a stock if the movement amounts to at least 0.15; movements of less than 0.15 are ignored. If a stock moves from 49 to 51⅛, the 2⅛ point rise would be considered "significant" because the rise amounts to 0.15 in the square roots of prices (the square root of 49 is 7.00 and the square root of 51⅛ is 7.15 – a rise of 0.15). Another stock selling at 25 needs to rise to only 26½ (1½ points) in order to have registered a "significant movement" (the square root of 25 is 5.00 and the square root of 26½ is 5.15 – a rise of 0.15).

> *Some of the essential ingredients in the Dow Theory deal with the penetration of resistance points and lines*

Some years ago we published, through the courtesy of Homer Fahrner a table of square roots which facilitated the square-root computations on stocks selling from $⅛ to $200. Copies of that table are now out-of-print, but in this Review we give another table which no longer makes necessary Mr. Fahrner's table for certain computations. For example, Column 2 states the amount of movement at various price levels which is equivalent to a 0.15 movement on a square-root scale. If a stock is selling at $2, we would plot all swings amounting to ⅜ or more; if the stock is selling at $10, we would plot $1 swings; if it is selling at $100, we would plot swings of $3 or more, etc. (In passing it may be observed that since stocks are actually traded in on a ⅛-point scale – ⅛ minimum between quotations – the table cannot give precise square-root proportions. However, we need not strive for hair-line precision.)

After we have charted the "significant" or 0.15 square-root movements, we can set up a method of deriving buy and sell signals on the basis of these movements. If we are interested in the orthodox Dow Theory principle of buying when the preceding Top is penetrated, and selling when the preceding Bottom is penetrated, we can go about getting signals in any stock by following this procedure:

1. **Chart the upswings and the downswings**

    An *upswing* is a rise of 0.15 or more. The high point of of an Upswing is called a *top*. (Use Column 2 of the table.)

    A *downswing* is a decline of 0.15 or more. The low point of a Downswing is called a *bottom*. (Use Column 2.)

2. **Cover shorts and buy** when prices rise 0.05 or more above the preceding. (Use Column 3 to convert 0.05 on the square-root scale into actual price movements.)

3. **Sell longs and go short** when prices decline 0.05 or more below the preceding *bottom*. (Column 3).

If you prefer to take quick, short profits in part of each of your commitments, reference to Column 7 is suggested. If you want to place stops, or limit losses, Column 6 may prove to be a good guide.

Traders using orthodox Dow principles may well make tests using the foregoing suggestions. It is possible that this "common-denominator" procedure is a "good fit" for many stocks.

THE USE OF SQUARE ROOTS WITH "NEW DOW PRINCIPLES"

It is written all over the face of stock and commodity charts that there is "something" which can be turned into profits if the trader operates on movements proceding from Double and Ascending Bottoms, Double and Descending Tops, and "Head-and-Shoulders" Tops and Bottoms. The problem is to find the best systematic ways to use the things we can "see" but somehow never define with considerable satisfaction. It appears that the authors of many texts on chart reading have "struggled" for precise rules and regulations. We too have grappled long years with the task of formulating precise methods, and sometimes it seems that the effort to make further improvements is a futile one. If the various problems are susceptible to better mechanistic solutions, it appears that some of those problems are best approached from a square-root outlook – since this procedure puts many stocks on a common-denominator basis, and the problems are therefore simplified to that extent.

Starting with this common denominator, we then need to formulate precise definitions, and finally we need to *count the cases* when these definitions work and when they do not work. Many of the texts (stock market courses, included) stop at what they "see" but cannot "define." Others give definitions but fail to count the cases where these definitions work and *don't work*. If we are to gain confidence, or at least understanding, in a method we should know quite precisely the rules of the method and how these rules have actually worked out in the past.

It is not our purpose here to set up a concrete, tested a-b-c or one-two-three method for trading in individual stocks or commodities. Rather, we hope at this time to stimulate further research in stocks and commodities along the line of principles stated in the New Dow Barometer. Table 3.1 on page 74 should prove helpful to investigators who care to engage in original research in specific stocks using principles from the orthodox Dow Theory and New Dow Barometer.

Variations in the suggested use of the table are, of course, permissable. Also, changes can be made in the figures given if such changes are believed to be more in keeping with individual stock behavior characteristics. The table cannot give effect to *exact* square root movements, as stocks are bought and sold on a $⅛ scale and not a square root scale. Furthermore, stocks are not "compelled" to move in exact conformity with the square-root law, or any other known and describable law. Indeed, some researches indicate that a "⅔ or ¾ power law" appears to be operating more effectively in stocks than the "½ power (square root) law." Then, too, stocks vary in their volatility, and perhaps an adjustment in the figures is necessary in individual cases to give effect to high and low "indexes of sensitivity" in specific stocks. (The Square Root Theory can be used, in the first place, to determine what these indexes should be). And, it is conceivable that the Square Root Theory may not be properly applicable to buying and selling problems involving the movements of *one stock over a period of time* (see D. W. Ellsworth, *"The Use and Abuse of the Square Root Scale for Charting Stock Prices," Annalist*, December 23, 1932), but we will hurry over this possible objection by stating simply that if it is valid to study chart phenomena on any other scale (arithmetic or log) it should be no less valid to study the same chart phenomena on a square root scale. In fact, it occurs to us that it is more appropriate to use the square-root scale in many problems in order to derive a single basic formula for all stocks, regardless of price levels, rather than a number of sliding-scale formulae designed to take care of each separate price level.

At any rate, there are problems to be solved in using square roots. We hope this table will provide other investigators with a handy working tool in getting at some of those problems.*

---

*For those interested in further studies in square-root technique, we suggest:
(1) The studies by Homer Fahrner, published in recent years in *Investor's Future*.
(2) Our own latest work, *One-Way Formula*.

Table 3.1

1. WHEN PRICE IS:	2. CHART SWINGS OF: (0.15)	3. ENTER ON PENETRATION of last Top or Bottom (0.05)	4. ENTER ON MOVEMENT OF: (0.20)	5. PYRAMID ON MOVEMENT OF: (0.15)	6. LIMIT LOSS (0.25)	7. TAKE QUICK GAIN Square (0.15) Root
$	$	$	$	$	$	$
2	$\frac{3}{8}$	$\frac{1}{8}$	$\frac{5}{8}$	$\frac{3}{8}$	$\frac{3}{4}$	$\frac{3}{8}$
3	$\frac{1}{2}$	$\frac{1}{8}$	$\frac{3}{4}$	$\frac{1}{2}$	$\frac{7}{8}$	$\frac{1}{2}$
4	$\frac{5}{8}$	$\frac{1}{4}$	$\frac{7}{8}$	$\frac{5}{8}$	1	$\frac{5}{8}$
5	$\frac{3}{4}$	$\frac{1}{4}$	1	$\frac{3}{4}$	$1\frac{1}{4}$	$\frac{3}{4}$
6	$\frac{3}{4}$	$\frac{1}{4}$	1	$\frac{3}{4}$	$1\frac{1}{4}$	$\frac{3}{4}$
7	$\frac{7}{8}$	$\frac{1}{4}$	$1\frac{1}{8}$	$\frac{7}{8}$	$1\frac{3}{8}$	$\frac{7}{8}$
8	$\frac{7}{8}$	$\frac{3}{8}$	$1\frac{1}{8}$	$\frac{7}{8}$	$1\frac{1}{2}$	$\frac{7}{8}$
9	$\frac{7}{8}$	$\frac{3}{8}$	$1\frac{1}{4}$	$\frac{7}{8}$	$1\frac{1}{2}$	$\frac{7}{8}$
10	1	$\frac{3}{8}$	$1\frac{3}{8}$	1	$1\frac{5}{8}$	1
15	$1\frac{1}{8}$	$\frac{3}{8}$	$1\frac{1}{2}$	$1\frac{1}{8}$	$1\frac{7}{8}$	$1\frac{1}{8}$
20	$1\frac{3}{8}$	$\frac{1}{2}$	$1\frac{3}{4}$	$1\frac{3}{8}$	$2\frac{1}{4}$	$1\frac{3}{8}$
25	$1\frac{1}{2}$	$\frac{1}{2}$	2	$1\frac{1}{2}$	$2\frac{1}{2}$	$1\frac{1}{2}$
30	$1\frac{3}{4}$	$\frac{5}{8}$	$2\frac{1}{4}$	$1\frac{3}{4}$	$2\frac{7}{8}$	$1\frac{3}{4}$
35	$1\frac{7}{8}$	$\frac{5}{8}$	$2\frac{1}{2}$	$1\frac{7}{8}$	$3\frac{1}{8}$	$1\frac{7}{8}$
40	$1\frac{7}{8}$	$\frac{5}{8}$	$2\frac{1}{2}$	$1\frac{7}{8}$	$3\frac{1}{8}$	$1\frac{7}{8}$
50	$2\frac{1}{8}$	$\frac{3}{4}$	$2\frac{7}{8}$	$2\frac{1}{8}$	$3\frac{1}{2}$	$2\frac{1}{8}$
60	$2\frac{3}{8}$	$\frac{7}{8}$	$3\frac{1}{4}$	$2\frac{3}{8}$	4	$2\frac{3}{8}$
70	$2\frac{5}{8}$	$\frac{7}{8}$	$3\frac{1}{2}$	$2\frac{5}{8}$	$4\frac{1}{4}$	$2\frac{5}{8}$
80	$2\frac{3}{4}$	$\frac{7}{8}$	$3\frac{5}{8}$	$2\frac{3}{4}$	$4\frac{1}{2}$	$2\frac{3}{4}$
90	$2\frac{7}{8}$	1	$3\frac{7}{8}$	$2\frac{7}{8}$	$4\frac{7}{8}$	$2\frac{7}{8}$
100	3	1	4	3	5	3
140	$3\frac{1}{2}$	$1\frac{1}{4}$	$4\frac{3}{4}$	$3\frac{1}{2}$	6	$3\frac{1}{2}$
180	$4\frac{1}{8}$	$1\frac{1}{2}$	$5\frac{1}{2}$	$4\frac{1}{8}$	7	$4\frac{1}{8}$

An example of experiments using Table 3.1:

Column

1. If a stock is selling near $50 (between, say, 45 and 55),
2. chart all swings amounting to $2⅛ or more (high-low prices, perhaps, rather than closing prices).
3. If you should not buy on the basis of the above, then buy on ¾ penetration of the preceding Top.
4. Get an Original Buy Signal (reversal signal) on a rise of $2⅞ above a Double Bottom or an Ascending Bottom, or on a rise of $2⅞ above the Preceding Bottom if the rise starts from a Lower Bottom.
5. Having obtained an Original Buy Signal, pyramid, or buy again, on a rise of $2⅛ above an Ascending Bottom.
6. Limit loss on each trade to a maximum of $3½ (or, perhaps, use $¾ -column 3- as a stop-point below the Bottom from which the rise started).
7. Take a quick profit of $2⅛ in half or more of each commitment, letting the balance of the trade ride until closed out by a reversal signal or until a stop is caught (the stop can be progressively raised as new Bottoms are made – the stop being placed $¾ under the latest Bottom).

3. If you should not buy on the basis of the above, then buy on ¾ penetration of the preceding Top.

QUICK PROFITS IN
FAST-MOVING STOCKS

Do you often let paper profits fade away? How many times have we bought a stock and soon thereafter had the opportunity to take a good profit – but failed to do so? Isn't it true that too often we allow the opportunity for a gain to slip away, and then we finally close out our position with a loss?

If that has been your fortune too, you may well give serious consideration to the table on the next page. The information in this table is based on scientific observations derived from investigations into the Square-Root Theory – but you need not concern yourself with the facts of that Theory in order to use the table.

Suppose you buy a stock at $30, and in a few days or weeks you have the opportunity to sell it at $33. If you sell your stock, your gross profit will be $3 per share (column Z). From this profit you will have to deduct approximately $⅝ for brokerage and governmental charges for buying and selling the stock (column Y). This will leave you a net profit of $2⅜ or 7.91 per cent (column X) on your purchase price of $30. Such a profit is, I think, very satisfactory if you held the stock for only a short period of time – certainly it is much more desirable than allowing a paper profit to turn into an actual loss.

Of course, if one is to take quick profits in this manner, he will have to forego the possibility of making a "big killing" in any single trade. Some traders will, therefore, prefer to take a quick gain in part of his commitment (say, in half of it) and then let the remainder "ride" for a possible large gain if the movement proves to be one of the big ones. Other traders will prefer to take quick gains in all of his trades, provided he can make many such trades over the course of a year. This trader will permit the magic of compound interest to work miracles in the growth of his original capital.

Naturally, the "catch" to all of this is in the *timing* of the commitments into the market and in the *selection* of the stocks in which to trade. If the timing of your purchases (and short sales, if you engage in them) is reasonably accurate, and if your stock selections are good, well, your problem is solved! Merely take from 4 to 20 per cent net gain per trade, as indicated in the Table, and before long you, and the income-tax collector, should be happy indeed!

Sometimes I wonder if the problems of commitment-timing and stock-selections are of first importance. It seems to me that the main difficulty has been in ourselves – the human element with all its negative qualities such as impatience, fear, greed, and wishful thinking. If you will look back at past experiences, perhaps you will find that you have seldom bought at the very top of movements – usually a profit has been available for the taking, but the difficulty has been in actu-

the difficulty has been in actually taking the profit

ally *taking* the profit. Our mechanical trading plans certainly provide the opportunity for gains in a large majority of instances, but I must admit that it takes a considerable amount of humility and self-discipline to follow simple automatic procedures.

Be that as it may, here is a table which, if followed faithfully in conjunction with a reasonably good timing method, will provide quick gains, particularly in fast-moving stocks such as those listed on pages 78 to 81.

Table 3.2

WHEN PURCHASE PRICE (OR SHORT-SALE PRICE) IS NEAREST*:	X THE DESIRED NET GAIN IS:		Y APPROXIMATE** ROUND TRIP OVERHEAD	Z (X+Y) TAKE GROSS GAIN
	$	%		
5	1	20.00	¼	1¼
10	1⅜	13.75	⅜	1¾
15	1⅝	10.83	½	2⅛
20	1⅞	9.37	½	2⅜
25	2⅛	8.50	½	2⅝
30	2⅜	7.91	⅝	3
35	2⅝	7.52	⅝	3¼
40	2¾	6.87	¾	3½
50	3	6.00	¾	3¾
60	3⅜	5.62	¾	4⅛
70	3⅝	5.17	¾	4⅜
80	3¾	4.68	⅞	4⅝
90	4	4.44	⅞	4⅞
100	4¼	4.25	⅞	5⅛

*If purchase (or short-sale) price is at midpoint of two intervals, use the highest price. Example: If you buy at 7½ , use the figures following 10: $1⅜ Desired Net Gain, etc.

**Only approximate allowance can be made for overhead as Federal tax is based on par value of individual issues, and also stocks move in intervals of 12½¢ (⅛) while commissions are computed to the exact 1¢. Overhead here stated is per share, trading in 100-share lots.

FAST-MOVING STOCKS

The stocks listed here have generally been fast-moving. They have usually moved up faster than the "average stock" percentagewise, and they have also ordinarily shown greater percentage declines. Research into the volatility of many of these stocks goes back as far as 1932. Represented in the list are stocks which are sometimes considered by investment analysts as being highly speculative, as well as other stocks which are considered to be more seasoned or conservative issues. Regardless of their "investment ratings," these stocks generally move up and down rapidly in their major and intermediate swings.

The stocks are arranged by groups. If the groups continue to "rotate" as they have often done in recent years, this will provide a convenient reference list to fast-moving stocks in various groups. The list is not intended to be all-inclusive, but it is well representative of the high-volatile stocks. Thus, if the automobile group becomes particularly active, there is a choice of stocks which should participate well in the movement. By following the rotation of groups, the trader might take quick, worthwhile profits in each of several groups during the course of a single general-market movement.

Aircraft – manufacturing

Avco	Curtiss–Wright	No. Amer.
Boeing	Douglas	Martin
Con. Vultee	Lockheed	Republic

Airline – transportation

American	Eastern	Transworld
Capital	Northwest	Western

Automobile & truck

Chrysler	Kaiser	Reo
Gen. Mot.	Mack	Studebaker
Graham-Paige	Nash (now	White
Hudson (now	American Motors)	Packard
American Motors)		

Automobile equipment

Bendix	Cont. Motors	Elec. Auto-Lite
Borg Warner	Dana	Hayes Mfg.
Budd	Eaton	Young, S W

Building & supplies

Amer. Rad.	Crane	Stone & Webster
Carrier	Flintkote	US Plywood
Celotex	Masonite	Walworth
Certainteed	Nat. Gypsum	

Coal

Lehi Valley	Pittston

Chemical

Commercial Solvents

Containers

Crown Cork & Seal	National Can

Drugs

Bristol–Myers

Electrical-radio-television

Admiral	Philco
Emerson Elec.	Radio Corp.
Gen. Cable	Sparks Withgtn.
Magnavox	Westinghouse
	Zenith

Farm machinery

Caterpillar	Minn–Moline
Case, J. I.	Oliver
Deere & Co.	

Investment companies

Adams Express	Gen. Amer. Inv.
Allegheny	Tri-Continental
Amer. Int.	US & For. Sec.

Liquors

Schenley

Machinery
Amer. Mach. & Fdry.
Blaw–Knox
Chi. Pneu. Tool   Fairbanks Morse
Dresser Ind.   Foster Wheeler
Ex-Cell–O

Meat packers
Armour   Wilson

Office & business equipment
Remington–Rand   Nat. Cash Reg.

Metal & mining
Aluminum Co.   Kennecot
Amer. Smelting   Nat. Lead
Anaconda   St. Joseph Lead
Inspiration   Revere Copper
Amer. Zinc, Lead & Smelt.   Vanadium

Oils
Houston   Richfield
Mission   Skelly
Phillips   Sunray

Paper & paper products
Container   Int. Paper
Crown Zellerbach   St. Regis Paper

Railroads
Atlantic Coast Line   Kansas City Southern
Baltimore & Ohio   Lehigh Valley
Boston & Maine   Louisville & Nashville
Chicago & Northwestern   Missouri Kansas Texas
Chicago Great Western   New York Central
Chicago Milwaukee & St. Paul   New York Chicago & St. Louis
Delaware & Hudson   Northern Pacific
Delaware Lackawana & Western   St. Louis & San Francisco
Erie   Southern Pacific
Great Northern, Preferred   Southern Railway
Gulf Mobile & Ohio   Texas & Pacific
Illinois Central

Railroad equipment
Amer. Car & Fdry.   Baldwin Locomotive
Amer. Locomotive   Pressed Steel Car

Retail stores
Allied Stores   Mont. Ward
Gimbel Bros.   Rexall Drug
Spiegel
West. Auto Supplies

Rubber
Firestone   Goodyear
Goodrich   US Rubber

Soft drinks
Canada Dry   Pepsi-Cola

Steel & iron
Armco   Interlake Iron
Allegheny Ludlum   Jones & Laughlin
Bethlehem   Republic
Crucible   US Steel
Follansbee   Youngstown S. & T.

Textiles
American Woolen   Industrial Rayon
Burlington Mills   Textron
Celanese   United Mer. & Mfg.

Theatres
Paramount   Twentieth Cent. Fox
Radio-Keith Orp.   Warner Bros.
Technicolor

Utilities
Amer. Water Works   Int. Tel. & Tel.
Columbia Gas Sy.   United Corp.
Elec. Bond & Share   Western Union

THE THRUST METHOD IN STOCKS

The research on the method was conducted with the thought constantly in mind that it should serve the busy business man, or professional man, who has little time for recording statistics and charting stocks, and no time for elaborate statistical analyses. It should not require over one hour each week-end for charting the weekly high, low and closing prices of 20 to 30 stocks and interpreting the price actions of those stocks. (The Sunday issue of some metropolitan newspapers gives the weekly ranges and closing prices of New York stocks, as does *Barron's* which is published Monday morning.)

If you are plotting the weekly figures on your own charts, it is preferable that you continue using them as you are accustomed to your own charts. But, they must be drawn so that you can read them accurately to the "last ⅛ of a dollar," as this is a mechanical method and the rules for buying and selling are stated to the "⅛ point." If you do not already have your own charts, you can purchase a set, but if you do this make sure that the price scales are drawn so that you can read the prices accurately. I do not sell charts but, on request, I can direct you to a publisher of charts.

The charts should be diversified among various stock groups – motors, rails, steels, oils, stores, electronics, aircrafts, etc. A minimum of perhaps 20 stocks should be charted. If you can afford the time to chart 40 or 50 stocks, the extra effort will likely prove to be to your advantage. The list should include at least one stock from each of several groups. If you will do this, it is quite certain that you will have a signal to enter into a position in one or more stocks near the start of every important general-market movement. Furthermore, if the groups continue to rotate as they have often done in recent years, it is possible that you will get signals first, for instance, in the motors, then later in the oils, still later in the rails, etc. In other words, it is entirely possible that you will profit in two or more stocks during the same major rise or decline in the general market.

Of course, this method, like any method, does not always bask in the sunshine. It too knows disagreeable days. Yet, I feel that in the great majority of stocks a net gain is almost a certainty over a "reasonable period of time." It is difficult to define what is a "reasonable period of time" because at times some stocks are dead and trendless and it may take years to jar them into a profit-making movement. So, let us simply say that if a stock participates in what is generally conceded to be a major bull or bear market movement, the Thrust Method should surely yield a pleasing net profit in that stock.

The method *is simple*. If you will make the effort to understand it – write and ask questions if necessary – I believe that it will open up for you a new field of analysis which is both fascinating and profitable.

CHART WEEKLY PRICES

The first step, of course, is to select the stocks we want to follow and then to keep our charts up-to-date.

In the fast-moving, ever-changing commodity markets it is necessary, for best results, that we use daily data. In stocks, fortunately, we can reduce the labor in charting by using weekly data. Some students of the Thrust Method have experimented with daily data in stocks, using the same procedures, and have obtained some excellent results. However, stocks prepare for their movements in a more leisurely manner than commodities, and weekly data will afford sufficient opportunities without considerable expenditure of time in charting. Weekly data, too, has the advantage in that it smoothes over some of the irregularities – "whipsaws" – which are inherent in the nature of the more sensitive daily data.

The ultimate purpose of any trading method is, of course, to make profits. The greatest potential profits reside, obviously, in those stocks which are in the habit of moving vigorously, both up and down. The Thrust Method should also give profitable signals in the slower-moving, more conservative issues but our interest is in trying to obtain maximum gains. We naturally prefer, for tax purposes, to hold a stock longer than six months, but we are willing to sacrifice this advantage, whenever necessary, in the interest of larger net gains. In other words, we do not object to in-and-out trading whenever the signals dictate such a procedure. We are interested mainly in *profitable action*; consequently, we devote our main attention to those stocks which have long demonstrated their inclination toward *activity*. We are not concerned with whether these issues possess the attributes of "dignified investments;" we are willing to buy and sell the "cats and dogs" if it appears likely that we can profit in them.

In another study, "Quick Profits in Fast-Moving Stocks," I give a list of 170 stocks which have generally been fast-moving. Likely it required thousands of man–hours to compile that list. I merely spent a few weeks in going over the tabulations of other investigators and from these tabulations I made a "consensus" of their findings. If all of the authorities agreed that a stock has had volatile characteristics for years, that stock was included in my list. You may find many of your favorite stocks on the list and it is suggested that you watch them for signals by the Thrust Method.

I hesitate to point out any specific stocks which have performed exceptionally well by the Thrust Method. All stocks probably have losing streaks from time to time and if I were to emphasize certain spectacular issues, I might do so at an inopportune time. The Thrust Method seeks its net gain over a series of trades embracing a reasonable period of time. It is interesting to note that in 70 stocks which I personally watched from January, 1953 to August, 1954 only one showed a disappointing overall record, although most of them registered single losses from time to time. I have also made visual chart observations in many stocks as far back as 1943 and have tabulated detailed records in a few of them. All of this has given me the feeling of certainty that the Thrust Method is grounded in sound principles. Improvement can undoubtedly be made in the mechanical rules, but fundamentally it seems that we are working on a solid foundation.

So, it is suggested that you select your own stocks and put them under observation. Whatever stocks you select will likely yield gains over a reasonable period of time. You may even discover some "spectacular issues."

DETERMINING THE BAROMETRIC SWINGS AND THEIR TOPS AND BOTTOMS

Let us assume that we have just finished the weekly chore of charting the weekly high-low-closing prices, so our charts are now up-to-date and we are looking for opportunities for profits.

Our problem now is to determine, for each stock, whether prices are likely to go higher or lower and the point at which we should buy or sell. To solve this problem we need, first, to relate a stock's present prices to its prices in the recent past. We need to discover first whether prices are now strong or weak in respect to what they have been in the recent past.

Of course, we might simply glance at a chart and draw a conclusion as to whether a stock is now stronger or weaker than what it has been recently. A novice might correctly conclude that the trend is now up if prices have been moving upward for several weeks. But, what will he do when a declining week comes? He then may be badly mistaken if he then infers that the underlying trend is down. Or, if he reasons that the reaction is only a temporary one, he may also be wrong. He will certainly be confused when he is confronted with a series of up and down weeks; and he will be entirely lost when a stock simply stops in its tracks and moves in a manner which on the surface appears to be aimless and trendless.

Above all, we need a *specific method* of analysis; we cannot just "look" at our charts and make trustworthy deductions. Chart readers have always "found" in "looking" at their charts the very things that they were looking for. Charts can become the means of providing "reasons" for our emotions and wishful thinking. If you "want" the market to go up, just turn to your charts and to the many miscellaneous theories of chart reading. You will likely find for yourself satisfying reasons why the market "should go up." Another fellow, at the same time and using the same charts, but inclined to be bearish, will likely find just as good reasons why the market "should go down." Unless we employ a definite, concrete, systematic procedure, we had just as well abandon charts and turn to "analyzing fundamentals" – and heaven help deliver us from the risks of that hazardous occupation!

So, let us take the first step in setting up a definite, methodical procedure for analyzing our charts. This first step is to determine a stock's "barometric swings." We call these Upswings and Downswings, and the high points (Tops) and the low points (Bottoms) of these swings are very important to us in analyzing a stock's current position-buy, sell, or hold.

Now, there are numerous ways of setting up Upswings and Downswings, and I have experimented with many of these. Not any single method is entirely satisfactory. We could, for example, set up very sensitive swings, and in so doing we could buy at practically every important bottom and sell almost always at every important top. Here is how that would be done:

How to buy at the bottoms of bear markets
and
How to sell at the tops of bull markets

We can buy almost any active New York stock near its bear market low and sell it near its bull market peak! That sounds rather stupendous, but it's a fact – though, unfortunately, it entails troubles. As an illustration, all we need to do is to make a "swing chart" of every $1 movement, and then buy when the top of the last upswing is penetrated upward by $1 and sell when the bottom of the last downward swing is pierced downward by $1. Such a "$1 swing chart" *might* look like the picture to the left of Figure 3.1, but very probably it will look more like the picture to the right – and therein we see the flaws inherent in setting up very sensitive swings.

Fig 3.1 $1 swing chart

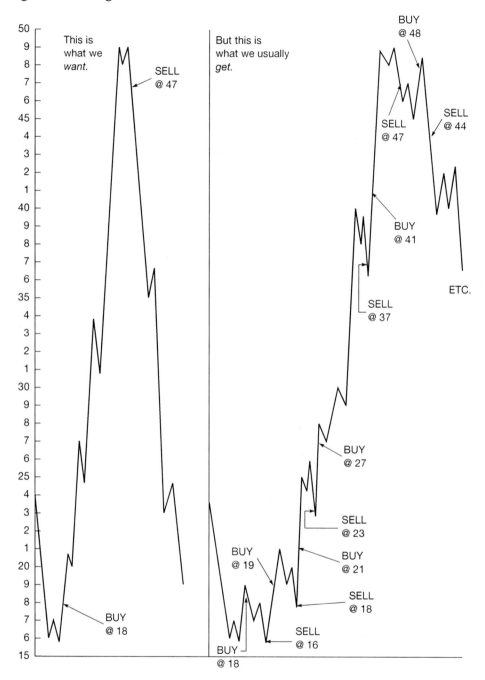

Comment on Figure 3.1

In the chart of "$1 swings," we are reviewing the old orthodox Dow principle of buying when the last top is penetrated upward and selling when the last bottom is penetrated downward. This procedure has little to do with the Thrust Method (though, we do use it at times as a "last resort"), but let us continue a little farther with the review in order to illustrate the difficulties and importance in setting up appropriate Upswings and Downswings.

Instead of charting swings of "$1 or more," we could chart swings of "$2 or more." This would eliminate some of the whipsaws and, as compensation, we will often buy at higher prices and sell at lower prices than those which can be obtained by using the $1 swings. If we ignored all swings unless the movement amounted to, say, "$5 or more," we could do away with many of the whipsaws but also we would often find ourselves buying far above bottoms and selling far below tops.

Can't we find some "in-between figure" which would give executions in most stocks reasonably close to bottoms and tops, and at the same time do away with many of the whipsaws? Well, as of date, I don't know of any such figure and doubt very much whether we can ever find one. It doesn't seem sensible that we should use some one figure for all stocks regardless of price level or price activity.

Let us for a moment glance at the chart of General Motors which I have used for advertising purposes. The General Motors formula was "discovered" early in 1953 and it has been working very well ever since. (Some of my prospects don't think so as they write indignantly that the chart shows whipsaws and one could do better by buying at the bottom and holding on to the top. Unfortunately for you and me, they do not make clear how they go about accomplishing the latter feat.) Here, through trial-and-error I found that when General Motors was selling above $40 satisfactory results could be obtained by charting swings of $3⅝ or more. I selected $3⅝ because it appeared to be the best single figure I could find for General Motors when it is above $40. Likely that figure should be raised when the stock moves higher and higher just as I lowered it to $2⅝ when the stock goes under $40. If I were to conduct the same research in Chrysler, or in Northern Pacific, or in any of hundreds of other stocks, I would likely find that $3⅝ is not the best figure to use. Chrysler probably has its own "best figure," Northern Pacific likely has an entirely different "best figure," etc., and likely there should be some "give-and-take" to all of these "best figures" in order to allow for differences in price level and activity from time to time. So, you can see that there would be no end to the research we could do – if we had a staff of a few hundred workers – on this initial problem of setting up the proper swings for each stock.

Instead of charting the swings on an arithmetic basis, I have also tried using the percentage basis. I have tried 1%, 2%, 2½%, 5%, etc. But, here again we run into difficulties. Low-priced stocks do not fluctuate percentagewise the same as high-priced stocks. During the same period of time a volatile stock may out-distance a slow-mover by many percentages. If we are going to use the percentage scale for measuring swings, we are right back to the old problem of finding the right percentage for each stock and each price level.

So, the suggestion has been made to "use the 'square-root scale' and this will equalize the various price levels at which different issues sell." In a study, "The Dow Method Applied to Your Own Stocks" (now out of print) I adopted this procedure. I'm not sure that this is the right answer. Surely it considers that all stocks have the same mobile nature, and obviously this is not true.

It seems that nothing is entirely satisfactory so I have adopted a plan which, though it too has defects, is simple; it can be used in all stocks and commodities; it gives recognition to the "sensitive" swings as well as the longer swings, and it seems to make some automatic adjustment for the "speed" of various stocks.

. . . At this point I am going to direct you to the study "Gains in Grains." You may not be interested at present in commodities, but nevertheless the *same principles and methods apply to both*. In the first printing of this paper on stocks I practically duplicated the paper on "Gains in Grains", making the word "stock" appear where "wheat" (or "grain") appeared in the commodity paper, and also changing the wording to "weeks" rather than "days" since we are using weekly data (instead of daily data) in stocks.

There were certain little differences in the stock method but these were very minor and I am sure they will cause no difference in the net profit from the method in the long run. A couple of these differences are pointed out in the "Work Sheet" at the end of this paper. Even these ("Test of Bottom," "Test of Top," and "Thrust") need not be used in the stock method as the definitions for grains should do equally as well over a period of time. My recent study in "One-Way Formula" has convinced me that if a method works well in grains on a daily basis it is likely to work even better in stocks on a weekly basis.

So, turn now to "Gains in Grains" and as you read think of dollars instead of cents, and think of weekly data instead of daily data. You may even become interested in commodity trading! I assure you that it is more exciting than stocks. But, whether or not you become interested in commodities, you will learn in "Gains in Grains" a good way to get *Buy and Sell Signals* by "The Thrust Method in Stocks."

The *Operating Plan* is, however, different in stocks. So, after you learn how to get the Buy and Sell Signals return then to the following explanation on the Operating Plan in stocks.

CLOSE OUT TRADES BY AN OPERATING PLAN

A specific method of trading in stocks must include these two ingredients:

1. An automatic barometer for detecting the trend of prices from week to week.
2. A systematic plan of operation by which actual purchases and sales are made.

In other words, we must know: (1) "how things look today," and (2) "what to do about it." In preceding pages we took up the first of these and we are now ready to consider the second problem.

Market fluctuations must, of course, always be viewed in terms of probabilities – even though we may not attempt to express the probabilities in precise mathematical language. The future is strewn with risks. Would it not be a blessing if we could eliminate the unknowns of the future? I guess not – for a known future would make a dull present. The fascination of living would crumple if the future could be definitely predetermined. We do not wish to eliminate the unknowns of the future; we wish merely to avoid unnecessary risks.

This can be done in stock trading by eliminating as far as possible the future from our method. If we buy today and secure a reasonable paper profit tomorrow, we should somehow protect that profit. When we limit our losses, when we take steps to protect our paper profits, we are then exerting a measurable degree of independence over the unknowns of the future. We are operating to *grasp* the opportunities usually presented to us by today's trend signals.

As one studies and studies the past, trying to lay hands on the "Utopia Method," the realization becomes clearer and clearer that the wise trader will reconcile himself to the fact that he must make a sacrifice somewhere along the line. We might attribute this fact to "the law of compensation," to "the equality of action and reaction," to "the give-and-take in life" which seems to be the natural order of things. Whatever the reason may be, we will *never* get all we want from market operations – we must be willing to give up one advantage in order to secure another advantage.

If the trader desires to make a profit in nearly all of his trades, it seems he will have to be satisfied with relatively small profits in single trades. The small profits may come at frequent intervals thereby permitting the magic of compound interest to multiply his capital rapidly. But, if he desires mostly gains, and only infrequent losses and break-even trades, it appears he will have to be content with small gains in the individual trades. He will likely have to sacrifice the occasional "big killing" which the market offers from time to time.

On the other hand, if the trader desires to ride along with the movements and take, from time to time, substantial gains in single trades, he will have to be willing to endure more individual losses and break-even trades. After he buys and a small paper profit is soon shown, he has his choice whether to take that profit or to try for a larger profit. If he decides to try for the larger profit, he must necessarily risk losing the present profit which is available for the taking. Quite often the larger profit does accrue, but also, quite often, the present paper profit is sacrificed and the trade breaks even or turns into a small loss. The trader cannot have everything he wants; he must be willing to make sacrifices.

It seems that we might sensibly divide our total trading capital into two parts, "Fund L" and "Fund S". Fund L would be for "long-term trading." riding the main trend movements with the expectation of large profits from time to time *and* the expectation of some losses and perhaps several break-even trades over a period of time. Fund S would be for small, quick-profit trading, and it would provide for recovering the losses entailed by Fund L, and in fact, in the long run it would provide for a net gain over and above the temporary losses which will likely accrue to Fund L. Hence, whatever happens – whether the movement be long or short, sizeable or small – we should have an excellent chance to either gain or break even in the single trade. (Of course, there are times when *both* lots will lose.) But, even this plan imposes a sacrifice too. It usually turns out better in the long run to employ *all* of the fund in Fund L – if the trader is willing to suffer a greater number of losses and break-even trades, he will ordinarily net a greater gain (because of the occasional large gains).

So, it all boils down to a decision which each trader must make for himself. If he seeks only the big gains which do come from time to time, then he must be prepared to endure the discouraging small losses and break-even trades. If he hopes to win in nearly all of his transactions, he must be willing to forego the possibility of a large gain in a single movement. If he resolves to combine both types of operations, then he must be willing to sacrifice the greater profit he could make eventually by putting his entire capital into Fund L.

My own opinion is that most traders need, above all else, "peace of mind." He cannot lose or break even in many of his trades, or he will soon abandon his barometer (even a good one) and start searching again for a better method. It seems that it is our task to reduce the probability of loss in single transactions to a minimum, and, at the same time, to offer a fair chance for a large gain and a good chance for a small gain in each single transaction. If the trader can make a "one-base hit" most of the time when he goes to bat and an occasional "home run," he may possibly find peace-of-mind in his trading operations. Dividing your trading fund into two equal parts, Fund L and Fund S, may give this.

In "Gains in Grains" several operating plans are presented for the reader's consideration. The same could be done in stocks, but at this time I am outlining briefly only one plan. It is not a "perfect plan," but nevertheless it has been tested successfully in past market and, above all, it *is a concrete plan*. The trader must possess a definite plan of operation; he cannot survive, except through luck, if he has no blueprint to follow.

Close out trades

On original Reversal Signal, place half of capital in Fund S and half in Fund L. In all commitments limit loss to amount listed in Column 4 of Work Sheet, on page 93.

Take Quick Profit (column 5) in Fund S in above first trade on Reversal Signal. After taking this profit, enter into another Fund S trade on next Repeat Signal. In this trade take profit amounting to figure in Column 7 if and when said profit is available. If this trade is closed out with profit, try again for another column 7 profit on the next Repeat Signal – and continue this procedure "indefinitely."

Try for large gain in Fund L. That is, "let it ride" with the view in mind that it might be closed out with a large gain. However, when Fund L shows a gross paper profit shown in Column 6, place a stop to break even.

Always close out both funds, and reverse your position, when Reversal Signal comes.

If loss is taken in either or both Funds and this is followed by another signal in same direction, follow the new signal regardless of the prior loss.

Record

Most of my work on the "Thrust Method in Stocks" has been done "Visually" – examining charts without compiling detailed records. However, I have tabulated every trade for a few stocks during the period 1946–1953. These records indicate:

1. A very substantial net profit will be shown over a "reasonable period of time" in most active stocks.
2. Reversal Signals will probably sustain small losses in about D of the reversal trades. At times these losses will be only nominal as Fund S will gain the amount that Fund L losses, and only the commission will be lost.
3. Repeat Signals which follow the original Reversal Signals are especially profitable. It appears that between 80 and 90% of these signals will be profitable if the trader will take the profits listed in Column 5 rather than Column 7. In Northern Pacific 90% of the Repeat Signals gave the profits listed in Column 7, but tabulations in General Motors, Celanese and US and Foreign Securities

Repeat Signals which follow the original Reversal Signals are especially profitable

indicate greater security in the individual trade if the trader will take the gains listed in Column 5. In the *long run* Column 7 will likely give the largest net gains, but from the viewpoint of profiting in the *next* trade Column 5 looks particularly attractive.

4. Losses will average less than the figures shown in Column 4 because Reversal Signals will many times close out trades with smaller losses than the maximum losses allowed by Column 4.

(1)	(2)			(3)	CLOSE OUT TRADES			
					(4)	(5)	(6)	(7)
						REVERSAL SIGNALS		REPEAT SIGNALS
					LIMIT LOSS	FUND "S"	FUND "L"	FUND "S"
WHEN PRICE IS NEAREST	"X" "TEST OF BOTTOM" "TEST OF TOP"			THRUST	IN ALL TRADES	TAKE PROFIT IN q-Σ OF TRADE	BREAK EVEN AFTER PAPER PROFIT OF	TAKE PROFITS
$ 5[a]	½	to	$1[b]	½	1¼	1¼	2½[c]	2½[d]
10	¾	to	1⅜	½	1¾	1¾	3½	3½
15	⅞	to	1⅝	¾	2⅛	2⅛	4¼	4¼
20	1	to	1⅞	¾	2⅜	2⅜	4¾	4¾
25	1⅛	to	2⅛	⅞	2⅝	2⅝	5¼	5¼
30	1¼	to	2⅜	1	3	3	6	6
35	1⅝	to	2⅝	1⅛	3¼	3¼	6½	6½
40	1⅜	to	2¾	1¼	3½	3½	7	7
50	1½	to	3	1⅜	3¾	3¾	7½	7½
60	1¾	to	3⅜	1½	4⅛	4⅛	8¼	8¼
70	1⅞	to	3⅝	1¾	4¾	4⅜	8¾	8¾
80	1⅞	to	3¾	1¾	4⅝	4⅝	9¼	9¼
90	2	to	4	1⅞	4⅞	4⅞	9¾	9¾
100	2⅛	to	4¼	2	5⅛	5⅛	10¼	10¼

[a] When price is mid-way between two price intervals, use the higher price.

[b] TOB is from $½ below to $1 above any of the last three Bottoms. TOT is from $½ above to $1 below any of the last three Tops.

[c] Close out this half of original trade by (1) Stop for maximum loss, (2) Stop at break-even point or (3) Reversal Signal, whichever comes first.

[d] If quick profit (Fund S) is taken in half of trade on original Reversal Signal, then re-enter market with this half of fund on next Repeat Signal. Take profit indicated or close out by Reversal Signal or for maximum loss. Continue to follow Repeat Signals whenever Fund S is inactive.

WORK SHEET – THRUST METHOD IN STOCKS

Part IV

GAINS IN GRAINS

THE USE OF MECHANICAL METHODS IN GRAIN TRADING

FOREWORD

We need not concern ourselves here with elementary facts and procedures on actual grain trading. The assumption is made in this text that the reader already knows *how* to buy and sell commodities – that he already knows such things as how to open an account with a broker; how to give buy and sell orders; the capital needed for trading and the broker's margin requirements; the meaning of such terms as "futures," "options," and "stop orders;" the advantages and disadvantages of commodity trading over stock trading – and knowledge of many other basic facts about grain trading is taken for granted in this text. Some brokers have prepared excellent treatises on these subjects and these publications will give the beginner all he needs in the way of background information on commodity markets. References to these free publications will be furnished on request.

Our concern here is in determining *when* to buy and sell commodities. Others have informed us clearly as to *how* we can go about buying and selling, but too little has yet been disclosed on *when* we should actually do our buying and selling. In other words, our subject here deals with methods of *timing* our purchases and sales.

During the course of this paper we should become acquainted with several trading methods. We shall start at the beginning of my commodity researches and work forward to my latest development. The latter method appears to offer excellent profit opportunities. It is not the "perfect method" which everyone seeks, but never finds. It has flaws and work is still being done to iron out some of its "kinks," but all in all it appears to offer a very good chance for consistent gains in grains.

The general principles underlying this method are applicable to all commodities as well as securities. It seeks to buy closer to Bottoms and to sell closer to Tops than has heretofore been possible with the use of automatic guides.

Because the prices of commodities reflect the knowledge, expectations, and feelings of all persons who influence those prices, any sound method of "forecasting" price movements must be grounded in the "natural laws of human behavior." It is likely that a trading method which is grounded in those laws, as well as based on the observable habits of market movements, will show a profitable record.

It appears, however, that in practice only a limited number of persons have the ability to follow such a method consistently enough to actually profit from it – no matter how precise the method may be. The record of gains usually reposes on paper only. This is so because of other "natural laws" or traits, inherent in human nature – impatience, intolerance, fear, etc.

Before embarking on an explanation of any specific barometer, it is desirable to consider first some of these fundamental concepts which have to do with human behavior, "automatic barometers," and "price forecasting." After that discussion dealing with a background of basic facts about ourselves and about our barometers, we may better determine the construction and most profitable use of such barometers in trading.

Good barometers should not die

I have seen many good friends of mine (speaking of mechanical barometers) die young. Many others with whom I enjoyed a speaking acquaintance through books, articles and instruction courses, also terminated their existence at a tender age. All unworthy associates, unfaithful barometers, departed, of course, from life rapidly and disastrously. Therefore I concluded that most mechanical barometers, good or bad, die young.

The life expectancy of a good mechanical barometer is such that barometers are a poor insurance risk. The lifeblood of a barometer flows through human veins, and as humans we seek a degree of perfection in our accomplishments which is impossible to attain today in the field of economic forecasting. We expect our barometer friend to make a hit nearly every time he comes to bat. Let him fail once and he is often condemned and always doubted; two straight strike-outs nearly always results in disqualification; three consecutive failures, even though small errors, invariably puts him on the bench forever.

This should not be so. A good mechanical barometer is merely an instrument which expresses, the best it can, outstanding characteristics in human behavior. We as individuals are of many types, but at times we deviate considerably from our own "usual self" or "individual personality." Individually and collectively we probably act in conformance with "natural laws." Human nature is not well understood yet. The psychologists and psychiatrists are making some progress, and perhaps the day will come when all the laws of life are known. (For example, studies at the University of Pennsylvania give evidence of a five-week cycle – from gloom to happiness – in the lives of many people.) But on the surface, and with the knowledge and measurements we now have, it seems that we are not consistent in our behavior. Sometimes we enjoy prosperity for several years; other times we allow depression to take over after only a brief period of elation. It is not possible yet, and probably never will be, to give a mathematical formula which expresses accurately the exact nature of human behavior. Our barometers, like ourselves, must behave imperfectly – even the good ones.

But, it is possible to give barometers which portray faithfully, over a period of time, *average tendencies* in the combined behavior of many people – and market prices are made by *many people*. I have known many of such barometers in past years, and to some of them I gave alluring names such as "Semaphore," "Technometer," "Stop-Go," "Barometer X," "Modified Dow Theory", "Follow-The-Trend," "ABC Barometer," "Timeter," etc.

As I look back today I can now see that some of these old friends let me down considerably, but most of them, not-withstanding their little and great imperfections, proved their goodness *in the long run*, but, I walked out on them after they made a mistake or two.

> *It is nonsense to state that grains, or stocks, should rise, or decline, to some future date*

I suppose I shall continue to go on believing that I am more perfect than a good barometer. Man is a stubborn cuss, forever overrating his own abilities.

Forecasting future turning points

Although this is a paper about "forecasting" price movements, the word "forecasting" is not a good one to express what we are trying to do. The term implies, in the minds of most persons, an attempt to predetermine future turning points. For example, we often hear and read such statements as these:

"The market should rise until such-and-such-a date."

"The market should rise to such-and-such-a price."

I believe it is nonsense to state that grains, or stocks, or business conditions, should rise, or decline, to some future date or to some future level. Yet, in the annual New Year "outlooks," and unceasingly throughout the year we witness thousands of unavailing attempts to unveil the future. The business tycoons, the professional counselors and services, or we the people, have never yet demonstrated any practicable consistency in being able to foresee *how far* any movement will go or *how long* it will last. Not one of us can give an answer, worthy of any attention, to such questions as:

"How long do you think the current rise (or 'decline') will last?" or

"How high (or low) do you think the current movement will go?"

The predetermination of future objectives in grains, stocks, or business, is not yet in the realm of scientific possibility. Fortunately, it is entirely unnecessary to engage in the precarious business of "forecasting," even though most persons will always cling to the hope that they, like God, will be able to foresee the future.

Following the trend

Yale, Vassar, and other institutions, have been "beating the stock market" for years without forecasting it. They do not care whether presently the market moves up or down; yet, in the long run they always win. They are conservative institutions and they win by "fighting." the trend – they buy more and more as prices decline lower and lower, and they sell more and more as prices rise higher and higher. As the market declines they "average down" their cost, and as it rises they "average up" their selling price. They are content with a *small* percentage gain at the end of several years – and they get it.

We who are less conservative, and more impatient, and have less money, than Yale or Vassar, should be able to do much better simply by being "friendly" instead of hostile, toward the trend. As individuals we seldom have enough millions to "fight the trend" therefore we should try to tag along with it; we should try to buy soon after it starts up and sell soon after it starts down. We should never attempt to anticipate its future movements; rather, we should wag our tail of devotion and turn our steps in whatever direction the master trend decides to lead us. There are good mechanical, "animal-like," ways of doing this. But, we usually don't follow those ways because we usually want to be THE MASTER. So, we usually go on losing and losing while Yale and Vassar, like the gambling palaces in Reno, go on winning and winning merely because they depend upon "natural laws" and mechanical instruments which do not try to forecast whether "black" or "red" will turn up on the next turn of the "wheel."

If we should resolve not to *forecast*, but to *follow*, the trend faithfully at all times, we could measure the probable direction of the underlying trend as it exists *today*, and then we could "ride along" with that trend until *tomorrow*. Then, when tomorrow comes, we could take another sounding of the trend's direction at that time, and again project that measurement ahead *one day* into the future. And so on – day by day. We would admit that we do not know, or even care to guess, where or when the trend will change its direction. The change might even come tomorrow, and if it does, we would be willing to take our gain, or loss, and follow the trend in its new direction.

Several authoritative studies demonstrate that there is a law of continuity, or momentum, operating in the markets. Today's trend is reluctant to reverse itself – it prefers to continue in the direction it is now moving. This means, from a practical viewpoint, that the *opportunity* for gain is nearly always present for the trader who will but be friendly with today's trend. The possible gain in a single trade may be small or large; we have no way of knowing in advance the potentialities in a single trade. But, we do know that over a "reasonable period of time" (say, the life of a future contract) the "law of averages" will give us a net gain, regardless of the outcome of any single trade.

A mechanical method of recognizing today's trend, coupled with an automatic procedure of buying and selling, plus a dependance upon the natural laws of momentum and probability, provides, I believe, an effective way of trading in the commodity and financial markets. Such a system and philosophy will relieve us from the dreadful task of trying to make forecasts by the common swivel-chair method of "analyzing" the maze of uncertainties in today's political and economic events. It relieves us from the responsibility of pretending that we have supernatural wisdom which permits us to foresee the future.

"Live one day at a time" is good philosophy for the trader in commodities and securities. Confucius stated it this way:

> "Every preconception is a mistake. Do whatever seems best in the circumstance of the moment, and as the situation demands."

Another authority, Jesus, gave us the same principle in these words:

> "Take therefore no thought for the morrow; for the morrow shall take thought for the things of itself. Sufficient unto the day is the evil thereof." – St. Matthew 6:34

In brief, it is not our task to forecast future trends; but, rather, it is our problem to recognize the presently existing trend, and upon this recognition to build an automatic trading procedure which gives "no thought for the morrow" but contends only with the "evils" of today.

Analyzing the fundamentals

How should we go about solving the problem of how to recognize the direction of today's trend? We could turn, as many do, to a broad analysis of the "fundamental factors" which ultimately may cause prices to move to higher or lower levels.

In referring to journals which delve into the world-wide wheat outlook, I read that there are such fundamental factors as:

Probable Production and Consumption.
Disappearance
Carryover
Exports
Acreage Allotments
International Wheat Agreement
Price Ceilings
Parity Prices
Government Price Support
General Price Level
General Business Outlook
The Weather
Insects

I am not grieved to state that I do not have the inclination to attempt to analyze the entanglement of statistics which must enslave the fundamentalist.

I do not know of any living fundamentalist who has made a livelihood in forecasting the price of commodities, although I grant that there must be some such rare individuals. I can, however, report facts and figures which show that the vast majority of grain traders lose money and I suspect that most of these traders are fundamentalists.

Therefore, I am herewith dismissing the subject of "fundamentals" with the thought that the "evils" in forecasting by fundamental factors must be very "sufficient," but, as for myself, I want no part in it.

Significant technical factors

There are three so-called "technical factors" which the trader may use in seeking to identify the direction of today's underlying trend:

1. The *price action* itself.
2. The *activity* of the price action (volume, breadth).
3. The amount of *time* involved in the action.

I believe that the first factor alone, price action, will disclose sufficient information to enable the trader to measure the direction of the basic trend. If one or both of the other two factors are included in the measurement, the probability of a correct interpretation of the existing trend might be enhanced; but for practical, profitable purposes, the inclusion of those two factors appears unnecessary. Particularly, I am sure that the market tells its own story, and the outside fundamental influences can well be ignored.

Certainly, fundamentals *do* influence prices. Therefore, it is certain that *prices will reflect* fundamentals. Why become involved in the complications created by many opposing fundamental factors? The *net result* of all of these influences is faithfully recorded in the market place for prices; consequently, market action is what we must study.

Robert Rhea, speaking of the stock market, stated the argument in these words:

> "The fluctuations of the daily prices of the Dow-Jones rail and industrial averages afford a composite index of *all the hopes, disappointments, and knowledge of everyone* who knows anything of financial matters, and for that reason the effects of coming events (excluding Acts of God) are always properly discounted in the market. The averages quickly appraise such calamities as fires and earthquakes."

We need not be concerned here with whether the Dow–Jones averages actually do everything which Mr. Rhea claimed for them. In the stock market there are various averages compiled, and the movements in some of these are likely more representative of the trend of the general market than are the Dow-Jones averages. Then too, there are hundreds of stocks to contend with in the stock market and individually they may not conform

in the market place, market action is what we must study

well with any "average trend" as depicted in market averages. In the wheat market, there is wheat and wheat alone; just one object not hundreds of them. I believe that the feelings and knowledge of all persons who influence wheat prices are reflected in wheat prices. Where else could they be reflected?

Technical factors are not "evil," but their proper interpretation is a most "sufficient" job "unto the day."

Our dependence upon human nature

It is, therefore, part of our task to measure, from day to day, the direction of the underlying trend as it is recorded in the market. At times this is a simple matter. A novice, reading the evening newspaper might conclude correctly that the trend is up today if prices have been going up noticeably for several days and the price today is also up. But, what will he do when a declining day comes? He may be badly mistaken if he then infers that the underlying trend is down. Or, if he reasons that the decline is not alarming, and probably is only temporary, he may also be wrong. He will certainly be confused when he is confronted with a series of up and down days; and he won't be very comfortable when the market simply stops in its tracks and moves in a manner which appears on the surface to be aimless and trendless.

Yes, that is a major part of our problem – to identify correctly the direction of the trend today. But, what happens if we are successful in recognizing today's trend? What comfort will that be since we have already concluded that it is impossible to know what will happen tomorrow – or next week, month, or year? The answer is we put out trust in "the natural law of momentum," and we couple that trust with a systematic procedure of buying and selling which recognizes also "the natural law of probability."

This law of momentum – sometimes called "inertia," "continuity" – simply means that once a movement starts the "natural thing" for it to do is to keep on going until it meets an "obstacle." The "obstacle" may be encountered tomorrow, or next week or month – we have no way of telling when – but usually it is not encountered before such time that the *opportunity for a profit* is made available. We should try, of course, to get in on the movement soon after its inception. But, even if we are quite slow in recognizing the start of a new trend, there is often enough profit opportunity left to warrant a trade in the direction of the trend.

In describing the *physical world*, the physicists define this law as "that property of matter by virtue of which it persists in its state of rest of uniform *motion* unless some force changes that state."

In the *mental and emotional world*, the same law operates. Man, considered collectively, imitates strong leadership. We may call it "mob psychology" or "public sentiment." Whatever name we give to the phenomena, it is certain that we do have "waves" in human action. We have waves in the style of clothes being worn, waves in the types of movies being shown and accepted, waves in the themes of best-selling books, crime waves, waves in political sentiment – and, yes, waves in market movements – all simply because it's "human nature" to respond to natural laws.

We need not go into details here to show that "the law of momentum" actually operates in commodity – and security – markets. We can, however, find contentment in knowing that this law has been carefully investigated by reputable, academic authorities. Its undeniable existence in the commodity and security markets has been reported on by the publications of The Econometric

Society, American Statistical Association, and Cowles Commission (University of Chicago).

If the law actually operates in the markets, then why don't we usually take a profit in our trades? There are at least three answers:

1. We, with our impatience, fear and greed, make the taking of profits extremely difficult.
2. Our measurements of today's trend are not perfect. The opportunity for a reasonable gain is usually, but not always, present.
3. Our "techniques" in trading procedure are not yet fully developed. We do not yet possess the best possible plans for taking, or protecting, our gains when they become available.

The latter point will now be discussed briefly in concluding this introduction.

Grasping our opportunities

We have long possessed methods which measure correctly, in the large majority of instances, the direction of today's trend. The old Dow Theory, if we had nothing else, gave the *opportunity* for gain in most of its signals. More recent developments often enable us to buy closer to Bottoms and to sell closer to Tops than was heretofore possible. Hence, today the opportunity for gain is greater than it has ever been before.

The important problem today is to set up a plan, or plans, of *securing the profits* which our trend methods make available to us. Many traders are not having too much trouble in getting *into the market* at prices which are potentially profitable, but are having trouble in getting *out of the market* with a "reasonable share" of the profit which usually is available. Too often we allow a satisfactory paper profit to dwindle down to practically no profit, or an actual loss. Sometimes we take a small profit and in doing so we sacrifice a much larger gain. Sometimes we try for the larger gain, but find ourselves regretting that we didn't grasp a small profit when the opportunity presented itself. At times, our stop orders are caught at the most inopportune moments, and at other times we find ourselves in embarrassing positions if we refrain from using stop orders.

Consequently, I believe that more research work today should be directed toward developing "techniques in trading" rather than "methods for signalling trends." Our present methods for signalling buying and selling points are certainly not the perfected tools we would like to possess, and we shall always continue to improve them, but even in their present state of development they offer excellent opportunity for gains. The main problem today is to set up a specific plan, a definite "trading technique" for grasping the opportunities for gains which these tools present to us from day to day – from swing to swing.

I believe that considerable progress has been made on this problem, as outlined later in this paper. Although much work is yet to be done, I feel very confident that the "Trend Signals" and the "Trading Techniques" already devised will provide pleasing profits in almost any grain contract in any year for the methodical trader who will but follow them faithfully through the life of the contract.

In summary, a "good barometer need not die," if we will:

1. Discipline ourselves in patience, tolerance, courage, humility, prudence.
2. Recognize the impropriety of attempting to foresee how far any movement will go or how long the movement will last.
3. Establish and follow a definite method for determining the direction of the existing trend.
4. Have confidence in the natural laws of momentum and probability to provide the opportunity for gain over a reasonable period of time.
5. Utilize a specific procedure by which trades will be conducted so that the opportunity for gain will be made secure.

THE EVOLUTION OF A TRADING BAROMETER

In the preceding section of this study we discussed the basic philosophy which must underlie the use of any methodical barometer if it is to be used successfully. Let us now approach the problem of setting up a new barometer which recognizes that basic philosophy. For purposes of identification, this new barometer will be called "The Thrust Method." It will be explained in complete detail later in this paper.

The present discussion will trace the evolution of "The Thrust Method." It is well that we become acquainted first with the principles involved in the more elementary methods. This will give us background to the more advanced techniques which are used in the Thrust Method. Incidentally, some of these earlier methods appear to be working quite well in the markets of today, so perhaps on their own merits they deserve attention.

"BREAKAWAY METHOD"

I published my first automatic method for trading in grains back in 1934 under the title "Breakaway Method." This method was quite simple. It merely plotted swings of 5¢ or more in prices and then proceeded to buy and sell in 1¢ penetrations of the Tops and Bottoms of those swings. See Figure 4.1.

Fig 4.1 The breakaway method

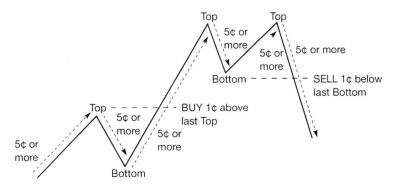

Daily high and low prices were used in determining swings of 5¢ or more. The high price (Top) of an upswing of 5¢ or more was considered an important "resistance point," and the low price (Bottom) of a downswing of 5¢ or more was considered a strong "support point." When prices were trending downward and then reversed and rose 1¢ above the last Top, a Buy Signal was given. A long position was then taken and the main trend was assumed to be in an upward direction as long as prices remained 1¢ or more above their last Bottom. When prices declined 1¢ below their last Bottom, the main trend was then assumed to be down and a short position was entered into at that time.

A definition of a "line" (sideways movement) was also included in this early procedure, but my recollection is that this definition caused many readers to be confused, so I won't bring it up again in this review of past barometers. Besides, the method depended largely on the 5¢-swings rather than on the line concept, so perhaps the latter had little bearing on the success or failure of the method.

Many tests were made with this method using it in conjunction with various "Operating Plans" (stop orders, etc.), and all of these worked out profitably. Some of these tests went back as far as 1925.

But, evidently after publication in 1934, I encountered difficulty with these 5¢-swings in actual practice. Perhaps I ran into two or three consecutive losses and therefore decided to let this barometer die in shame. (Page 17 points out this general attitude toward barometers which give two or more straight losses.) At any rate, I recall burning midnight oil during the late 1930s in frantic search of a formula that would give more satisfactory signals. This resulted in a paper entitled:

"A STUDY IN WHEAT TRADING"

This, the second of my commodity studies, was published early in 1939. The 5¢-swings were now reduced to swings of 2⅜¢ or more, and this reduction permitted buying closer to Bottoms and selling closer to Tops than was possible with the 5¢-swings.

Daily high and low prices were used in setting up the swings of 2⅜¢ or more. Movements within a single day were ignored. Swings of 2⅜¢ or more were used throughout the period tested, 1933–1938, except when prices were below 50¢ at which times swings of 2¢ or more were used.

The required penetrations of Tops and Bottoms in order to effect Buy and Sell signals varied according to this schedule:

Fig 4.2 A study in wheat trading

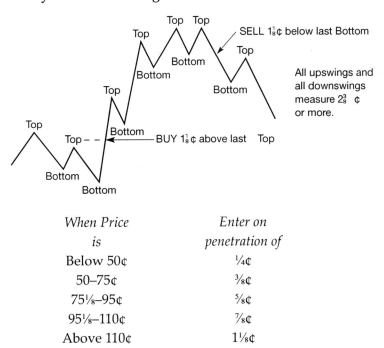

When Price is	Enter on penetration of
Below 50¢	¼¢
50–75¢	⅜¢
75⅛–95¢	⅝¢
95⅛–110¢	⅞¢
Above 110¢	1⅛¢

Following this method today with wheat, corn and soybeans above $1.10, the trader would enter into a long position when prices having been in a downtrend, reversed their downtrend and rose above the last Top by 1⅛¢.

A rather involved "Operating Plan" was set up to be used with this method. This will not be discussed here, but Plans similar to it will be outlined in a later section of this paper. One part of the problem of successful trading is to obtain reasonably good Buy and Sell Signals for purposes of *entering into trades*. An equally important part of the problem is know what to do about *getting out of trades*. How should losses be limited? How should paper profits be protected? When should profits be taken? What should be done about Repeat Signals? Should "pyramiding" be undertaken? These questions must be answered definitely by means of a predetermined "Operating Plan." If they are not answered, the trader is almost certain to encounter emotional storms and material losses. Like a ship without a compass, he will be lost most of the time.

The simplest "Operating Plan," if it can be called a "Plan," would be to buy when a Buy Signal is given and to hold that position until a Sell Signal is given at which time a short position would be taken. Losses would not be limited, paper profits would not be protected, and the eventual profit, if any, would be subject entirely to the fortunate occurence of a good Reversal Signal. It seems that most commodity traders follow just such a haphazard "Plan," and consequently it may be of interest to see how they would have fared in a recent wheat contract using the "2⅜¢ Swing Method" (1⅛¢ penetration above the last Top to give a Buy Signal and 1⅛¢ penetration below the last Bottom to give a Sell Signal). Also, a comparison of recent results of the "2⅜¢ Swing Method" with the earlier "5¢ Swing Method" may be interesting.

Table 4.1 shows the results in the March 1954 option in wheat. This option was chosen purely at random – it just happened to be the latest contract to expire at the time this recent testing was done.

Table 4.1 Record in March 1954 Wheat

5¢ Swing Method		2⅜¢ Swing Method	
2 Gains	58½¢	3 gains	64⅜¢
2 Losses	16⅜¢	5 Losses	18⅝¢
Gross Gain	42⅛¢	Gross Gain	45¾¢
Commissions	1½¢	Commissions	3¢
NET GAIN	40⅝¢	NET GAIN	42¾¢

Now, such profits are quite good and, undoubtedly, could be improved with the adoption of a sound Operating Plan to supplement the Signals. If the records were carried back to the time these methods were first published, very substantial net gains would likely be shown. But, of course, in our futile search for the perfect method, we are not content to rest with "imperfect methods." No doubt, the long-term record of these methods shows streaks of losses which would have discouraged the most faithful followers.

In fact, I must have run into just such a heartbreaking period soon after publication of the "2⅜¢ Swing Method" in 1939, for I find that my next publication on commodity trading was late in 1940. This was under the title:

"PERCENTAGE WHEAT METHOD"

It was obvious from the start of my researches that the same *arithmetic* rules should not be expected to apply to all grains regardless of their price levels. If 2⅜¢ is a satisfactory measure for the significant swings in wheat, then some figure smaller than 2⅜¢ should be an appropriate measure for the lower-priced oats. It would seem that a single measurement in *percentage* might give a satisfactory solution to this problem. Actually, it doesn't help considerably in setting up the important swings – when soybeans is $4.00, a 2% movement is a swing of 8 cents while a 2% swing in oats at 75¢ is only 1½¢, and this proportion doesn't seem to balance out properly in locating the guiding swings at various price levels.

At any rate, in 1940 I decided to be guided by the penetrations of Tops and Bottoms of Swings which amount to 3% or more. "Swing Charts" were set up in the same manner as just observed for the 2⅜¢ and 5¢ movements, only this time a movement had to progress 3% or more before it was considered to be an Upswing or a Downswing. Then, a Buy Signal was given when the last Top of one of these 3%-or-more swings was penetrated upward by 1¼¢ and a Sell Signal was given when the last Bottom was broken downward by 1¼¢. The concept of "lines" was also used in this study, as well as a definite Operating Plan, but these need not be discussed here in this historical summary of past barometers. It is sufficient to say that this method, using percentage swings instead of arithmetic swings, appeared to be an improvement over former efforts.

The record of this method, using it without any Operating Plan other than to buy and sell only on Reversal Signals, is indeed interesting as indicated below. However, this record in March 1954 Wheat is likely not typical of the results in many of the past grain futures. 3% swings appear to be too large in the higher-priced markets of today. Not many Tops and Bottoms are set up, and while this prevents many of the whipsaws which are inherent in the smaller swings, it also means that potential buying and selling points are often a considerable distance from current prices. This can cause much uneasiness on the part of the trader who having bought wheat at, say, $2.00 is obliged to wait until it declines to, say, $1.90 before a Reversal Sell Signal can be given. Or, if he buys wheat at $2.00 and thereafter it has a sharp rise so that he now has a paper profit of 50¢ per bushel, the selling point could very well be so far down that this paper profit would be practically all wiped out by the time a Sell Signal is given. It is clear that this method needs an Operating Plan which limits losses and protects profits.

3% Swings in March 1954 Wheat

2 Gains	63⅞¢
0 Losses	0
Gross Gain	63⅞¢
Commissions	¾¢
NET GAIN	63⅛¢

(Note: In these tests of the March 1954 contract in wheat, the assumption was made that a short position was taken on the *first day* the option sold. This assumption is valid because all the earlier options were already short at that time.)

The above ended my publications on grain trading until the present paper. However, this was not the end of *work* on the subject, as will be evident from the following remaining pages of this review of early investigations.

"2½% SWINGS IN 3 OR MORE DAYS"

During the years 1941–1942 I spent considerable time working on trading methods and techniques in commodity markets. Then, World War 2 came along and market research was suspended because of the more important, but less attractive, business at hand. The cost of this 1941–1942 research was financed by one man, and at that time it was not contemplated to publish the results. I am now grateful for his permission to give this outline of the main conclusions from that study. (The reader will not be burdened here with the voluminous details – technicalities, work papers and charts.)

The research period of the study covered the 12 years from January 1930 through December 1941. Two methods were evolved. The first sought to buy and sell advantageously on the penetrations of preceding Tops and Bottoms, in much the same manner as discussed in the foregoing earlier methods. The other method understood to buy and sell at more favorable prices – that is, to buy lower and to sell higher than is possible using the ordinary methods which depend essentially on penetrations of preceding supply and demand barriers for their signals. This second method, evolved in the researches of 1941–1942, is the forerunner of the present "Thrust Method," so it is well that we become acquainted with it for background information.

The buying and selling rules which I finally adopted were those rules which gave the maximum gains over the 12-year period, 1930–1941. In other words, through the process of trial and error, I *fitted* some rules to the 1930–1941 period. Obviously, the record is excellent for 1930–1941 period as the rules were *made to work* during that period.

Having thus found the best rules for the research period, I then proceeded to find whether the *same* rules would work equally as well, or nearly as well, in some *prior* period. If I found that the rules which were made to conform with the 1930–1941 period would also work quite well during a *prior* 12-year period it would be indicative that we would get profitable results in a *future* period. So, I tested the same rules for the 12 years in which the market was open during the years 1915–1929, inclusive (trading was suspended in commodity futures for nearly three years during this period – August 25, 1917–July 24, 1920).

I found, as expected, that while the methods did not give the excellent results of the formula-fitting period (1930–1941), they nevertheless made a creditable showing, and it was concluded that the prior performance (during 1915–1929) was about what we could expect of the methods in the future.

The supreme test of any method is, of course, "Will it work in the future?". At this time (June 1954, when the revised edition of this paper is being prepared) we have a little over 12 additional years (January 1943-June 1954) in which tests could be made of the 1941–1942 methods. I have not compiled any detailed record of this recent period, but have casually checked a number of options and have found net "gains in grains" in all of them. There were good times and there were trying times, but by the end of each option, there was always a net gain. The record of these methods extends, therefore, over nearly 30 years (1915–1954), about 12 of which have dealt successfully with the unknowns of the future. However, notwithstanding all this, the methods do not appear to offer all we can expect from methodical trading procedures. The same objections which we found in the "3% Method" appears also to be present here – mainly, that the "significant" Tops and Bottoms are set up too infrequently, and signals might, therefore, be long delayed after an important movement gets under way.

Penetration of Tops & Bottoms of 2½%–3-day swings

A cursory inspection of a price chart will give a general picture of past trends. But, such a view of the past is barely helpful when our purpose is to judge *today's trend*. We need first to cut off from our view the "insignificant movements" of the past. We wish to focus our attention on only "significant past movements in their relationship to present prices. Our purpose is to correlate present prices with past prices in such a way as to detect whether the present trend of prices is up or down.

> *The swings which gave the best signals were those which measured at least 2½%*

Therefore, in order to confine our attention to the *main essentials*, and not to the erratic details, we first set up on our chart the important past Upswings and Down-swings and their Tops and Bottoms. We have already mentioned ways in which attempt: have been made to do this (5¢ swings, 2⅜¢ swings, 3% swings). In my 1940–1941 research I tried out a considerable variety of "swings" from 1¢ to several cents, from 1% to 6%, and I also now included the *time element* in the definitions of swings.

I finally came to the conclusion that the swings which gave the best signals during the years 1930–1941 were those which measured at least 2½% *provided they occupied at least three trading days.* (Swings of 6% or more which occurred in less than three days were also considered meaningful, but these were relatively few in number and can be ignored in this discussion.) In order to set up an Upswing, for example, it was not necessary that the market rose three *consecutive* days. There could be declining days between the Bottom and Top, but it was required that the time elapsed between the Bottom and the Top was at least three trading days, and that during this time the market rose at least 2½%. Hence, movements of one or two days were ignored (unless the move was 6% or more).

These "2½%-3-day Swings" do not seem suitable to me today. It will be shown in the "Thrust Method" that the smaller, more sensitive, swings can be utilized advantageously. However, let us continue with the background and learn how these 1940–1941 methods were constructed. The first of these methods can be illustrated by Figure 4.3.

Fig 4.3 2½%-3-day swings

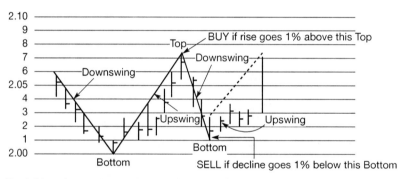

Each Upswing and each Downswing amounts to 2½ % or more and occupies at least 3 trading days.

An elaborate Operating Plan was set up to be used with this method. This Plan limited losses, protected profits, gave effect to Repeat Signals, and provided for a way of deciding whether a trade should be conducted on a quick-run or a long-term basis. But, as mentioned before, we shall consider Operating Plans later in the paper. Our purpose now is simply to point out former methods of recognizing changes in the main trend – Reversal Signals.

Let us look again at the recently expired March 1954 Wheat Future and see how this method fared in it. Again we shall not bother with an Operating Plan but shall assume that the trader followed the dangerous practice of buying on a Buy Signal and this was held, come what may, until a Sell Signal was later given, at which time he went short and held on until a new Buy Signal was given, etc. Furthermore, we are again going to assume that the trader went short on the first day of the March 1954 wheat option for the reason that all the other wheat options were short at that time – and, still furthermore, we are going to assume that an open position toward the end of the contract would be disposed of at the closing price on the last day of the contract. Now, these things would seldom be done in actual practice – a trader rarely gets into an contract on the first day it appears on the board and he seldom ever holds on to a commitment until the very end of a contract. However, for purposes of *testing the efficiency* of a method these assumptions are entirely justifiable. A grain contract, unlike a share of stock, does not have a continuous life, and if we are to test a single grain option, we must make some reasonable assumptions. While the trader would not trade in March Wheat from the start to the end of its life, the overall record in March Wheat during its full life is indicative of the results the trader might expect in any of the wheat options during the same period.

"2½%–3-Day Swings" in March 1954 Wheat"

2 Gains	50⅜¢ per bushel
0 Losses	0
Gross Gain	50⅜¢
Commissions	¾
NET GAIN	49⅝¢

Of course, if the point must be reemphasized, the reader should not infer that a net gain of about 50¢ per bushel is the usual result. Some contracts have done better, some have done decidedly worse, and all seem to result in a net "gain in grains."

Here are a few interesting and perhaps very important, "by-products" which came from the investigation of this method.

Buying after Double Bottoms and selling after Double Tops

I found that a Buy Signal was particularly effective if it was preceded by a Double Bottom. I considered that a Double Bottom pattern was present if the last Bottom was 2¢ or less, either above or below, the preceding Bottom. See Figure 4.4.

> *I found that a Buy Signal was particularly effective if it was preceded by a Double Bottom*

Fig 4.4 Buying after a Double Bottom

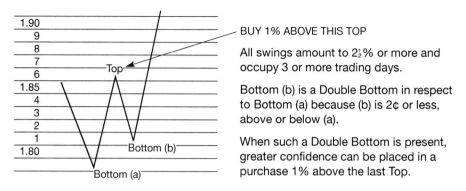

BUY 1% ABOVE THIS TOP

All swings amount to $2\frac{1}{2}$% or more and occupy 3 or more trading days.

Bottom (b) is a Double Bottom in respect to Bottom (a) because (b) is 2¢ or less, above or below (a).

When such a Double Bottom is present, greater confidence can be placed in a purchase 1% above the last Top.

The situation is similar in case of a Double Top formation before the penetration of the last Bottom. See Figure 4.5.

Fig 4.5 Selling after a Double Top

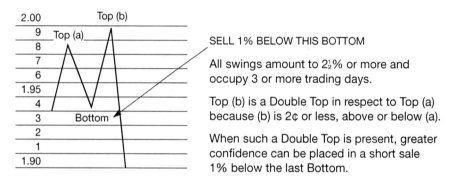

SELL 1% BELOW THIS BOTTOM

All swings amount to $2\frac{1}{2}$% or more and occupy 3 or more trading days.

Top (b) is a Double Top in respect to Top (a) because (b) is 2¢ or less, above or below (a).

When such a Double Top is present, greater confidence can be placed in a short sale 1% below the last Bottom.

The above rules were checked in wheat during the years 1921–1941. Using a definite Operating Plan which limited losses and protected profits, it was found that 92½% of the trades which followed such Double Top or Double Bottom formations were profitable. This compares with 86% of the trades being profitable which were not preceded by the Double Top or Double Bottom formation.

Buying when Double Tops are penetrated and selling when Double Bottoms are penetrated

The situation in this "by-product" is somewhat different. We now wait until a Double Top is set up, and then we buy 1% above the highest of these two Tops. A Double Top is defined in the same manner – the last two Tops must be within 2¢ of each other.

Fig 4.6 Buying when Double Tops are penetrated

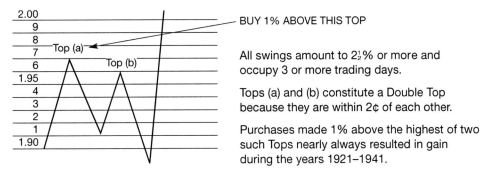

BUY 1% ABOVE THIS TOP

All swings amount to $2\frac{1}{2}$% or more and occupy 3 or more trading days.

Tops (a) and (b) constitute a Double Top because they are within 2¢ of each other.

Purchases made 1% above the highest of two such Tops nearly always resulted in gain during the years 1921–1941.

Fig 4.7 Selling when Double Bottoms are penetrated

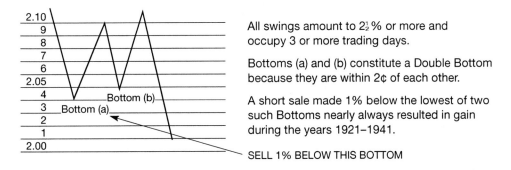

All swings amount to $2\frac{1}{2}$% or more and occupy 3 or more trading days.

Bottoms (a) and (b) constitute a Double Bottom because they are within 2¢ of each other.

A short sale made 1% below the lowest of two such Bottoms nearly always resulted in gain during the years 1921–1941.

SELL 1% BELOW THIS BOTTOM

During the years 1930–1941, 40 of these "Double Top" or "Double Bottom" trades were entered into, and 39 of these turned out profitably. During 1921–1929, there were 31 of such trades and 28 of these resulted in gain. Such a record borders on the miraculous. Figure 4.6 shows a Double Top preceding the penetration of a Double Bottom – and this was almost a "sure thing" for profits during 1921–1941. I have not yet made a count of how such formations are working today, but I am certain that they are well worth investigating. This will be done during the course of present investigation.

Market orders vs stop orders

Another interesting sidelight of the 1940–1941 research came as a result of a test on whether a trader should buy and sell by means of "stop orders" or by "market orders." In buying 1% above the last Top, the purchase could be engineered either by(1) placing ahead of time an "open stop order" to buy at the calculated price or by (2) waiting until prices rose to the calculated price and then placing an order to buy "at the market." The latter would assume that the trader was in close touch with the market during trading hours, and throughout these commodity studies I have not wanted to make that assumption. Many of us cannot, or prefer not, to watch the market during the day; we would rather do our chart work, make our calculations, and place our orders, after the market closes or before it opens the following day.

Therefore, if we are willing to buy wheat if it rises to, say, $2.00, the question is should we place (1) an "open stop order" to buy at that figure or should we (2) wait until the day wheat actually sells at $2.00 or more, and then place an order to buy "at the opening" the following morning?

It was found that 54% of the trades favored executions by open stop orders, while 46% of the trades favored waiting until the opening of the following morning before buying or selling. Over the 1930–1941 period, the total net additional profit gained through using open stop orders was 48¢ per bushel. Although this is not considerable extra profit over a 12-year period, the advantage of "stop orders" over "opening orders" becomes more apparent when we look at some of the single transactions – in one trade a purchase would have been made 12⅛¢ higher if the trader had postponed buying until the opening following the day of the signal.

Today there appears to be a distinct tendency toward strong or weak openings, depending upon the direction of the prevailing trend. I would say that the evidence today is very favorable toward the use of "open stop orders" rather than "market" or "opening orders."

Buying on rise from Double Bottom

In all of the methods so far discussed, we are utilizing the old Dow Theory principle of buying when prices rise above a former Top and selling when prices decline below a former Bottom. Now at times this is quite satisfactory, but much too often it puts the trader into an uneasy position of having bought after a considerable rally. Likewise, selling is often not done until after the market has had a very sharp decline.

The practical trader has long sought for methodical ways of buying closer to Bottoms and selling closer to Tops. This brings us to the "Thrust Method" which will be outlined in detail in the next section of this paper. At this point, we shall merely glance at a technique which I used back in 1940–1941. This dealt with a rise from a Double Bottom to give a Buy Signal and a decline from a Double Top to give a Sell Signal.

In this case I changed the definition of Double Bottoms and Double Tops from 2¢ to 2%. When grains are above $1, this gives a wider price range in which the existence of Double Tops and Double Bottoms is possible. Also, I defined a Double Top so that it would embrace either of the *two* preceding Tops, instead of simply the one preceding Top. The same was true in respect to the definition of a Double Bottom – it now gave recognition to the *two* preceding Bottoms, rather than the last Bottom alone. Here is how the Double Bottom concept was used:

A possible Double Bottom exists today if the Low Price in the current Downswing is within 2% (above or below) either or both of the two preceding Bottoms. In such case, BUY if prices rise 3 or more days and 2½% or more above the Low Price. (Rise must occupy at least 3 days and amount to at least 2½%.)

Fig 4.8 Buying on rise from Double Bottom

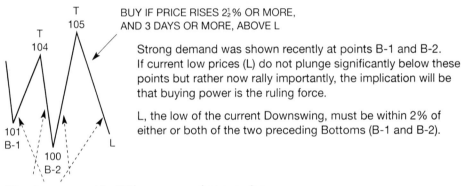

BUY IF PRICE RISES 2½% OR MORE,
AND 3 DAYS OR MORE, ABOVE L

Strong demand was shown recently at points B-1 and B-2. If current low prices (L) do not plunge significantly below these points but rather now rally importantly, the implication will be that buying power is the ruling force.

L, the low of the current Downswing, must be within 2% of either or both of the two preceding Bottoms (B-1 and B-2).

All swings amount to 2½% or more and occupy 3 or more days.

Selling on decline from Double Top

The same procedure, in reverse, was used for determining Sell Signals on declines from Double Tops.

A Possible Double Top exists today if the High Price in the current Upswing is within 2% (above or below) either or both of the two preceding Tops. In such case, SELL SHORT if prices decline 3 or more days and 2½% or more below the High Price. (Decline must occupy at least 3 days – not necessarily consecutive days – in which time decline must be at least 2½%.)

Fig 4.9 Selling on decline from Double Top

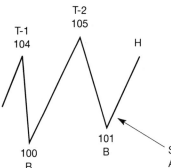

H, the high of the current Upswing, must be within 2% of either or both of the two preceding Tops (T-1 and T-2).

Forceful supply as shown recently at points T-1 and T-2. If current high prices (H) cannot rise importantly above these former highs, but rather prices now decline significantly, the evidence will be that sell-power is the dominant force.

SELL IF PRICE DECLINES 2½% OR MORE, AND 3 DAYS OR MORE, BELOW H.

Summary and acknowledgments

I am quite convinced that all of the foregoing past research was not in vain. In fact, I am very sure that if I had, during past years, followed consistently any of these former methods, a very substantial net gain would now be shown. But, it is the nature of man to work for improvements. You, or I, are never going to evolve the "perfect" commodity method, but nevertheless we shall probably keep on trying.

Before turning to the "Thrust Method," a word should be added here about charts. The reader has likely observed that we are dealing with "precision instruments." The "last ⅛ of a cent counts;" therefore our charts must be carefully drawn so that we can read them to the "last ⅛." If the reader already has such charts, he should continue using them as he is accustomed to his own charts. If he wants to make up a set of charts, data for years back can be obtained from the US Department of Agriculture. If he prefers the easier way, to buy a set of charts already made, I can, on request, direct him to a publisher of charts. (In passing, I hope I will be pardoned for mentioning that I do *not* receive any "commission" from the sale of products or services of others – although I frequently recommend the works of others to my clients.)

No statement of past research would be complete without an acknowledgment of the great assistance I have received from other students of market action – Ainsworth, Cole, De Mandel, Drew, Edwards and Magee, Fahrner, Gann, Jackson, Livermore, Rhea, Wyckoff – just to mention a few.* Their writings have influenced much of our present-day thinking. Sometimes I feel that

---

Editor's footnote: The great market minds mentioned here should, with a goodly number of others, some day go on commemoration scroll that does deserved honor to their monumental contributions to technical analysis.

there isn't much more known today about technical analysis than was known years ago. Quite often I have made a "new discovery," only to find later that someone else found the same things years ago. Such experiences are shocking to one's ego, but this is compensated by the consolation of knowing that the things which appear new and important today were actually working successfully in the markets of years ago.

If I have made any original contribution in the field of technical analysis, it is perhaps in trying to make *order* out of disorder. In one of my publications, I gave an explanation of "115 Barometers." This sort of thing may have some academic value, but from the point of view of *actual trading*, such a conglomeration of ideas is hardly helpful. It is easy enough to look *back* and see that we *should have used* "such-and-such a rule;" but in looking *ahead* the trader needs a *definite, methodical plan* and not a great smattering of information from which he can select that which pleases the whims of his feelings and intellect. I hope that this study will be helpful into putting the reader's commodity activities on a systematic basis.

I should too at this point express my appreciation for current help in research work. I have been receiving some very constructive assistance in the problems before us, and I expect that the present "Thrust Method" will soon step aside for something better. In the meanwhile, I feel confident that it will lead to "Gains in Grains," which, after all, is the matter in which we are interested today.

Finally, I'd like to mention my sincere thanks to the many clients who have for years "footed the bill" for these research efforts, and a special note of appreciation to Mr. Franklin P. Jackson and Mr. Homer Fahrner who have kindly recommended my studies to their clients.

THE THRUST METHOD

The Thrust Method will require a little study. On first reading it may seem complicated, but such is not the case. Once the method is set up on a chart, it can be followed easily in a minute a day per chart.

Each day, *after the close,* you simply chart the high, low and closing prices for that day. After that is done, you will be able to see almost instantly whether any "Signal Patterns" are present which might lead to the opening of a new trade on the following day. You will also be able to see whether prices moved during the day in such a manner as to require a change to be made in any orders now placed with your broker on a transaction not yet closed out. Hence, almost at a glance, you will know what orders, if any, to telephone to your broker for the following day. Having thus taken care of the "evils of today" in a few minutes, you can then go about your regular business or pleasure, and let tomorrow take care of itself.

UPSWINGS & DOWNSWINGS, TOPS & BOTTOMS

Our ultimate aim, at any time, is to determine whether our market position should be long or short, and, of course, to profit from that position.

We must also know the points at which recent Tops and Bottoms occurred

We take a long position on the presence of *Buy Pattern* followed by a *Thrust* above those Buy Patterns. And, we take a short position on the presence of *Sell Patterns* followed by a *Thrust* below those Sell Patterns.

A first step, therefore, is to look at our daily price chart and determine whether any Buy Patterns, or Sell Patterns, are now present. But we cannot determine this until we first know (1) whether prices are now in an Upswing or in a Downswing, and (2) whether prices are now above or below recent Tops or recent Bottoms.

In other words, as a very first step we must "size up" the current price action in relation to its recent action. We must first know whether prices are now in an Upswing or a Downswing, and we must also know the points at which recent Tops and Bottoms occurred in order to relate current prices to those Tops and Bottoms. After we have taken that step, we will then be ready to determine whether any Buy Patterns, or Sell Patterns, are present in the current price action.

The Thrust Method recognizes that the small, minor swings are important for deriving buy and sell signals at favorable prices. Using minor swings, as well as the larger swings, we automatically set up a considerable number of Upswings and Downswings so that it is unlikely that any important details will be lost. This permits us, at times, to buy close to Bottoms and to sell near the Tops.

Also in watching the minor swings, we are enabled often to get "Repeat Signals" during the long movements in a given direction. Very often when the market reacts temporarily against its main trend, the minor reaction will signal another trade in the direction of the main trend. These "Repeat Signals" can be used either for trading for additional quick, short-term profits or for "pyramiding" operations with the larger profits in view.

Moreover, the particular method proposed here of establishing Upswings and Downswings, and their Tops and Bottoms, makes it unnecessary to revise the rules for various price levels or for various mediums for trading. The procedure is "universal," and can be applied to any commodity, or any security, at any price.

Upswings and Tops

An UPSWING *starts* when a day's high and low prices rise above the respective high and low prices of the latest Downswing.

Prices then remain in an Upswing – regardless of the appearance of daily price action – until such a day that the high and low prices decline below the respective high and low prices of the highest day of the Upswing.

The highest price in an Upswing is called a TOP.

Downswings and Bottoms

A DOWNSWING *starts* when a **day's** high and low prices decline below the respective high and low prices of **the** highest day of the latest Upswing.

Prices then remain in a Downswing – regardless of the appearance of daily price action – until such a day that the high and low prices rise above the respective high and low prices of the lowest day of the Downswing.

The lowest price in a Downswing is called a BOTTOM.

Illustration

The above definitions seem to me to be too "wordy" for the simple matter now being considered. Figure 4.10 will probably make the definitions clear.

Fig 4.10 Upswings, Downswings, Tops and Bottoms

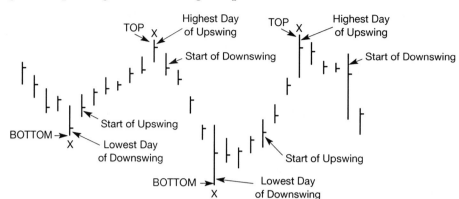

(Tops and Bottoms can be conveniently marked on charts with the letter "X".)

In "The Evolution of a Trading Barometer" we learned of other ways of determining Upswings and Downswings and we began to realize the importance and difficulties in this matter. In the stock market, Dow theorists often disagree about what past Tops and Bottoms should be considered important as the guiding lights for their signals. In either stocks or grains we shall always have the same trouble unless we adopt a definite, mechanical procedure for recognizing Upswings and Downswings and their Tops and Bottoms. A method which readily adapts itself to both stocks and grains, regardless of price level, and which gives recognition to the minor swings, seems to me to be the best yet proposed.

Sometimes these minor swings are too "sensitive" – "Xs" appear on a chart marking "swings" which actually don't look like swings, and unfortunately these, at times, lead to whipsaws. At other times these very "swings" are the sole means of deriving signals at very attractive prices. So, "sensitively" is both an asset and a liability. I am sure that the favorable balance is on the asset side of the ledger.

> **We shall always have the same trouble unless we adopt a definite, mechanical procedure**

The main objection, as I see it, to this plan of determining the Upswings and Downswings comes when a wide-ranged "outside day" is followed by a series of "inside days." My definition of swings does not take care of this situation when it occurs which, fortunately, is not frequently:

Likely it is too early in the paper to present "technicalities" such as the above, so I suggest that the reader does not ponder long on the difficult points at this time. These should become very clear in due time.

Fig 4.11 Outside day followed by inside days

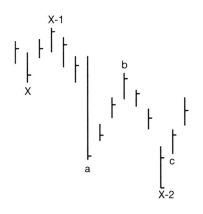

Since 'b' did not go above the high of 'a' there is no Upswing from 'a' to 'b'. The entire movement from X–1 to X–2 is a Downswing and the Upswing starts at 'c'.

This means, according to our definition, that 'a' is not a Bottom, and 'b' is not a Top, and they should therefore be ignored in determining present Signal Patterns *from past Tops and Bottoms.* (It will be seen later that while 'a' cannot be used as a 'Bottom', it is still useful for measuring 'Narrow Range" and determining "Inside Range." Also, such a day as 'b', though it is not a "Top," it might be useful as a "Narrow Range" or an "Inside Range.")

SIGNAL PATTERNS WHICH LEAD TO BUY AND SELL SIGNALS

Having set up the past Upswings and Downswings, and their Tops and Bottoms, we now relate the present market action to these past movements. We look for certain formations, or patterns, in today's price action, relative to preceding action, which may lead the way to a buy or sell signal *tomorrow.* Briefly, these patterns are:

Buy patterns	Sell patterns
1. Test of Bottom (TOB)	1. Test of Top (TOT)
2. Closing-Price Reversal (CPR)	2. Closing-Price Reversal (CPR)
3. Narrow Range (NR)	3. Narrow Range (NR)
4. Inside Range (IR)	4. Inside Range (IR)
5. Penetration of Top (PT)	5. Penetration of Bottom (PB)

These are the signal-producing phenomena, price patterns, which we have chosen to use as offering good opportunities for gains. If two or more of the first four Patterns are present today and this is followed tomorrow by a "Thrust," the opportunity for a gain is considered to be very favorable. These four Patterns often provide the means for us to buy very close to Bottoms and to sell very near the Tops. When these four patterns do not get us in early in a movement, we then fall back on the procedure explained in Figure 4.2. Hence, there is little chance that we will be left behind on the sidelines during the course of a large trend movement. In fact, if the trend movement is large, we will usually have *repeated* opportunities to get aboard the movement (through "Repeat Signals"). Of course, the path is not strewn only with roses; we run into thorns – losses – from time to time along the way.

> **We shall show how these patterns produce automatically their buy and sell signals**

We now define each of these patterns *mechanically*. After that is done, we shall then show how these patterns produce *automatically* their buy and sell signals.

"BUY PATTERNS"
(PATTERNS WHICH MAY LEAD TO HIGHER PRICES)

Test of Bottom (TOB)

A "Test of Bottom" is present when the *lowest price in current Downswing* is within 1¢ above or below either of the two preceding Bottoms.

Fig 4.12 Test of Bottom

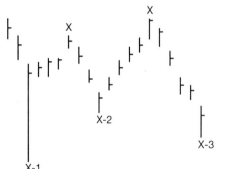

A TOB is present if:
(1) X-3 is 1¢ or less above either X-1 or X-2,
           or if
(2) X-3 is 1¢ or less below either X-1 or X-2.
(Of course, a TOB is present if X-3 is equal to either X-1 or X-2.)

All students of market action are well acquainted with the formations known as "Double Bottoms," "Ascending Bottoms," "Head-and-Shoulder Bottoms," "Complex Bottoms," etc. I have chosen to use the term "Test of Bottom" which embraces somewhat the various bottom formations. Recent Bottoms (X-1 and X-2) represent the points at which buying support actually came into the market, while the current low price (X-3) is that point at which support *may* be forthcoming again. Will strong buying power appear again near the price, or prices, at which support was obtained recently? If a TOB is present *today*, and if strong buying power is evidenced *tomorrow* by virtue of a "thrust" above today's high price, we will have at least that much evidence that the momentum favors the upside. (The term "thrust" will be defined later.)*

(At this place it seems appropriate to make a parenthetical observation: The textbooks and market courses usually do not venture to make *precise* definitions of "Double Bottoms" or any of the other price patterns. It is imperative, however, that our rules be stated *mechanically* if we are to test the actual efficiency of our observations. If they are not stated mechanically, we will be mere subjects of all the pitfalls of human reasoning and wishful thinking. We can always find "reasons" for a movement *after* the movement is over – a non-mechanical system can boast 100% accuracy over any *past* market period because there are plenty of "rules" to draw from and some of them are bound to work. It is more difficult to know what particular rule, or rules, to select *now*. If we are to test this method, or any method, we must insist upon *precision*. Our mechanical rules are likely not the best that can be found, but nevertheless they are, and must be, *precise*.)

Closing-Price Reversal (CPR)

A "Closing-Price Reversal" is present when the closing price on the lowest day in current Downswing is above the closing price of the preceding day.

Fig 4.13 Closing-Price Reversal

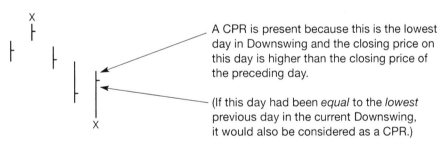

A CPR is present because this is the lowest day in Downswing and the closing price on this day is higher than the closing price of the preceding day.

(If this day had been *equal* to the *lowest* previous day in the current Downswing, it would also be considered as a CPR.)

A better term for this pattern might be "Bottom-Day Reversal." After the first printing of this paper, I found some students marking their charts with "CPRs" every time the market closed higher (or lower, it didn't seem to make much difference.) To qualify as a Buy Pattern, the higher close must come on the *lowest day of the Downswing* (or on a day equal to the lowest day).

---

*The Author knew here that he was dealing with a powerful analytical tool that while known to many in the technical analytical field, it was little appreciated. The reader is encouraged here to use what should be known as the Dunnigan/Jackson Thrust Methodology definition and take it as a starting point to further develop the Thrust concept; the results should prove worth it.

Some newspapers give "split prices" for the closes. If you chart both of these prices, then to qualify as a CPR both of the prices for today's close should be

> *To qualify as a Buy Pattern, the higher close must come on the lowest day of the Downswing*

above the highest of the split price in yesterday's close. Some chartists prefer to use only one figure for the close – either the first or last figure, if used consistently, should serve just as effectively in the long run as the "split closes." Most newspapers only give one figure for the close, so there is no choice but to use it. (I don't feel that this observation is too important but several readers of the first edition made inquiry about it.)

The Closing-Price Reversal pattern has been observed by many market technicians. It appears to have been an excellent indicator in the old days, and it appears to be working just as effectively today. *However*, if prices are now in a major downtrend, I certainly wouldn't care to buy simply because a CPR appeared on a low day. After the CPR comes, *insist upon a THRUST upward* before considering the bullish implications. If you buy every time in a major decline when a CPR appears on a low day of a Downswing, you will be inviting some major disappointments. (For *Repeat Signals* the story of CPRs is different – in this case we do not have to wait for a "thrust" – as will be explained later. We are talking now about a *Reversal* Buy Signal during a major decline when our position has been on the short side.)

The "reason" why the CPR pattern is often a good one might be explained this way: The closing price is considered by many persons to be the most important price during the day. It is the "evening-up" or "balancing" price of the day after the give-and-take of supply and demand has been spent. It supposedly represents the best net opinion of everyone as to the value of a grain for that day. Consequently, if during a day wheat drops into new low ground for the current Downswing, or if it hovers at old low ground for the current Downswing, and then spurts up to close higher than it did the day before, the implication is bullish. A reversal in sentiment may have occurred, and if this is confirmed later by other evidence, we would be willing to buy.

Narrow Range (NR)

A "Narrow Range" is present when any daily range in current Downswing is ½ or less of the largest daily range from the Top of current Downswing. See Figure 4.14a.

Fig 4.14a Narrow Range

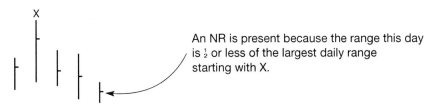

An NR is present because the range this day is $\frac{1}{2}$ or less of the largest daily range starting with X.

Also, a "Narrow Range" is present when any daily range in current Upswing is ½ or less of the largest daily range from the Bottom of current Upswing. See Figure 4.14b.

Fig 4.14b Narrow Range

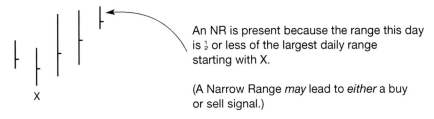

An NR is present because the range this day is $\frac{1}{2}$ or less of the largest daily range starting with X.

(A Narrow Range *may* lead to *either* a buy or sell signal.)

Students of stock and commodity prices have long recognized "rest periods" in the markets – "lines," "trading areas," "consolidation areas," "apexes in triangles," etc. They have observed that prices eventually break away from these rest periods and move, one way or the other, in a spirited manner. The "mob," "mass psychology," slows down, it is uncertain, it hesitates, it awaits leadership. Sooner or later, the leadership asserts itself, and eventually the mob joins in on the movement – often too late.

We use a narrowing of the range to indicate inactivity, hesitation, indecision. Then, as an indication of powerful "leadership," we use a one-day *thrust* in prices – an emphatic one-day breakaway past markets when supplemented with other considerations which will be explained later.

Inside Range (IR)

An "Inside Range" is present when the range for a day, in either an Upswing or a Downswing, is within (neither above nor below) the price range of the preceding day.

Also, an "Inside Range" is present when each of the daily price ranges for a series of consecutive days is within the price range of the day preceding the start of the series.

Fig 4.15 Inside Range

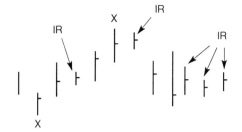

Each of the days marked "IR" is an "Inside Range" and *may* lead to *either* a buy or sell signal.

"Inside Range" has the same "logical inference" as "Narrow Range." In fact, Inside days are often also Narrow-Range days – although this is not required. A day which is inside of the range of the previous day (or a series of days all inside the range before the start of the series) marks a time of hesitation, a slowing-down in the price movement, a moment of indecision. The breakaway (thrust) from such a day, or days, may give the clue as to whether supply or demand is the ruling force.

Penetration of Top (PT)

A "Penetration of Top" is present when price rises above the last Top by any amount.

Fig 4.16 Penetrating of Top

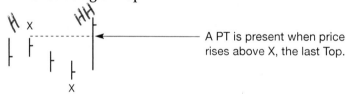

A PT is present when price rises above X, the last Top.

This is our "last-resort pattern." We do not like to use it and most of the time we don't have to. Usually a signal to buy will come before this pattern is needed. In other words, we will ordinarily buy at a lower price than is possible through the PT pattern.

The "reasoning" underlying this pattern is quite generally understood. It is the old Dow-Theory principle which we reviewed in Part III of this paper. The last Top is the spot where forceful supply just recently exerted itself. If the demand now becomes so urgent that it can push through the supply which again may be encountered at that spot, the implication may prove to be that the buying power now exceeds the selling pressure.

"SELL PATTERNS"
(PATTERNS WHICH MAY LEAD TO LOWER PRICES)

Test of Top (TOT) ST OF UT , SOT oR creek holds

(handwritten: (1) (2) (3))

A "Test of Top" is present when the highest price in latest Upswing is within 1¢ above or below either of the two preceding Tops.

Fig 4.17 Test of Top

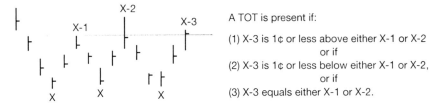

A TOT is present if:

(1) X-3 is 1¢ or less above either X-1 or X-2
      or if
(2) X-3 is 1¢ or less below either X-1 or X-2,
      or if
(3) X-3 equals either X-1 or X-2.

"Test of Top" embraces, to some extent at least, the well-known patterns, "Double Top," "Descending Top," "Head-and-Shoulder Top," and "Complex Top." Recent Tops (X-1 and X-2) represent the points at which selling pressure actually came into the market, while the current high price (X-3) is that point at which pressure *may* again be exerted. If a TOT is present *today*, and if strong selling pressure is evidenced *tomorrow*, by virtue of a "thrust" below today's low price, we will have evidence that the balance of power favors the downside.

Closing-Price Reversal (CPR)

A "Closing-Price Reversal" is present when the closing price on the highest day of latest Upswing is below the closing price of the preceding day.

Fig 4.18 Closing-Price Reversal (TOP DAY REVERSAL) UT

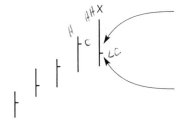

A CPR is present because this is the highest day in Upswing and the closing price on this day is lower than the closing price of the preceding day.

(If this day had been *equal* to the *highest* previous day in the current Upswing, it would also be considered as a CPR.)

A better descriptive term for this pattern would probably be "Top-Day Reversal," but we shall continue with the present terminology because many readers of the first printing of this paper have adopted it. To qualify as a "sell CPR" the lower close must come on the *highest day of the Upswing* (or on a day equal to the highest day.) Hence, merely because the market closed lower today than yesterday would not necessarily make today a CPR. Some few readers have inferred that when the market closes higher it is a "buy CPR" and when it closes lower it is a "sell CPR" – hence, nearly every day became a CPR of some sort. Of course, this is not true, and, though there is no change in my present drawings and definitions of "CPRs," I hope this additional explanation will help those who have been confused. A "buy CPR" must come *on the lowest day (or equal low) of a Downswing*. A "sell CPR" must come *on the highest day (or equal high) of an Upswing*.*

If you use both of the split prices for charting the closing price, then to qualify as a Sell-Pattern CPR both of the prices for today's close should be below the lowest of the split price in yesterday's close.

The "logic" behind the "top-day reversal" (CPR) is something like this: If today wheat rallies into new high ground for the current Upswing, or meets its former high for this Upswing, and then declines to close lower than it did yesterday, the implication is that traders are not enthusiastic about valuing wheat at the higher prices. They make a test at the higher values, but the test fails – the net consensus of opinion is that wheat isn't even worth what it closed at yesterday. If this bearish attitude is later supported by other similar evidence, we will be justified in looking for lower prices.

Narrow Range (NR)

(Same as Narrow Range in "Buy Patterns" – see Figures 4.14a and 4.14b.

Inside Range (IR)

(Same as Inside Range in "Buy Patterns" – see Figure 4.15.)

Penetration of Bottom (PB)

A "Penetration of Bottom" is present when price declines below the last Bottom by any amount.

---

*The highest day *at a particular date* may not later prove to be the actual high day; nevertheless if the highest day *to date* has a lower close, it *is* a "sell CPR."

Fig 4.19 Penetration of Bottom

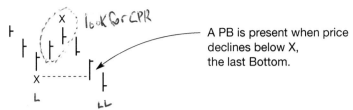

A PB is present when price
declines below X,
the last Bottom.

This is our "last-resort pattern" for getting a Sell Signal. Usually Sell Signals come at earlier and higher prices than is possible with the use of this pattern; but when those more attractive signals fail to come, we fall back on this pattern.

The preceding Bottom represents a potential demand point. Buying power may show itself again at that point (in the event of a TOB followed by an upward Thrust), but if this fails and prices instead decline below the last Bottom, the implication may well be bearish.

Summary of buy & sell patterns

The foregoing are the price patterns, or formations, which we are going to depend upon to produce "gains in grains." There is nothing startlingly new about these patterns. They secured the favorable recognition of competent market analysts many years ago. About all this writer has done is to "mechanize" those patterns and, frankly, I'm not too well pleased yet with my "mechanizations". Notwithstanding that, I feel confident that if these patterns are used in a methodical manner, they will fulfil the title of this paper and produce for any trader "Gains in Grains." Whether you, or I, can actually use them in a methodical manner is a highly questionable matter (see "The Use of Mechanical Methods in Grain Trading"), but the possible solution to that comes under the subject of psychology or, perhaps, psychiatry, and that is outside of the scope of this study.

The matter before us now is to set up a very definite procedure for using these patterns. Readers who have followed my ideas in recent years are well aware that a considerable variety of procedures could be set up, but I am not going to burden you with a review of all of these in this paper. Our main ever-present problem seems to be: "How can we reduce the number of losses – whipsaws – so that we can have greater confidence in the single trade at any single time?" We can (and I am sure it has been long demonstrated) obtain a good net profit over a period of time. But, how can we enter into the very next trade with a high expectation that it will turn out profitably? Well, I have some present ideas on that, and they will be brought out in the course of this treatise.

They deal with the taking of quick, short profits, and I believe they will work for the man who is willing and able to trade on that basis. Many of us, however, would like to "ride" the big movements. If that is your preference, you should then be prepared to take a larger number of losses. At any rate, the balance of this paper is devoted to giving the best ideas I have today on the subject of trading procedures.

HOW TO BUY

The presence of a Buy Pattern is not sufficient in itself to produce a Buy Signal. However, one or more Buy Patterns must be set up before a Buy Signal is possible.

In order to get a Reversal Buy Signal (reversal from bear to bull trend), we ordinarily require the presence of two Buy Patterns. Furthermore, we require a Thrust on the day following the second of these Patterns. (The occasional exception to this is in the case of Figure 4.27. This is explained in Rule 3.)

Rather than to state the rules in formal language, I'll try to explain the rules clearly by visualizing a possible scene.

Let us assume that you are home, you have an evening newspaper, and from the commodity quotations on the financial page you have charted today's high, low and closing prices for each of the commodities in which you are interested. Let us further assume that you are now short and are looking for a spot to cover your short position and to go long. (The way in which to go short is told later under "How to Sell.")

Rule 1 HL

You are now short, prices are in a Downswing, and you are looking for an opportunity to buy. If you could buy on the very *first day* that prices start moving into a sizeable Upswing, the experience would obviously be pleasant. Such an experience is quite often possible using this rule.

First, look at the *last Bottom* on your chart. Was there a TOB or a CPR at that Bottom? If one of these Buy Patterns was present at the last Bottom (or if both of them were present), then prices have already given *preliminary indication* that they "want to rise." Potential strong buying power was shown because of the fact that a TOB, or CPR, prevailed at that Bottom.

It makes no difference how much prices moved above the last Bottom. (The amount of "thrust" above that Bottom is immaterial.) The important thing now is whether there was a TOB or a CPR at the last Bottom. Let us assume that there was.

Now look at the current Downswing. Did today show the lowest price to date in the present Downswing – or was the low price today equal to the lowest prior price in this Downswing? And, if today registered the lowest price in the present Downswing, was this low price *above, or not more than 1¢* below* HL *the last Bottom?*

Because of the TOB or CPR at the last Bottom, you have reason to believe that there was strong buying power at that Bottom. But, in the present Downswing, if the low price goes much below that last Bottom (more than 1¢), it would not be logical to assume that the buying power at the former Bottom is still existent. If, however, prices stay above the last Bottom, or do not decline below the last Bottom by more than 1¢, you have reason to believe that the strength at the last Bottom is still a potential force today.

But, this in itself is not sufficient to warrant you to take a long position. You are seeking to get the odds definitely in your favor, and therefore you will not buy simply because there was a Buy Pattern at the last Bottom and the present decline stopped today at a price above or slightly below that last Bottom. For all you know, the price tomorrow may plunge several cents below the last Bottom,

and you therefore seek more evidence of strength in the present price structure.

> **Insist that there be a Thrust tomorrow above the high of today's price range.**

This additional evidence is given in two ways: First, you insist upon a TOB or a CPR today and, second, you insist that there be a Thrust tomorrow above the high of today's price range. If there is a TOB or a CPR, or both, today (today being the lowest day in the current Downswing), you have another indication of potential buying power. But, you want to see that potential buying power become an actuality – you want to see a *Thrust* tomorrow above today's high price. If that, too, comes to pass, you will then say that the odds

---

*I am now making one revision in the various rules given in the first edition of this paper; namely, I am changing the figure here from 1/2¢ to 1¢. This is being done for two reasons: (1) 1¢ appears to be working better in recent markets and, (2) the figure "½¢" caused many readers to be confused. These readers were mixing up the present concept with the concept of a TOB. The latter uses 1¢ so readers found it difficult to reconcile why we could not use Rule 1 if prices were more than ½¢ below the last Bottom. Actually, at this time we are only trying to define whether we can use the last Bottom for purposes of getting a Signal Pattern. In the case of stocks, we state that we cannot use the last Bottom if the current low price is *any amount below* said last Bottom, and we can use the last Bottom if the current low price is equal to or *any amount above* said last Bottom. On reflection it will be seen that this part of the procedure isn't concerned with the possible presence of a TOB. At any rate, I trust that the new definition will be easier to handle. Rule 1 in commodities is now applicable if the low price in the current Downswing is *any amount above*, or *not more than 1¢ below*, the last Bottom.

are in your favor, and you will be willing to cover your short position and go long. (In fact, you probably should place a stop order with your broker to buy tomorrow in the event prices rise above today's high price by the required amount of Thrust.)

Thrust

We need now to define "Thrust." Here again, many definitions could be set up. The one I have chosen makes automatic allowance, within limits, for differences in price level and for the activity of prices at various times. Other things being equal, the size of the daily range seems to vary with the price level and/or the activity of prices. Oats sell at a lower price than wheat, and the daily range in oats is usually less than the daily range in wheat. Occasionally though, oats becomes unusually active, compared with wheat, and at those times the daily range in oats is likely to be larger than the daily range in wheat. Therefore, the price range makes automatic adjustment for price level and price activity.

This provides us with a good basis for measuring "Thrust" – or how much prices should rise above today's high price in order to give authority that the movement is important. We should expect that a small rise in oats will have as much significance as a larger rise in wheat, unless, for reasons of its own, oats is relatively more active at this time.

Consequently, after seeing that the current situation is "all set" for a possible Buy Signal tomorrow, you will look at today's range for the amount of Thrust which must take place tomorrow in order to produce a Buy Signal.

The rule is: Tomorrow's prices must rise above today's high price by an amount equal to today's range; but if today's range is less than ½ cent, use ½ cent, and if today's range is more than 1½ cents, use 1½ cents. (If today's range is between ½ cent and 1½ cents, use today's range. If today's range is ½ cent or less, use ½ cent. If today's range is 1½ cents or more, use 1½ cents.)

To ask the market to give evidence of a reversal *in a single day* may seem to be a severe requirement – and it is. Sometimes the market refuses to do this, and when it does fail to give an emphatic one-day sign of reversal, we must wait until such time that it does. Fortunately, our method is so set up that the one-day "thrust" shouldn't be long delayed if the movement is to prove a worthwhile one. The market usually doesn't just slowly "drift" to substantially higher or lower levels. Sooner or later it emphasizes its chosen direction by *a substantial thrust in a single day*. If the Thrust does not take place after early signal-producing Patterns are set up, then it is likely to take place later, after one of the other Patterns appear in current prices. If it should fail to occur in all instances, then we can still ride part of the movement, if it is a long one, by resorting to the old Dow Theory principle – Penetration of a Top (PT) or Bottom (PB).

Summary and Illustration of Rule 1

In order to effect a Reversal Buy Signal we need two Buy Patterns plus a Thrust on the day following the second of these Patterns. Rule 1 is used in an attempt to buy on the very first day of an Upswing. Since two Buy Patterns are required, we look, under this rule, to the last Bottom for one of these Patterns and then we look to the current low price for the other Pattern. However, we cannot use this rule if the current low price is more than 1¢ below the last Bottom – the current low price can be any amount above the last Bottom (giving effect to the "Ascending Bottom" formation), or it can be equal to the last Bottom ("Double Bottom"), but it can't be more than 1¢ below the last Bottom. If the current low price in the present Downswing is more than 1¢ below the last Bottom, we will then have to turn to Rule 2 for a possible Buy Signal – that is, we will be unable to use the last Bottom as a means of getting one of the two required Buy Patterns.

[handwritten: spring in down trends fail is why.]

1. There must be a TOB or a CPR (or both) at the last Bottom.
2. Today must be the lowest price in the current Downswing.
3. The low price today must be above the last Bottom or not more than 1 cent below it.
4. There must be a TOB or a CPR (or both) today.
5. There must be a Thrust tomorrow above today's high price by an amount equal to today's range (minimum Thrust, ½ cent; maximum Thrust, 1½ cents).

Fig 4.20

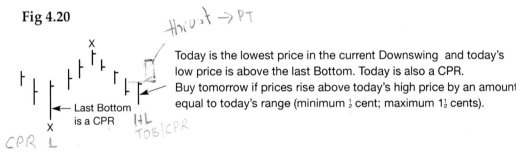

[handwritten: thrust → PT]

Today is the lowest price in the current Downswing and today's low price is above the last Bottom. Today is also a CPR. Buy tomorrow if prices rise above today's high price by an amount equal to today's range (minimum ½ cent; maximum 1½ cents).

[handwritten labels: X, Last Bottom is a CPR, CPR L, X, TOB/CPR, H+L]

In Figure 4.20, the last Bottom and today's low price could each be a TOB – or one could be a TOB and the other a CPR. Also, today's low price could be as much as 1 cent below the last Bottom.

[handwritten: indicates demand present]

Rule 2

Rule 1 can give a Buy Signal on the *first day only* of an Upswing. Sometimes it does just that. But, when a Thrust doesn't follow immediately after the low day of a Downswing, you turn to Rule 2 for guidance. Also, if conditions were such that Rule 1 could not give a Buy Signal, you employ Rule 2 (for instance, if the current low is more than 1 cent below the last Bottom – or if no TOB or CPR is set up).

In Rule 2, as in Rule 1, *two* Buy-Pattern *days* are needed. You may have two Buy Patterns in a *single day* (for example, a TOB and a CPR), but this is considered only *one Pattern* day. You need still another Buy-Pattern day in order to make conditions ripe for a Buy Signal.

So, you look at your chart again. Maybe the low day in the current Downswing is a TOB. Or perhaps it's a CPR – or maybe an NR. If the low day is one of those Patterns and if it is followed the next day by an IR, you again have a chance to buy at a very attractive price – should the next Upswing prove to be a large one. For example:

Fig 4.21

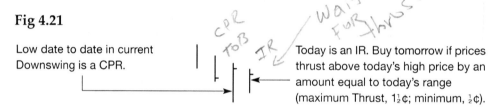

Low date to date in current Downswing is a CPR.

Today is an IR. Buy tomorrow if prices thrust above today's high price by an amount equal to today's range (maximum Thrust, 1½¢; minimum, ½¢).

The low day, in Figure 4.21, could be TOB and today could be an NR instead of an IR. The same rule would apply: buy tomorrow if prices thrust above today's high price by an amount equal to today's range.

Or, the situation might appear where there are two days of equal low prices and each of these days has a separate Buy Pattern. For example, see Figure 4.22.

Fig 4.22

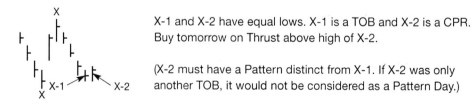

X-1 and X-2 have equal lows. X-1 is a TOB and X-2 is a CPR. Buy tomorrow on Thrust above high of X-2.

(X-2 must have a Pattern distinct from X-1. If X-2 was only another TOB, it would not be considered as a Pattern Day.)

If there is a Buy Pattern on the low day, as illustrated in Figure 4.22, you have a chance to buy very early in an Upswing. But, what if there is no Buy Pattern on the low day? You can still get a Buy Signal some time during the course of the Upswing if two or more separate Buy Patterns appear and the last of these is followed by a one-day Thrust. In this case, the Buy Patterns might take the form of two IRs, or two NRs, or one IR and one NR. For example, see Figure 4.23.

Fig 4.23

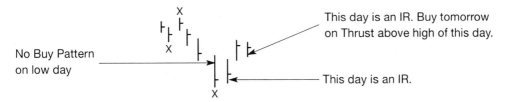

No Buy Pattern on low day

This day is an IR. Buy tomorrow on Thrust above high of this day.

This day is an IR.

Sometimes a complication arises when there is a series of IR days, all within the range of the day preceding the start of the series. Such a series of IR days is considered as *one* Pattern. During such a series, prices are "at rest" or making a "line," weighing the bullish and bearish factors. Such a rest period should not be given double importance, so we consider a series of such IR days as a *single Pattern*, and still another Buy Pattern is necessary in order to pave the way for a Buy Signal. For example, see Figure 4.24.

Fig 4.24

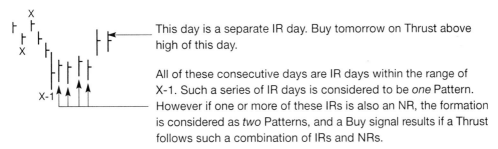

This day is a separate IR day. Buy tomorrow on Thrust above high of this day.

All of these consecutive days are IR days within the range of X-1. Such a series of IR days is considered to be *one* Pattern. However if one or more of these IRs is also an NR, the formation is considered as *two* Patterns, and a Buy signal results if a Thrust follows such a combination of IRs and NRs.

In the case of two NRs, it has been found best to apply this rule: the second NR must be at a higher price level than the first NR, then buy on Thrust above the second NR.

What if there is no Thrust after the second Pattern is set up? In that case you merely wait for another Pattern to be set up *in the same Upswing*, and you then require a Thrust after that Pattern. Sooner or later, during the course of the Upswing, a Thrust will usually occur after two or more Patterns have been established. But, when this does not occur, or when no Patterns have been set up (or only one Pattern has been set up), you turn to Rule 3 as a last resort for an almost certain signal.

Fig 4.25

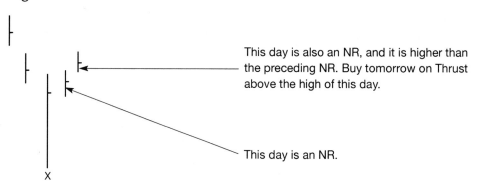

This day is also an NR, and it is higher than the preceding NR. Buy tomorrow on Thrust above the high of this day.

This day is an NR.

One more point which may need clarification: After a new low is made in a Downswing never look back in the Downswing for a Buy Pattern. When a day proves to be a new low day, that is the place to start looking for Buy Patterns.

Fig 4.26

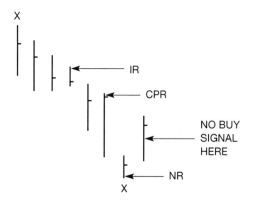

IR

CPR

NO BUY
SIGNAL
HERE

NR

An NR is made on the low day of the Downswing. But, you cannot combine this NR with the previous IR, or the previous CPR, of the Downswing in order to effect a Buy Signal.

Each time a new low is made, start looking at that point for the Buy Patterns.

Rule 3

A Buy Pattern is established by this rule when the last Top is penetrated by any amount. Prices move above the last Top and this gives a Buy Pattern on the day in which the penetration occurred. A Thrust must then occur above the high price of the Pattern day. This Thrust can take place *anytime* during the course of the *same* Upswing – it need not take place in a single day.

> *A Buy Pattern is established by this rule when the last Top is penetrated by any amount*

Fig 4.27

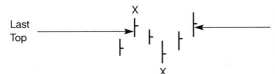

This day penetrates above the last Top. Buy anytime during current Upswing if prices rise above high of this day by an amount equal to this day's range (maximum Thrust, 1½¢; minimum, ½¢).

HOW TO SELL

Let us say that you are now in a long position through the operation of one of the foregoing three rules. The question now is: What are you going to do about it? This, as already stressed, is the BIG question.

Things happen fast in commodities. You can "make or break" in much less time than is required in the stock market. One of the poorest Operating Plans, I believe, is to sit back and do nothing other than to wait for a Reversal Signal to close out your present position. I know that there is an old adage that states:

> "Limit your losses and let your profits ride." But that bit of counsel stops short in that it doesn't tell you how far to let your profits ride . . . nor, for that matter, how to limit your losses.

In the next two sections of this paper we shall outline some concrete Operating Plans. There is no limit to the possible varieties of Operating Plans, and no one yet has worked out the elusive "best plan." The reader may decide to adopt one of the plans explained later. But, let us assume now that you are just going to hold on to your purchase until the time a Reversal Sell Signal is given, and at that time you will not only sell but you will go short.

You have probably already concluded that Sell Patterns and Sell Signals are much the same as Buy Patterns and Buy Signals. That is correct, the only difference being that we are now going downhill instead of up.

Rule 1

You have bought and prices are now in an Upswing. If possible you would like to sell on the very first day of a Downswing. Therefore, if prices are now below, or not more than 1¢* above the last Top, look first at that Top and see if there was a TOT or a CPR (or both) at that Top. If either or both of these Patterns were present you already have one Sell Pattern set up for you. If today is the high day (or equal high day) in the current Upswing, and if this day is either a TOT or a CPR,

---

*See footnote on page 135.

or both, the second of the required two Sell Patterns is also set up, and all that remains for the issuance of a Sell Signal is a downside Thrust tomorrow.

1. There must be a TOT or a CPR (or both) at the last Top.
2. Today must be the highest price in the current Upswing.
3. The high price today must be below the last Top or not more than 1 cent above it.
4. There must be a TOT or a CPR (or both) today.
5. There must be a Thrust tomorrow below today's low price by an amount equal to today's range (minimum Thrust, ½ cent; maximum Thrust, 1 – ½ cents.)

Fig 4.28

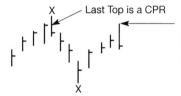

X   Last Top is a CPR

X

Today is highest price in current Upswing and today's high price is below last Top. Today is also a CPR. Sell tomorrow if prices decline below today's low price by an amount equal to today's range (minimum, ½ cent; maximum, 1½ cents).

In Figure 4.28, the last Top and today's high price could each be a TOT – or one could be a TOT and the other a CPR. Also, today's high price could be as much as 1 cent above the last Top.

Rule 2

Let us assume now that conditions did not work out right for a Sell Signal by Rule 1:

1. the current high price was more than 1¢ above the last Top, or
2. no TOT or CPR was set up at the last Top, or, perhaps at the current high price, or
3. there was no Thrust on the first day of the decline.

In any of these events, you turn to Rule 2 for guidance.

You can still sell at a very attractive price (assuming the ensuing decline proves to be a large one) if there are two Sell Patterns set up at the approximate peak of the current Upswing. See Figure 4.29 and Figure 4.30.

Fig 4.29

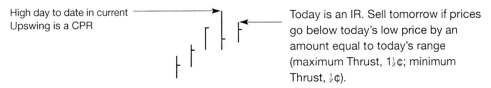

High day to date in current Upswing is a CPR

Today is an IR. Sell tomorrow if prices go below today's low price by an amount equal to today's range (maximum Thrust, 1½¢; minimum Thrust, ½¢).

The high day, in Figure 4.29, could be a TOT and today could be an NR instead of an IR. The same rule would apply: Sell tomorrow if prices thrust below today's low price by an amount equal to today's range, observing, as always, maximum and minimum limits for the amount of Thrust.

Fig 4.30

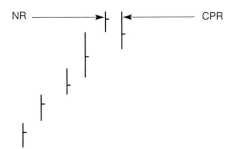

NR   CPR

Here we have two days with equal highs in the current Upswing. The first of these is an NR and the second is a CPR. Since each of these Patterns is different, sell tomorrow in the event of a Thrust below today's low price.
(Two different Patterns in a *single day* would not qualify as two Sell Patterns. There must be *two distinct Pattern days*.)

Perhaps you will not be so fortunate as to sell on the first day of a large decline. You may have to wait until the decline gets farther along in the Downswing. See Figure 4.31 and Figure 4.32.

Fig 4.31

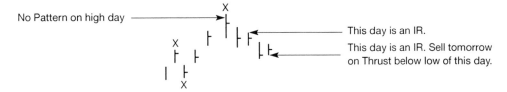

No Pattern on high day

This day is an IR.

This day is an IR. Sell tomorrow on Thrust below low of this day.

Fig 4.32

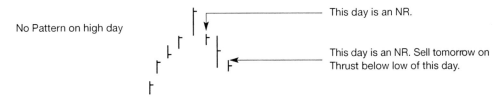

No Pattern on high day

This day is an NR.

This day is an NR. Sell tomorrow on Thrust below low of this day.

The other points under this rule are similar to those already considered under buying directions:

A series of IRs, all within the range preceding the start of the series, is considered to be *one* Pattern day. But, if one or more of these IRs is also an NR, we then consider the series as *two* Patterns and proceed to sell in the event of a Thrust below any current day in the series.

When a new high is made in an Upswing, never look back at that Upswing for Sell Patterns. Each time a new high is made, start at that point looking for Sell Patterns and not at some point lower down in that Upswing.

Under Rule 1 only can you "borrow" a Pattern from the previous Upswing and that Pattern must be on the extreme high day of that Upswing. Under Rule 2, you cannot combine a Pattern in one swing with a Pattern in another swing. The two Pattern days must occur in the *same swing*.

You can see that quite a variety of things can happen, any one of which would give you a Sell Signal under Rule 2. But if all of these fail, and the down movement proves to be a large one, you will still be able to resort to Rule 3 for a Sell Signal.

Rule 3

A Sell Pattern is established by this rule when the last Bottom is penetrated downward by any amount. A Thrust must then occur below the low price on the day of penetration. This Thrust can take place *anytime* during the *current* Downswing – it need not occur in a single day.

Fig 4.33

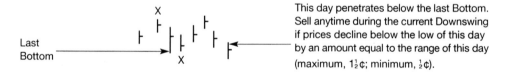

Last Bottom

This day penetrates below the last Bottom. Sell anytime during the current Downswing if prices decline below the low of this day by an amount equal to the range of this day (maximum, 1½¢; minimum, ½¢).

REPEAT SIGNALS

Once a trend movement sets in, bull or bear, Repeat Signals then provide the means for further gains. These Repeat Signals are extremely interesting and we shall comment on them more at length when we come to consider Operating Plans. It appears that the probability of loss in a single trade can be reduced to a minimum by means of operating on Repeat Signals. It will be shown later, when we review the record of the Thrust Method, that the original Reversal Signals are likely to provide the greatest gains in the long run (due to large single profits from time to time) but the Repeat Signals are more trustworthy from the standpoint of whether or not any single trade will be profitable.

Let us assume that you just bought on a Reversal Buy Signal as explained in the preceding pages. If that signal is going to result in a large profit, or even a fairly good profit, it will likely be followed by one or several Repeat Signals. During a long trend-movement, our method often indicates over and over again, after minor reaction, to join in and ride along with the movement. It is not uncommon for the method to shout repeatedly at us: "Get aboard." Of course, all movements must eventually terminate, so the odds may be against the last Repeat Signal in a major bull or bear movement, but even so the combined probabilities of all the Repeat Signals seem highly favorable.

If the Reversal Buy Signal (on which you just bought) is going to prove unprofitable, it may never be followed by a Repeat Buy Signal. This suggests that we might wait for the first Repeat Buy Signal before acting in order to reduce the probability of loss in the single trade. It also suggests that we might operate with one or more funds – putting only part of our capital into the market on the appearance of the original Buy Signal and then adding to the commitment if Repeat Signals follow. This might take the form of "pyramiding" for the possible very large gains, or it might take the form of "scalping" for the likely small gains. Yes, Repeat Signals provide the means for added adventure in commodity speculation.

At any rate, you are now long and we will assume that you want to buy some more in the event of a Repeat Buy Signal. Here is the procedure and thought behind it:

When you bought originally you demanded that the market show some very emphatic evidence that it had reversed its trend from the down to the up side. You insisted that *two* Buy Patterns put in their appearance and then you required that the market follow this up with a *full-range Thrust in a single day*. The market did all this for you, so now you have good reasons for believing that the main trend is up and you become less demanding in respect to any Repeat Signals the market may give.

Let us assume that after you bought the market continued to move up. This may be one of the large bull movements but, of course, you know from experience that no major movement is straight in one direction only. Interruptions – reactions – occur from time to time. If you can buy some more on the *Bottom* day of the next reaction – or on the Bottom day of any of the following reaction –

you will obviously be pleased with your "technique." Such pleasant experiences are very often provided for through our old friend, "CPR." See Figure 4.34.

Fig 4.34 Closing price reversal

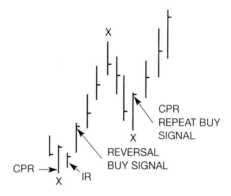

Two Buy Patterns – CPR and IR – are set up and these are followed by a Thrust to give a Reversal Buy Signal.

Watch all subsequent Downswings for a CPR. When the main trend is up, a Repeat Buy Signal is given immediately on the appearance of a CPR during any Downswing.

The rule is to buy at the close of the day in which the CPR appears or at the opening of the following morning.

It is surprising the number of times a CPR does appear on the Bottom day of a minor reaction (Downswing) during a major rise. But, of course more often than not this will not happen and therefore we need to provide for other ways of getting in on the opportunities afforded by Repeat Signals. One of these ways is to buy when a TOB appears and this is followed the next day by an IR. Here we buy on the first day after the current low day of the Downswing, and this too puts us in the market at a very attractive price when the main trend is on the upgrade.

Fig 4.35 TOB followed by an IR

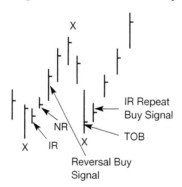

Two Buy Patterns – IR and NR – are set up and these are followed by a Thrust to give a Reversal Buy Signal.

Watch all subsequent Downswings for a TOB followed by an IR. When a Reversal Buy Signal has alredy been given (and we assume therefore that the main trend is up) a Repeat Buy Signal is given immediately on the appearance of a TOB followed the next day by an IR.

The rule is to buy at the close of the IR day or at the opening the following morning.

You can also buy again (Repeat Signal) on the appearance of a TOB on the low day of a Downswing if this is followed the next day by a *one-half range Thrust*. Here again we become lenient in our demands on the price action. Since it has already given good evidence that the main trend has turned to the upside, we now ask for only *one* Buy Pattern and this to be followed the next day by a ½-range Thrust. (If the range is 1½¢, the required Thrust for tomorrow is ¾¢ – use, as before, ½¢ minimum and 1½¢ maximum Thrust.)

Fig 4.36

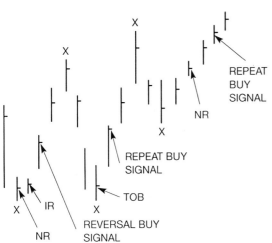

Two Buy Patterns – NR and IR – lead to the original Reversal Buy Signal. This is followed by a short rally and then a reaction (Downswing). The low day of this reaction tests one or both of the last two Bottoms (TOB) and this is followed the next day by a ½-range Thrust to give a Repeat Buy Signal. (½ of the range of the TOB day is used as the measurement of the amount of upside Thrust which must occur the next day in order to produce a Repeat Buy Signal – always keeping in mind the maximum and minimum limits.)

Observe too that the NR in the next Upswing gives a Repeat Buy Signal when on the following day prices rise above the high of NR day by an amount equal to ½ the range of the NR day (IR, alone, also gives Repeat Signals in the same manner as NR.)

Just a few other points about Repeat Signals, and I think the procedure is covered:

1. Do not act on a Repeat Signal in the *same swing* which gave the original Reversal Signal. The Reversal Signal may come at a low level in an Upswing and then higher up in the same swing an IR or an NR may produce a "Repeat Buy Signal." Do not act on the latter.

2. Do not act on two Repeat Signals in the same swing. You may get a Repeat Signal on the basis of a CPR on the low day of a Downswing, and later in the same Upswing you may get another Repeat Signal on the basis of a Thrust above an NR day. Do not act on this second Repeat Signal. We are always trying to buy as low as possible, so act only on the first signal which appears in a swing. (In fact, I'm inclined in practice to ignore all Repeat Signals

unless they come on the Bottom day – CPR – or very close to the Bottom day, such as TOB followed by IR.)

3. Ignore all Repeat Signals based on Penetration of last Top (PT) or Penetration of last Bottom (PB). These are definitely too far away from the inception of the movement. There are safer opportunities in the other Patterns.

Repeat Sell Signals are similar to Repeat Buy Signals as you will observe from Figure 4.37. Here we go short on a Reversal Sell Signal and then on the Top day, or soon after, of the minor rallies (Upswings) we seek to go short again for repeated profits.

"ALL THE ANSWERS"

This is an appropriate place to add some thoughts on an important matter. These thoughts are directed especially to the beginner and to those few clients who think I know "all the answers."

As I work on charts, trying to unravel the mysteries of price movements, I can see scores of unsolved problems. No person or organization is likely to do the great amount of work which must be done if we were to obtain all the "right answers" – at least, the work will never be done in our time. With what we know today we can lay down sound basic principles and the right general approach. But, the particular rules and procedures which we use are certainly not highly developed instruments.

When, for example, we use 1¢ as the measurement to establish a TOB or a TOT, we are frankly doing a lot of guess-work. In going over past charts of wheat and corn, the 1¢-measurement works out reasonably well, but it certainly is not necessarily the best measure which can be found. If 1¢ is appropriate for wheat and corn, then it would seem that some smaller figure should be used for oats and some larger figure for soybeans and, perhaps, rye. I don't know the right answer to this, and while I have ideas on it, I think your judgment in untested matters is just as good as mine. And, when you multiply this little problem by many others – what the Thrust "should be," the "best" definition of a Narrow Range, the "best" Operating Plan for maximum gains, etc. etc. – well, that leaves a lot of unfinished work for our descendants.

Therefore, while I'd like to be helpful in answering all questions, I must warn you that I do not possess tested, scientific knowledge on many, many things. I can emphasize basic principles and I can give you concrete procedures. The first (principles) *must be sound*; the second (procedures) must be imperfect because we do not possess the knowledge today to make them otherwise.

Fig 4.37 Repeat sell signals

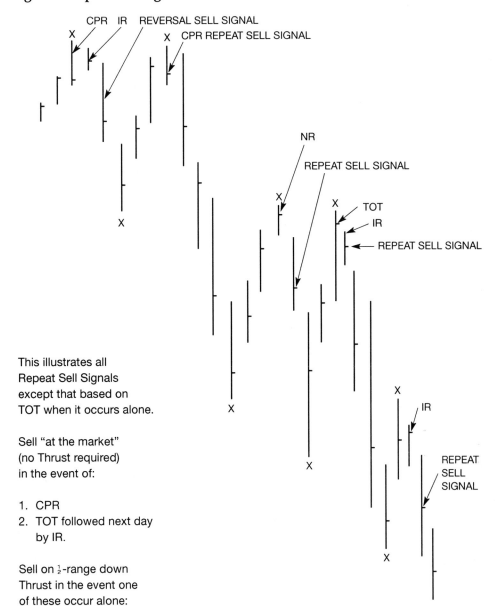

This illustrates all
Repeat Sell Signals
except that based on
TOT when it occurs alone.

Sell "at the market"
(no Thrust required)
in the event of:

1. CPR
2. TOT followed next day
   by IR.

Sell on ½-range down
Thrust in the event one
of these occur alone:

3. TOT
4. NR
5. IR

The principles underlying our methods are more important than the actual mechanical rules

The principles underlying our methods are more important than the actual mechanical rules that we can use in applying those principles. It is, I believe, a sound *principle* "to follow the trend and not try to anticipate the trend." It is, I believe, a sound *principle* "to attach importance to a TOB or a TOT." It is, I believe, a sound *principle* "to require *two* Pattern days (except in Rule 3) before a Reversal Signal." And so forth. The point I am trying to drive home is to look at *principles* first, and then try to express those principles mechanically the best you can, knowing that whatever mechanical expressions you give will fall short of your hopes.

"Knowledge is power"

My method, or any method, will certainly disappoint you if you depend upon it blindly. Almost certainly at some future time it will take a few consecutive losses as it has done from time to time in past periods. I believe in the Thrust Method and think, like any father, that it's the finest brain-child around today. But, when this child gets into one of its ugly moods, and starts knocking the record for a few straight losses, I know you will want to "kill the brat." I am very sure that if you are going to have success with any method you must first make that method *your method*. You must dig in and do some work on your own. You must convince *yourself* that the rules *will work for you if* you stay with them over a reasonable period of time. In other words, you must be *your own counsellor* – you must, to repeat the slogan I've used since 1930, "Make Your Own Forecasts."

So, don't simply take my word for things and start plunging into the market. Do some more reading on the subject. *"The Golden Harvest"* by Franklin Paul Jackson will give you ideas not even mentioned in this study. Another good one is *"Technical Analysis of Stock Trends"* by Robert D. Edwards and John Magee, Jr. (stock market techniques are applicable to commodities). If you can locate a copy of Ralph M. Airnsworth's old book *"Profitable Grain Trading"* you should read it. Another good old-timer is George Cole's *"Graphs and their Application to Speculation."* In fact, if "a little knowledge is a dangerous thing," you should begin now to learn what the other fellow has to say about "Signal Patterns," "Buying and Selling Rules," "Operating Plans," etc. If you don't have time for all this, and prefer to go along with my ideas on the subject, then at least get some past charts and do some experimenting of

Get some past charts and do some experimenting of your own

your own. If you become sufficiently acquainted with the Thrust Method so as to feel you know its good and bad points, you will then be better able to maintain your faith during those stormy days which come to all methods.

Miscellaneous technical points

When you get into past or current charts, you will observe, from time to time, certain "technicalities" that require special definitions or rules not covered in the foregoing explanation of the Thrust Method. Just how these things are handled is not usually a matter of considerable importance, but it is important, I believe, that they be treated, whenever they occur, in some *consistent manner*.

In my own researches, I have to adopt *consistent mechanical rules*. If I did not do this, I would probably change the rules from time to time in order to obtain the results that I would like to obtain. It is easy enough to go over a back chart and set up rules that will work almost perfectly *for that particular chart*. (Some popular texts do just that.) But, when those same rules are applied to *another chart*, the resulting picture is often unpleasant.

In other words, whatever rules you decide upon, *be consistent in using them*. If you change the rules at will, you had just as well abandon mechanical rules entirely and depend upon your "good old judgment" or "common sense". In that way, you will fool yourself in back-testing, and perhaps, if you happen to be a publisher of methods like I am, you will fool a few readers. But not for long, because when you get your judgment (or when I get mine) working in the present market, with the future not yet recorded on our charts, the truth will soon come to light – "common sense" is a poor guide to follow.

But this doesn't mean that we can concoct a set of mechanical rules that will explain, and predict, all the inconstancies of price movements. It does mean that we are forced to use imperfect tools; and if we choose to use them, we should use them in a uniform manner. PRINCIPLES MUST BE RIGHT; the particular rules which express these principles can only be roughly right, but, right or wrong, they should be adhered to strictly.

Therefore, the manner in which I handle various "technical points" is not too important; it is only important that (1) I stick to principles and (2) I stay consistent in my procedure. The latter is extremely difficult to do in *actual trading*, but it *must be done in back-testing the efficiency of a method*, and I am sure it *should be done in actual trading* (even if you or I can't seem to do it). Here are just a few "technicalities" which you will run into in your charts. If you don't understand them, make up your own technical rules. They will probably serve just as well:

1. If there are two or more days of equal Tops (or equal Bottoms), use the *last* of these days for establishing Upswings and Downswings.
2. If a Top (or Bottom) has two or more days of equal highs (lows), use the range of the *last* of these days for measuring NR.
3. If an upside Thrust gives a Reversal Buy Signal and later the same day a downside Thrust occurs, the original short position before the Upside Thrust should be reentered into.

   Or, if a downside Thrust reverses a long position, and later the same day an upside Thrust occurs, the long position should then be reinstated. (These things happen *rarely*.)
4. If you have a choice of two or more days for measuring Thrust, use the day that gives the most favorable execution. (This happens occasionally when more and more Patterns are being set up and these are not followed immediately by Thrust.)

And now, having set up a specific method for entering *into* the market, let us turn to a consideration of methods for getting *out* of the market.

THE GROWTH OF OPERATING PLANS

A specific method of trading in grains must include these two ingredients:

1. An automatic barometer for detecting the trend of prices from day to day.
2. A systematic plan of operation by which actual purchases and sales are made.

In other words, we must know: (1) "how things look today," and (2) "what to do about it." In preceding pages we took up the first of these and we are now ready to consider the second problem.

Market fluctuations, commodities or stocks, must, of course, always be viewed in terms of probabilities – even though we may not attempt to express the probabilities in precise mathematical language. The future is strewn with risks. Every venture in life, no matter how carefully planned and started, will succeed or fail depending partly on numerous factors (hard work, ability, etc.) and partly on the winds of fortune which are beyond Man's control. Any farmer, any business man, any investor, can tell tearful tales of how well conceived plans and honest toil met disaster at the hands of the future. Would it not be a blessing if we could eliminate the unknowns of the future? I guess not – for a known future would make a dull present. The fascination of living would crumple if the future could be definitely predetermined. We do not wish to eliminate the unknowns of the future; we wish merely to try to reduce them to a minimum.

This can be done in stock and commodity trading by eliminating as far as possible the future from our method. If we buy today and secure a reasonable paper profit tomorrow, we should somehow protect that profit. When we limit our losses, when we take steps to protect our paper profits, we are then exerting a measurable degree of independence over the unknowns of the future. We are operating to *grasp* the opportunities usually presented to us by today's trend signals.

As one studies and studies the past, trying to lay hands on the "Utopia Method," the realization becomes clearer and clearer that the wise trader will reconcile himself to the fact that he must make a sacrifice somewhere along the line. We might attribute this fact to "the law of compensation," to "the equality of action and reaction," to "the give-and-take in life" which seems to be the natural order of things. Whatever the reason may be, we will *never get* all we *want* from market operations – we must be willing to give up one advantage in order to secure another advantage.

If the trader desires to make a profit in nearly all of his trades, it seems he will have to be satisfied with relatively small profits in single trades. The small profits may come at frequent intervals thereby permitting the magic of compound interest to multiply his capital rapidly. But, if he desires mostly gains, and only infrequent losses and break-even trades, it appears he will have to be content with small gains in the individual trades. He will likely have to sacrifice the occasional, "big killing" which the market offers from time to time.

On the other hand, if the trader desires to ride along with the movements and take; from time to time, substantial gains in single trades, he will have to be willing to endure more individual losses and break-even trades. After he buys and a small paper profit is soon shown, he has his choice whether to take that profit or to try for a larger profit. If he decides to try for the larger profit, he must necessarily risk losing the present profit which is available for the taking. Quite often the larger profit does accrue, but also, quite often, the present paper profit is sacrificed and the trade breaks even or turns into a small loss. The trader cannot have everything he wants; he must be willing to make sacrifices.

It seems that we might sensibly divide our total trading capital into two parts, "Fund L" and "Fund S." Fund L would be for "long-term trading," riding the main trend movements with the expectation of large profits from time to time *and* the expectation of some losses and perhaps several break-even trades over the life of a future contract. Fund S would be for small, quick-profit trading, and it would provide for recovering the losses entailed by Fund L, and, in fact, in the long run it would provide for a net gain over and above the temporary losses which will likely accrue to Fund L. Hence, whatever happens – whether the movement be long or short, sizeable or small – we should have an excellent chance to either gain or break even in the single trade. (Of course, there are times when *both* lots will lose.) But, even this plan imposes a sacrifice too. It usually turns out better in the long run (over the life of a grain future) to employ *all* of the fund in Fund L – if the trader is willing to suffer a greater number of losses and break-even trades, he will ordinarily net a greater gain (because of the occasional large gains) by the end of a future contract.

So, it all boils down to a decision which each trader must make for himself. If he seeks only the big gains which do come from time to time, then he must be prepared to endure the discouraging small losses and break-even trades. If he hopes to win in nearly all of his transactions, he must be willing to forego the possibility of a large gain in a single movement. If he resolves to combine both types of operations, then he must be willing to sacrifice the greater profit he could make eventually by putting his entire capital into Fund L.

My own opinion is that most traders need, above all else, "peace of mind." He cannot lose or break even in many of his trades, or he will soon abandon his barometer (even a good one) and start searching again for a better method. It seems that it is our task to reduce the probability of loss in single transactions to a minimum, and, at the same time, to offer a fair chance for a large gain and a good chance for a small gain in each single transaction. If the trader can make a "one-base hit" most of the time when he goes to bat and an occasional "home run," he may possibly find peace-of-mind in his trading operations. Dividing your trading fund into two equal parts, Fund L and Fund S, may give this.

Some of the following Operating Plans give consideration to two such funds – L and S. Later, when we take up the S/R Operating Plan, we shall consider the advisability of operating with three funds – L, M and S. None of these plans is a perfected device. Better ones could undoubtedly be worked out if we had "frequency distributions" showing how grain prices actually behave for many past years. Then, "probability tables" could be set up and from these we could learn the most likely expectation of a present movement. Until such a study is made, if ever, one of the following plans may meet your needs in actual trading. I am listing them in a sort of chronological order as plans I have considered and done research on in past years.

PLAN #1 – BUYING AND SELLING ON REVERSAL SIGNALS ONLY

Let us dismiss this procedure at the very start for it subjects us to the very thing we are trying to avoid. If we buy today and then wait for a Reversal Signal before selling, we are placing ourselves fully in the hands of the uncertain future. At times our losses will be unduly large, and we will often see worth-while paper profits turn into real losses. Tests of this plan in both commodities and stocks lead me to believe that the trader might expect losses in nearly half of his trades if he waits for Reversal Signals before closing out. The gains will average considerably higher than the losses so that over a series of trades there will be a substantial excess of dollar gains over dollar losses. Yet, most traders will not be able to follow faithfully a method which loses nearly half of the time. The trader needs, above all, a reasonable feeling of security in *each* of his trades. Regardless of what system is set up to derive Buy and Sell Signals, it appears that Operating Plan #1 is a bad one. A popular application of this plan follows.

PLAN #2 – BUYING AND THEN PLACING STOPS UNDER LAST BOTTOMS

In "The Evolution of a Trading Barometer" we reviewed a few methods which buy when the last Top is penetrated upward and sell when the last Bottom is pierced downward. Methods of this type are popular among many traders. Even those traders who use "advanced techniques" often attach considerable importance, for stop-order purposes, to the breaking of recent Bottoms and Tops.

Fig 4.38 Buying and placing stops under last Bottoms

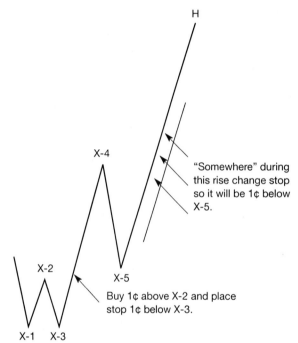

H

X-4

"Somewhere" during this rise change stop so it will be 1¢ below X-5.

X-2

X-5

Buy 1¢ above X-2 and place stop 1¢ below X-3.

X-1   X-3

Under this plan purchase is made when the last Top is penetrated upward by a "significant amount." A stop is then placed below the last Bottom (at which point a short-sale position would also be entered into). If the rise continues and higher Bottoms are made, the stop is raised progressively so that it is always below the most recent Bottom.

A couple of questions about this plan are: (1) How high above X-5 do prices have to go before the stop is changed to "1¢ below X-5?" (2) When the high is reached at H, are we going to take a chance on losing all of the profit with our only protection being a stop below X-5?

In the Thrust Method we provide for this type of stop-order protection and Reversal Signals through Rule 3 (based on PB and PT), so it may seem that we are not being consistent when we criticize this popular method. Actually, though, Rule #3 is our biggest headache and I wish there were some way we could do away with it. It comes in handy every once in a while when a long trend movement is not preceded by a Rule 1 or Rule 2 signal, so it appears that we are forced to keep Rule 3 "for better or for worse."

So, I am not trying to advocate that the beginner or advanced student abandon the idea of watching recent resistance points as potential areas for Reversal

Signals and stop-order protection. But, I *am* advocating that these students look honestly at their charts and count the number of times that *a penetration of a Bottom marks the near-low of the downward movement* and also to count the times that *a penetration of a Top marks the near-high of the upward movement*. It is surprising the number of times we should BUY, not sell, when a former low point is broken downward. And, it is surprising the number of times that we should SELL, *not buy*, when a former high point is penetrated upward. Or, is it surprising? After all, don't most of the popular methods, including Dow Theory, often buy at the top of a movement and sell at the bottom?

In my forthcoming study (to be started soon on completion of the rewriting of this paper and "The Thrust Method in Stocks") I hope to do something about the perplexing situation involved in penetrations of Tops and Bottoms. I hope to find definite ways of knowing whether to buy or sell when Bottoms and Tops are pierced. If, for example, I should sell when a Bottom is broken I will want the movement to continue on downward. And, if I should buy soon after a new low is made, I will want the movement to start upward. I think there are definite cues in price action which will permit the doing of this in many instances – but the testing of these ideas remains to be done and, therefore, this matter has no place in the present Thrust Method.

> *It is surprising the number of times we should BUY, not sell*

(Incidentally, we need not consider as a separate plan, "Selling and then Placing Stops Above the Last Tops," as this would be just a repetition, inversely, of the above.)

PLAN #3 – TAKE 2½¢ GROSS PROFIT; LIMIT LOSS TO 5¢

This was tried in the early "Breakaway Method" published back in 1934. The formula was simply to take a 2½¢ gross profit just as soon as it became available and to limit any loss to 5¢. The profit-loss ratio may seem out of line but the purpose was to avoid being stopped out during temporary setbacks. Besides, the losses sometimes did not run as high as 5¢ – Reversal Signals sometimes came before the maximum 5¢ loss was incurred. This plan showed 25 profitable trades and 3 unprofitable trades from January 1930 to July 1934. The net profit per bushel over the period was only 37 cents, but here was a method of winning 90% of the time. This is a simple formula, and I feel quite sure that if anyone wants to try it today in wheat, corn, soybeans or rye, using the Thrust Method, he can expect gains in grains in nearly 90% of his trades.

PLAN #4 – TAKE 5¢ GROSS PROFIT; LIMIT LOSS TO 4½¢

This method resulted in 87½¢ net profit over the 1930–1934 period or more than twice as much as Plan #3. However, as compensation, only about two-thirds of the trades were profitable (35 gains and 17 losses). The formula was:

1. Enter market on Breakaway Signal.
2. Take a 5¢ gross profit or 4½¢ gross loss.
3. If a profit is made in a long commitment, repurchase after the first 1¢ rise following a decline of 2¢ or more from the high of the move.
4. If a profit is made in a short sale, sell short again after the first 1¢ decline following a rise 2¢ or more from the low of the move.
5. If a loss is made in either a long or short trade, reenter the market on the next Breakaway signal, and again follow the foregoing procedure.

PLAN #5 – AFTER 2½¢ PROFIT, FOLLOW UP WITH STOP

This appears to be the best trading plan developed in connection with the Break-away Method. There were 26 profitable trades and 3 unprofitable trades for a net of 77⅜¢ per bushel in wheat during the period, January 1930 to July 1934. This plan limited the loss to 5¢ (plus commission). When 2½¢ gross profit was registered, a stop was placed to insure a 1¢ net profit. Then, if the movement continued so that an 8¢ gross profit was shown, the stop was moved in order to gross 2¢ profit. Thereafter the stop was always kept 6¢ under the extreme of the movement – if 10¢ paper profit was shown, the stop protected 4¢ of this profit, etc. Of course, as in all plans, Reversal Signals were always followed if these came before stops were touched off. This plan is undoubtedly still working today, but the chief objection to it is that too many trades will be stopped out with a mere 1¢ gain.

PLAN #6 – LONG-PROFIT vs QUICK-PROFIT TRADING

Something new was added in "A Study in Wheat Trading," published in 1939. The decision was now made to let some trades "ride" and to take a "quick profit" in others, depending upon the price action. The rules varied according to price level, but for illustrative purposes we shall assume that the price is above $1.10 and purchase is made 1⅛¢ above the Top of the last 2⅜¢ swing (see Figure 4.2). The question before us now is whether to let the trade ride or to try for a small but quick profit. I decided back in 1939 to let the trade ride for a possible large profit if any of these conditions were present:

1. If at the time the purchase is made, a Bottom was already set up within 4¢ of the purchase price.
2. If after the purchase is made, prices decline below the purchase price by 1¢ or more.
3. If after the purchase is made prices start rising but then decline and a new Bottom is later established.

Each of these conditions requires a recent reaction in prices. Such a reaction might be construed as a "healthy correction," and the market, therefore, might be in a position for an extended drive. But, if there has been no reaction recently, or if there is no reaction soon after entering the market, then prices might be due for a correction – therefore, try for a quick profit only.

If the trade was a "ride trade," this procedure was followed:

1. Limit loss to 4¢ (plus commission).
2. After 2¢ paper profit, place stop for ½¢ gross profit.
3. After 3¢ paper profit, place stop for 1¢ gross profit.
4. After 4¢ paper profit, place stop for 1½¢ gross profit.
5. After 10¢ paper profit, place stop for 5¢ gross profit.
6. If prices continue to move up strongly so that a large paper profit is shown, but no Bottom is set up within 15¢ of the current high price, keep a stop 10¢ below the highest price reached.
7. If closed out by the execution of one of the above stops, enter the market again on next penetration of a Bottom or Top, and start all over again with above procedure.

If the purchase was on a "quick-profit" basis, this procedure was followed:

1. Limit loss to 4¢.
2. Take 2½¢ gross profit.
3. If profit is taken, buy again ⅜¢ above the high of the day which gave the profit.
4. If loss is taken, start over again and buy, or sell, on 1⅛¢ penetration of last Top or Bottom.

Over the years 1933–1938 this method showed 96 gains and 17 losses for a net gain of $2.48⅞ per bushel in wheat. Profit in a single trade ran as high as $1400, but many of the ride trades were closed out with only minor net profits (1¢ or less). It appears that the later objection, using short stops, would be particularly prevalent today.

PLAN #7 – ANOTHER METHOD OF LONG-PROFIT vs QUICK-PROFIT TRADING

Turning to the 1941–1942 studies, these conditions were established for deciding whether to try for a quick profit or to let the trade ride for a possible large profit:

Let Trade Ride

1. If a Bottom has been set up within 5% of the purchase price (or if a Top has been set up within 5% of the short-sale price).
2. If a Bottom has been set up within 5 days of the date of purchase (or if a Top has been set up within 5 days of the date of sale).

Try for Quick Profit

If neither of the above conditions are present at the time the purchase (or short sale) is made.

Assume that we have just made a purchase. If a downswing has occurred which set up a Bottom recently (not more than 5 days ago) the probability of an early reaction is diminished – therefore, let the trade ride. Or, if the last downswing culminated near the buying day (within 5% of it), the likelihood of an early set-back is also diminished – so, let the trade ride. But, if the last Bottom is quite a distance away in time (more than 5 days) or in extent (more than 5%), the likelihood of a near-by reaction is enhanced – therefore, try only for a quick profit. With prices above $1.20, the desired quick profit was 3¢. If this profit is taken, and the movement continues in the same direction, the trader would reenter ¾¢ above the high of the day which closed out a long position – or ¾¢ below the low of the day which closed out a short position.

Here is the schedule for handling "ride trades."

1. Limit loss to 8¢ (losses averaged 4¢, no 8¢ loss was taken).
2. After gross paper profit of 2¾¢, place stop for 1/2¢ gross gain.
3. After 4¾¢ paper profit, place stop for 2¢ gain (all figures gross).
4. After 12¢ paper profit, place stop for 5¢ gain.
5. Take 20¢ net profit whenever available.
6. Always, of course, close out in event of Reversal Signal.
7. If closed out of a position with a profit, and no Reversal Signal occurs, reenter ¾¢ above the high of the rally which preceded the decline which stopped out the trade. (Or, if position was short, sell again ¾¢ below the low of the decline which preceded the rally that closed out the trade.)
8. If closed out of a position with a loss, wait for new trend signal before reentering the market.

This shows 148 gains and 17 losses over the 1930–1941 period. This is about 90% gains; however, many of them were for only ½¢ gross. Total amount of gains was $4.29 per bushel after deducting commissions. Total losses, including commissions, was 71¢ per bushel. Net gain per bushel, $3.58.

Possibly today it would not be too effective to apply the 5% rule in deciding whether to let the trade ride or to try for a quick profit. With soybeans at $4.00, for example, this would mean that the last Bottom could be as much as 20¢ away from the purchase price and the trade would be considered as a "ride" one. Possibly, 3% would be more effective at such higher price levels.

PLAN #8 – TAKE 2% NET PROFIT; LIMIT LOSS TO 2¼%

This plan is another of several which were tried in the 1941–1942 studies. The idea here was simply to take a 2% net profit or a 2½% loss (plus commission) whichever came first. Due to Reversal Signals the losses averaged less than 2%. A little over three-fourths of the trades proved profitable, and the plan averaged about 30% net profit per year on an outright basis or 150% per year on a 20% margin. (A test was also made limiting the loss to 2½% placing a stop to break even after a 1% paper profit, and then letting the trade ride until closed out by Reversal Signal. This gave larger profits in the long run, but nearly half of the trades were closed out at the break-even point.)

PLAN #9 – TRADING WITH TWO FUNDS

If the trader likes the idea of trading with two funds, one for the shorter profits (Fund S) and one for the larger profits (Fund L), a variety of plans can be set up. For example, he might employ half of his capital in the foregoing Plan 3 and half in Plan 5. Or, he might use Plan 8 for Fund S and the "ride" section of either Plan 6 or 7 for Fund L.

Here is another plan which merits consideration. This summary applies to grain prices between $2.00 and $2.75. For other price levels see schedule which follows.

Capital is divided into two parts for trading in two lots of 5,000 bushels each – one for Fund L and one for Fund S.

When a Reversal Signal comes

1. If you are in the market in a direction opposite to the signal, close out that position.

2. Make a new trade in one lot (Fund L).

3. Limit loss to 5 cents gross.

4. After 4 cents gross paper profit; place stop to break even.

5. If you are not closed out by (3) or (4), take 10 cents gross profit when available, or close out by Reversal Signal if this comes before 10 cents gross profit.

6. If you are closed out at a loss, start over again and require Reversal Signals before entering into new trade.

7. If you are stopped out even, or at a profit enter into 1 lot (Fund L) on next Repeat Signal and again follow (3), (4), and (5).

When a Repeat Signal comes

1. Enter into one lot (Fund S) if the above Fund L trade shows a gross paper profit of at least 2 cents at the price at which the Repeat Signal is given. If the original trade does not show a gross paper gain of at least 2 cents, we ignore the Repeat Signal. In other words, we want the market to move in our favor before incurring farther risk.

2. Limit loss to 5 cents gross.

3. After 4 cents paper profit (gross), place stop to break even.

4. If trade is not closed out at a loss or even, take 5 cents gross profit when it becomes available – or close out on Reversal Signal if this comes before 5 cents profit.

5. Enter into a new trade on another Repeat Signal if a 5 cents gross profit was taken in the preceding Repeat-Signal trade. Ignore the Repeat Signal if you are now holding a Repeat-Signal lot awaiting a 5 cents gain.

6. If you are closed out of a Repeat Signal at a loss, require a full Thrust before entering into a new trade in the same direction.

WHEN PRICE is:	REVERSAL SIGNALS – Fund L			REPEAT SIGNALS – Fund S		
	LIMIT LOSS	BREAK EVEN AFTER PAPER GAIN	TAKE PROFIT	LIMIT LOSS	BREAK EVEN AFTER PAPER GAIN	TAKE PROFIT
Below $1	3¢	$2\frac{1}{4}$¢	5¢	3¢	$2\frac{1}{4}$¢	3¢
Between $1 $1 – 1.99\frac{7}{8}$	4¢	$3\frac{1}{2}$¢	6¢	4¢	$3\frac{1}{2}$¢	4¢
Between $2 – 2.75$	5¢	4¢	10¢	5¢	4¢	5¢
Above $2.75	$5\frac{1}{2}$¢	$4\frac{1}{2}$¢	12¢	$5\frac{1}{2}$¢	$4\frac{1}{2}$¢	7¢

7. If you are closed out of a Repeat Signal even, or at a profit, require only one-half Thrust for new trade on Repeat Signal.

8. Follow only one Repeat Signal per swing.

OTHER PLANS

So you see many Operating Plans have been tried, and an infinite number of others could be tested. I wish I could point to the best plan. Maybe it is embedded somewhere in Operating Plan S/R which we will take up next. Perhaps you will prefer to work out some reasonable plan of your own, and in that event the ideas on these pages may prove helpful. In any event, I am sure that you should settle upon some definite plan. A methodical plan is a must; we cannot trust our "good old judgment" as we go along in the market from day to day.

We have only mentioned "pyramiding" and "scalping"* in this text. Pyramiding would mean the purchase (or short selling) of more and more lots on Repeat Signals as a long trend movement continued on. Each of the commitments in a pyramid could be placed on a separate long-term basis using one of the foregoing Fund-L plans, or some composite plan could be worked out whereby the entire pyramid would be closed out in the event of a reaction.

Many of the "scalping systems" presuppose a knowledge of the main trend. If the main trend is up, a scalper will usually try to buy on the minor dips and sell on the rallies. Actually, with our Repeat Signals, CPR and TOB plus IR, we are trying to do the same thing – and since these signals have been very successful, we can, if we choose, operate a scalping system of our own.

One of my readers (P.C.W.) is making a study of racing systems with the thought of testing some of these systems in commodities and stocks. This is not a matter to brush off lightly. Some brilliant mathematicians have devoted their talents to research on ways of beating the races and other gambling devices. I've often thought that if their skills were applied to the commodity or stock markets, where we can get the odds in our favor, some highly interesting Operating Plans would likely result. Perhaps Mr. P.C.W. will find one or more of such plans which I can pass on to you later.

---

*The term "scalping" for those who may be unfamiliar with its market usage here, the reference is to the measured taking of many tiny profits in very short-term trades regardless should the trade go much higher or much lower later. The scalper made his or her satisfactory profit and is happy with it.

OPERATING PLAN "S/R"

Operating Plan "S/R" appears to be the most satisfactory one developed in this text. It is not the "Perfect Plan" that we hope some day, somehow, will be revealed to us miraculously. But, it is a PLAN, and without a PLAN we are doomed to failure from the very start.

The S/R Plan is very precise, automatic. It can be used mechanically without injecting into it a mixture of your personal judgment or feelings. But, the mechanics of the Plan are such that you can revise them to suit your own ideas as to how the Plan can serve you most effectively. In fact, after explaining the Plan, I will suggest certain revisions, and you can carry on from there to still bigger and better improvements. It is still true that any plan must be *Your Plan*, not mine or the other fellow's if you are to use it faithfully.

"S/R" means "Square Root." "S/R" also means "Statistical Research." This Plan is built upon a foundation of "statistical research" plus the "Square Root Law."

I have done a considerable amount of research, delving into the price charts of past years with the hopes that I might discover the "ideal figures" at which to limit losses and accept profits. But, notwithstanding the time spent, I feel I have only scratched the surface of the problem. The job is really one for an institution with plenty of time and wealth on hand, and it is not likely that the job will ever be done in our time. The research "fundamentalists" are still in the large majority, producing as they do facts and figures which apparently have little or no use as a guide to future price changes. We "technicians" are a neglected lot, and must struggle along as best we can with our unfinished tools.

I feel, however, that my research has been productive of some rough and ready figures which work quite well "on the average." Curiously, these figures seem to tie in with the "square root law." This "law" has been quite definitely established as part of the explanation of the price movements of various stocks at different price levels. It is quite possible that the same "law" is in operation in commodity prices. I have a little "proof," very little, which makes me feel that if oats start at 81 cents and later sells at $1.00 (from 9 to 10, or 1 point, on a square-root basis, ignoring decimal points), during the same period of time, corn starting at $1.44 will tend to rise to $1.69 (12 to 13, or 1 point, on a square-root basis), and wheat selling first at $2.25 will tend to rise to $2.56 (or 15 to 16 – 1 point – in square roots).

Now, I don't want to go on record as claiming that various grains do tend to fluctuate relative to the square roots of their prices. It is entirely possible that the "square-root law" is reflected in commodity price movements just as it is in stock price movements. The evidence I have says that this is so, but this doesn't necessarily make it so! I have found, for example, when a grain sells around $1, a good "average figure" at which to limit losses is 3 cents. And, when a grain sells around $2.25, it is well, "on the average," to limit losses to about 4½ cents. Those figures came from considerable, though inadequate, *statistical research*. Curiously, they correlate quite well with the *square-root law*, as shown in the Tables to follow. It is possible that in using square roots as the basis of our Plan, we are getting about the same answers which would come from more and more years of tedious research. I wouldn't know about that, but I do know that we need a practicable plan, and that the S/R Plan is a good step in that direction. Here it is:

CAPITAL REQUIRED

The S/R Plan requires that you divide your trading capital into three parts:

1. Fund L – for long-term, large gains.
2. Fund M – for medium-term, medium gains.
3. Fund S – for small, quick gains.

As little as $500 (broker's minimum margin in opening an account) can set you up in business, using the Plan in job lots (1,000 bushels) in either oats or corn. To margin three job lots in wheat, rye, or soybeans will require a little more capital.

Table 4.2 Margin – for trading in 15,000 bushels (5,000 bushels in each Fund)

Commodity	Broker requires*		Deposit with Broker for Trading in 15,000 bushels** (add 33⅓% to required margin)
	Cents per bushel	Margin 15,000 bushels	
Oats	7¢	$1050	$1400
Corn	12¢	$1800	$2400
Wheat	20¢	£3000	$4000
Rye	20¢	$3000	$4000
Soybeans	25¢	$3750	$5000

*Margin requirements will vary from time to time and are not always the same among different brokers.
**If you prefer to trade in job lots (1,000 bushels in each of the three funds), divide these figures by 5. For example, $1000 should be adequate margin to trade in 3,000 bushels of soybeans, £800 for 3,000 bushels of wheat or rye, etc.

We shall assume that trading will be done in lots of 5,000 bushels, one 5,000-bushel lot for each of the three funds, or 15,000 bushels in all. The broker requires that we maintain adequate margin, so for a cushion or protection against early losses we will start the account by adding 33⅓% to the margin required by the broker.

PROCEDURE

Having more than satisfied the broker's margin requirements so that we are prepared to hold up under the misfortune of the maximum losses ever likely to come, we are now ready to start trading. For buy and sell signals we turn to the Thrust Method.

On a Reversal Signal we enter into *one* lot – 5,000 bushels. This is for Fund L in which we seek a large, "long-term" gain. (In commodities, where things happen fast, the expression "long-term" is a misnomer. Seldom is a trade held as long as six months, and it may be held only a day or two. But in comparison with the other two funds, the intention of Fund L is for large, "long-term" gains.)

If the original Reversal Signal is wrong, it is quite possible that no Repeat Signal will be given, and in that event a loss will be taken in only one lot. We must try to avoid taking a loss in the total fund at any one time. If we get into the middle of the stream during a whipsawing market, it will be much easier to take our losses to the tune of 5,000 bushels rather than 15,000. It is true that if we plunged everything into the original Reversal Signals whenever and wherever they occur, in the long run we would come out with the largest profit possible from our methods. But, it is also true that if we were to do this we would subject ourselves to the hazards of large losses, even though the losses be only temporary. Large losses breed discouragement, and discouragement leads to defeat – abandonment of the system. In an effort to gain poise and peace, we are willing to forego some eventual profits, and we use only one-third of our total capital in acting on a Reversal Signal.

We follow this trade through in accordance with the instructions in Table 4.3 and its Footnotes. If we buy wheat at $2.00, we then follow the instructions after the figure $1.95, this price being nearest to $2.00 of those prices listed. Immediately on entering the trade, we place an order to limit the loss to 4¼cents. If and when we get a 3½ cents paper profit, we change our stop to $2.00 so in the event of a reaction we will be closed out even, or nearly so since we will lose the commission cost, approximately ⅜ cents. If prices continue up to $2.07 so that a 7 cents paper profit is shown, we change our stop to $2.03½ so as to assure ourselves of 3½ cents gain or half the paper profit. If the rise continues so that 28 cents paper profit is available, we change the stop in order to be sure of 14 cents of this profit. In that event a Reversal Sell Signal will likely come before the stop is caught, and we will obtain a larger gain. In fact, trades in Fund L are generally closed by Reversal Signals with smaller losses and larger gains than those indicated in Table 4.3.

For the benefit of those who may be interested in knowing how the figures were derived from the "square-root law," this information is indicated in the Table. However, we need pay no attention to this in putting the Table to actual use. We need only have confidence that each figure expresses a tendency in price movements, and these tendencies are repeated often enough so that the figures will serve us profitably in the long run. They may lead to losses in the next trade, or the next few trades, but over the life of any grain future they should be expected to produce a net gain.

Having followed the original Reversal Signal by trading in one lot, we now watch our charts for Repeat Signals. Particularly, we watch for a CPR, or for an IR after a TOB (or, if short, for an IR after a TOT). If one of these Patterns comes, we will not require a Thrust, but will trade immediately at the closing price of the Pattern day, or at the opening the following morning if more convenient.

On the first Repeat Signal we enter into another lot of 5,000 bushels. This is for Fund M, in which we hope to get a "medium profit." We enter into this trade regardless of whether the original Reversal Signal shows a paper profit or loss at the time the first Repeat Signal is given. If prices have reversed themselves so that the original Reversal Signal shows a paper loss that is approaching the maximum, it is likely that no Repeat Signal will be given. But, this Repeat Signal may come at a higher or lower price than the original Reversal Signal, and, if it comes, we act on it immediately – assuming, of course, that the original Reversal Signal is still in effect and has not been nullified by an opposing Reversal Signal. We "ride" this 5,000 bushels in accordance with the instructions in the section of the Table under "Fund M." If we buy this additional 5,000 bushels at $2.02, we limit the loss to 4¼ cents; after 3½ cents gross paper profit, we place a stop to break even; and we take 7 cents gross profit if and when it becomes available.

Of course, when the first Repeat Signal comes, it is possible that the original Reversal Signal has already been closed out at a loss, or a gain, or at the break-even point. If this proves to be the case, we will then follow the first Repeat Signal for Fund L and then wait for the next Repeat Signal before engaging in

Table 4.3 Fund L – Reversal Signals

When you Enter Trade at Price Nearest:	Limit Loss To:	Break Even After Paper Gain of:	When Paper Gain Amounts to Figures Below, Place Stop to Protect ½ of Paper Gain					Square Root
$ .25	1½¢	1¼¢	2½¢	5¢	7½¢	10¢	12½¢	5
.35	1¾	1½	3	6	9	12	15	6
.50	2⅛	1¾	3½	7	10½	14	17½	7
.65	2⅜	2	4	8	12	16	20	8
.80	2¾	2¼	4½	9	13½	18	22½	9
1.00	3	2½	5	10	15	20	25	10
1.20	3¼	2¾	5½	11	16½	22	27½	11
1.45	3⅝	3	6	12	18	24	30	12
1.70	3⅞	3¼	6½	13	19½	26	32½	13
1.95	4¼	3½	7	14	21	28	35	14
2.25	4½	3¾	7½	15	22½	30	37½	15
2.50	4¾	4	8	16	24	32	40	16
2.90	5⅛	4¼	8½	17	25½	34	42½	17
3.25	5⅜	4½	9	18	27	36	45	18
3.60	5¾	4¾	9½	19	28½	38	47½	19
4.00	6	5	10	20	30	40	50	20
4.40	6¼	5¼	10½	21	31½	42	52½	21
Col. 1	Col. 2 30% of Col. 9	Col. 3 25% of Col. 9	Col.4 50% of Col. 9	Col. 5 100% of Col. 9	Col. 6 150% of Col. 9	Col. 7 200% of Col. 9	Col. 8 250% of Col. 9	Col. 9 Square Root of Col. 1

Square root figures are approximate.

Fund L – Operating Plan

1. When Reversal Signal comes, close out any opposing position.
2. Enter into new position in one lot.
3. Limit loss to amount shown in Column 2 (commission is additional loss).
4. After gross paper profit shown in Column 3, place stop to break even. (Do not make allowance for commission; place stop at entry price.)
5. After gross paper profit shown in Column 4, change stop in order to assure ½ of that amount gross profit if a reaction comes.
6. Change stop in the event that additional gross paper profit comes, as shown in columns 5, 6, 7, and 8; in each case changing the stop so that ½ of that amount of gross paper profit is protected.
7. Always close out trade if opposing Reversal Signal comes before any of the above stops are executed.
8. If closed out of a position in any manner and no Reversal Signal is given, enter into a new Fund L trade in one lot on next Repeat Signal and again follow the above procedure.
9. Do not enter into a new trade in the Delivery Month of any future.

the procedure reserved for Fund *M*. We hope at all times, to have Fund L working for us, just in case the movement proves to be one of those large ones where the profit potentials are tremendous.

If another Repeat Signal comes, and if at that time our paper position is profitable in *both* Funds L and M, we then enter into the market for our final 5,000 bushels. This is for Fund S, in which we seek a small but fast gain, according to the instructions in the section of the Table under "Fund S." This fund is not employed until both of the other funds are occupied in the market with a paper profit. If Fund L is in the market, and Fund M gets closed out, we will then enter into another Fund M trade before taking on a Fund S commitment. In other words, at all times we take our funds consecutively, L, M and S, and employ the S-Fund only if L and M are already profitably engaged in the market. This means that we are not going to incur any risks with our final 5,000 bushels until the market actually moves in our favor. The profits in Fund S are small, but tests show that they are very consistent. Moreover, I am inclined to believe that by "shopping" around the various options and commodities for Repeat Signals, Fund S can become a delightful source of excitement and income. In my tests of the Funds I have assumed that one sticks to one option only, and this means that Fund S was inactive much of the time. In practice, if a Repeat Signal for Fund S doesn't come in one option or commodity it may come in another – hence the Fund might be gainfully employed at nearly all times. More about this suggestion later in the paper.

The notes following Table 4.4 will make clear some points not brought out above.

RECORD

The foregoing Plan was tested in full detail in the May options of both wheat and corn in each of the years from 1947 through 1953. Spot tests were also made in oats, rye and soybeans. A net profit was shown in every future contract so tested. The following are the pertinent conclusions in respect to wheat and corn. Some of these conclusions suggest that certain changes may be in proper order in using the S/R Plan in current dealings.

1. Trading in all three funds, and following every signal in a contract, the net profit per contract, after deducting commissions, was:

   CORN: From $681 or 28% to $9625 or 401%. Average profit per contract was $4000 or 166% on $2400 investment at start of contract.

Table 4.4 Fund M and S, repeat signals

	FUND M REPEAT SIGNALS			FUND S REPEAT SIGNALS			
When you Enter Trade at Price Nearest:	Limit Loss To:	Break Even After Paper Gain of:	Take Profit	Limit Loss To	Break Even After Paper Gain of:	Take Profit	Square Root
$ .25	1½¢	1¼¢	2½¢	1½¢	1¼¢	1½¢	5
.35	1¾	1½	3	1¾	1½	1¾	6
.50	2⅛	1¾	3½	2⅛	1¾	2½	7
.65	2⅜	2	4	2⅜	2	2⅜	8
.80	2¾	2¼	4½	2¾	2¼	2¾	9
1.00	3	2½	5	3	2½	3	10
1.20	3¼	2¾	5½	3¼	2¾	3¼	11
1.45	3⅝	3	6	3⅝	3	3⅝	12
1.70	3⅞	3¼	6½	3⅞	3¼	3⅞	13
1.95	4¼	3½	7	4¼	3½	4¼	14
2.25	4½	3¾	7½	4½	3¾	4½	15
2.50	4¾	4	8	4¾	4	4¾	16
2.90	5⅛	4¼	8½	5⅛	4¼	5⅛	17
3.25	5⅜	4½	9	5⅜	4½	5⅜	18
3.60	5¾	4¾	9½	5¾	4¾	5¾	19
4.00	6	5	10	6	5	6	20
4.40	6¼	5¼	10½	6¼	5¼	6¼	21
Col. 1	Col. 2 30% of Col. 5	Col. 3 25% of Col. 5	Col.4 50% of Col. 5	Col. 2 30% of Col. 5	Col. 3 25% of Col. 5	Col. 4 30% of Col. 5	Col. 5 Square Root of Col. 1

Square root figures are approximate.

Fund M and S – Operating Plan

1. If you are holding a Fund L commitment (one lot), enter into another lot on Repeat Signal. This is for Fund M.
2. If you are not holding a Fund L lot (it having been closed out in some manner), enter into a Fund L trade on next Repeat Signal and then on following Repeat Signal make commitment for Fund M provided Fund L is still in market at that time.
3. Enter into one lot for Fund S on another Repeat Signal if at time this signal is given a paper profit exists for both Funds L and M.
4. Limit loss in each Fund to the amount shown in Column 2.
5. Place stop at break-even point after gross paper profit shown in Column 3.
6. Take gross profit for Fund M and S as designated in their respective Columns 4.
7. Close out if opposing Reversal Signal comes before stop is caught or profit-taking point is reached.
8. Whenever any Fund is closed out with gain, loss, or even, and the other Funds are occupied, enter on next Repeat Signal in the Fund just closed out, and follow again the procedure for that fund.
9. Always employ Fund L first, then M, and finally S.
10. If two or all of the Funds are closed out at a profit, enter again into one lot in each fund on next Repeat Signal and follow again the procedure for each individual Fund.
11. But, if two or all of the Funds are closed out even or at a loss, enter into only one lot on next Repeat Signal. Use Fund L first (if not already in Fund L). Then on following Repeat Signal take on new lot for Fund M, and finally on next Repeat Signal a lot for Fund S.
12. In a single Upswing or Downswing, use only the first Repeat Signal in that swing (sometimes there are more than one Repeat Signal in a single swing – use only the first one).
13. Do not follow Repeat Signals based on Rule #3.
14. Do not follow Repeat Signals in the Delivery Month of a future.

WHEAT: From $1400 or 35% to $7212 or 180%. Average profit per contract was $3689 or 92% on $4000 investment at start of contract.

From the above it is apparent that corn gives the better results. In May 1951 corn, the net profit in all three funds was $681 or 28% on original capital of $2400. In May 1948 corn the net profit was $9625 or 401% on original capital of $2400. The average net profit per contract over the seven year period was $4000 or 166% on $2400 capital. If the calculations were placed on a "cumulative basis" – starting off in 1947 with $2400 capital and adding more and more bushels as the fund grew – I daresay that the profits by the end of 1953 would be astronomical. Such figures look good in print, but somehow we don't seem to get that kind of results in practice. I think it is more practical to feel that we have a good chance of averaging over 150% each year in corn. But, in case anyone wants to build dream castles, $2400 original capital will compound to $1,464,337 in seven years at 150% annual return!

2. The original Reversal Signals prove the most profitable in the long run due to large gains from time to time. But, the odds are not very favorable insofar as the individual transaction is concerned. In corn there are about two gains for each loss, and about 13% of the trades result in neither gain nor loss. The probabilities for success in the single trade are even less in wheat. When the final score on Reversal Signals is added up, corn shows about 7 cents gain for each 1 cent loss, and wheat about 5 cents gain for each 1 cent loss. So, these signals turn out well in the end, though rather dangerous in single trades.

3. The odds are very favorable in the S-Fund – over five out of six of these signals result in profits and average around 10 cents profit for each 1 cent loss. The M-Fund too does much better than the original Reversal Signals both in number and amount of gains relative to losses.

4. This suggests that we can enhance the chances for success if we wait for the first Repeat Signal before acting. When a Reversal Signal comes, we could close out our present position, and then step aside and wait for a Repeat Signal. If no Repeat Signal comes soon after the Reversal Signal, it is likely that the Reversal Signal was in error and a loss would have been taken in it. If a Reversal Signal does come, we could then enter into two lots, and follow Fund L in one of them and Fund M in the other. Sometimes the first Repeat Signal is at a better price than the original Reversal Signal. If it should come at a price considerably worse than the Reversal Signal it could be ignored in favor of some other Repeat Signal in some other commodity.

5. If we are willing to forego the opportunity of occasional large profits as offered by Fund L as well as the medium profits of Fund M, and if we will be satisfied with frequent small profits, then I think we can get the laws of chance so highly in our favor that we will be operating on as close to a "sure thing" as will ever be possible in commodity trading. It appears that this can be done by simply acting on Fund-S Repeat Signals and taking gross profits as listed in Columns 3 of the Tables. If we buy wheat at $2.00, for example, we would limit the loss to 4¼ cents and we would take 3½ cents gross profit just as soon as it became available. The losses would average considerably less than 4¼ cents due to the appearance of Reversal Signals before the 4¼ cents stops were caught. There would be no break-even trades. And, in watching all the futures in each commodity, there would be frequent trading signals. Frequently there would be opportunities in different commodities at the same time – the three lots could then be diversified in three commodities. I do not have calculations on the relative long-term merits of this plan as compared with the S/R Plan, but this suggestion looks very inviting from the viewpoint of few losses. In corn about 6 out of 7 trades result in gains over the 1947–1953 period. Wheat, in this case, does even better, with 7 out of 8 trades resulting in gains and the losing trades averaging about 1½ cents per bushel including commissions. The idea is worth more than a second thought.

6. Rye and soybeans are more volatile than the other commodities. Shouldn't something be added to the figures in the Tables to give effect to this extra volatility? Yes – but you do your own "adding" as this is one of the many answers I do not have. The same applies to TOTs and TOBs. If "1 cent above or below" is a good measure of a TOT for corn selling at $1.60, obviously some figure greater than 1 cent should be used in soybeans selling at $3.00. Your judgment is as good as mine as to what figure to use. The need for a "universal" or "one-way" formula is apparent. Perhaps I can work out such a formula. In the meanwhile, the mechanical rules as presented in the many foregoing pages have worked in the past without adjustment for particular commodities. I think they will continue to work in the future.

ODDS AND ENDS ON COMMODITY TRADING

The following pages are devoted to miscellaneous matters which appear important in commodity trading. First a few words, in general, about the Thrust Method in commodities and about present plans.

On three occasions, since publication of the first printing of this paper in 1952, I have issued a three-months "Coaching Service" for readers of "Gains in Grains" The purpose of this service was to give instruction in the use of the Thrust Method in actual, current markets. No such service is being issued at the present time as I believe that present readers of "Gains in Grains" are now able to follow the method without my help. I have never yet issued an advisory service, or a telegraphic service. Some day I may try my hand at that sort of thing for the possible benefit of the business or professional man who does not have time to personally follow the market. But, if at all possible, I think everyone should become *his own counsellor* – should make his own trades by methods which he personally understands.

I am sure that these former "Coaching Letters" have amply demonstrated that the Thrust Method is very likely to give a pleasing net profit over the life of any commodity option. The letters certainly demonstrated that all is not "gains" – the method runs into bad periods from time to time in which small whipsawing losses are taken. But, almost invariably it has come back strong, recovered its losses, and wound up the contract with "gains in grains." (The only exception I know to this is in a couple recent oats contracts where the movements were so small that it was hardly possible to profit – even then, the net loss was very small.)

My present work (starting in July, 1954) is to develop a "ONE-WAY FORMULA" and to publish the results of this new research in the form of "PROGRESS REPORTS." The Thrust Methods, as we are now using them in commodities and stocks, present difficulties which can be surmounted if we have a *single, unchanging formula for all stocks and commodities.*

I expect to do away entirely with the present necessity of changing the rules to fit the commodity or stock under observation. Tables will no longer be needed to determine Patterns, Signals, Stop-Loss Points, and Profit Points; the price action of the chart alone will tell the whole story. Largely through a methodical use of price ranges and price swings. I am confident that a ONE-WAY FORMULA is practicable.

Also, I expect to improve on our present mechanical signals. For example, the #3 Signals (penetrations of Tops and Bottoms) can obviously be improved. Often when a former Top is exceeded that is the place to *sell*, not the place to buy. All of us know that Dow Theory and similar methods often buy at the top of a movement and sell at the bottom. I believe I've discovered a way of recognizing whether the penetration of a Top, or Bottom, means a "climax reversal" or a "continuation of the movement." This needs further testing, but it appears now that we shall soon have a good tool which will often prevent us from being deceived by "new highs" and "new lows." We shall often know when a new high is made whether that marks a "climax," the place to sell, or whether the movement is likely to continue farther. And, when a new low is made, we shall often know whether to buy or whether to expect still lower prices.

> *Through a methodical use of price ranges and price swings, I am confident that a ONE-WAY FORMULA is practicable*

We can improve also on other points in our present procedure. For instance, a "Test of Top" (or "Test of Bottom") should be the same for soybeans as it is for oats, it should be the same for both a low-priced stock and a high-priced stock. I have a simple plan in mind (using price ranges) for accomplishing this. And, to mention one more thing, it seems to me that we can learn where to place our stops and where to take our profits simply by observing the size of typical recent swings in the stock or commodity under observation. All of this is a part of ONE-WAY FORMULA, an unchanging procedure for analyzing any chart at any time.

The PROGRESS REPORTS will be issued at the rate of about two each month, and will continue until the work is completed. Liberal use will be made of current charts in actual stocks and commodities for illustrating all new points. This will be "advanced technique" exclusively for readers of "Gains in Grains" and/or "The Thrust Method in Stocks." ONE-WAY FORMULA will not be widely publicized, and I firmly believe it will surpass anything heretofore done in the way of a methodical trading plan in either stocks or commodities. It will likely be my final publication on commodity and stock market methods as I expect to do this work well and have nothing left to say when it is completed.

THE THRUST METHOD IN COTTON

Upswings and downswings: Same as in Chapter 3 of "Gains in Grains".

Signal patterns: The Patterns are the same as explained in Chapter 3. Two Pattern Days are required for Reversals (except for Rule 3), one Pattern Day for Repeats.

TOB and TOT: Within 10 points of either of last two Bottoms (Tops).

Rule No. 1: Current low must be above or not more than 10 points below last Bottom. Current high must be below or not more than 10 points above last Top.

Thrust: Use the same procedure as explained in Chapter 3. If Signal Pattern is set up today, the amount of Thrust required to produce a signal is:

- *Reversal signal:* Use today's Range with a maximum of 25 points and a minimum of 15 points.

- *Repeat signal:* Use one-half today's Range with a maximum of 15 points and a minimum of 10 points. (No Thrust required for CPR – or TOB plus IR – or TOT plus IR.)

Suggested operating plan

Confirmed signal
1. Limit loss to 50 points (plus commission).
2. After 35 points paper profit, place stop to break even (commission is lost).
3. After 75 points paper profit, place stop for 25 points gross profit.
4. After 100 points paper profit, place stop for 50 points gross profit.
5. Take 200 points gross profit when available.

Repeat signal
1. Limit loss to 50 points (plus commission).
2. After 35 points paper profit, place stop to break even (you lose commission).
3. After 75 points paper profit, place stop for 25 points gross profit.
4. Take 100 points gross profit when available.

Hold only one Repeat trade at one time. This is, wait for present Repeat trade to be closed out with loss or gain before entering into another Repeat trade.

MULTIPLE QUICK PROFITS

We confess that it is extremely difficult for us to be contented with "fast, small profits." Our charts in both stocks and commodities are shouting at us: "Repeat Signals with their quick-multiple gains offer the sure road to market success." The record on paper is clear: through Repeat Signals we should expect a profit eight times in every ten trades; we should expect that the two losses will average much smaller than the eight gains; and by watching several stocks or commodities, we should expect these Repeat Signals at *frequent intervals.*

Truly a "MULTIPLE-PROFIT PLAN." And, yet when it comes to the individual trade, we often find that wishful thinking takes over. We start building dream castles and find ourselves hoping that this particular trade will prove to be one of the "big ones." So, likely as not we proceed to ignore the highly favorable odds for a quick gain and set our sights on big game.

> *"Repeat Signals with their quick-multiple gains offer the sure road to market success"*

We are sure that many of our readers also suffer from this common disease – "enlargement of the profit complex." Most of the mail we receive indicates that our readers share with us the hope for a killing in each trade. But, the road to recovery from this disease is clear, if we will just take it.

C. W. B. prescribed the right medicine in a letter he kindly wrote us on February 9, 1954:

> "Have just received your S/R Operating Plan. My eye was at once caught by your remarks concerning the possibilities of concentrating on short term profits. This has long been a firm conviction of mine. That is, that he who jumps in and out (according to some carefully preconceived plan) will eventually come out of the game with more marbles – and more fun – than the long term boys.
>
> "I know the above is contrary to long-established belief. However, figures don't lie and neither does an attractive bank statement.
>
> "I'm pleased to find that many of your methods are much like ones I have employed for a good and profitable period . . . though I must confess that mine were not so highly refined as yours. Hence, a bit of spot checking quickly reveals additional profits I might easily have banked."

Yes, Repeat Signals *can* become a source of lucrative income. It is true that no single profit looks particularly attractive. But, if we add together many of these small profits, the potentials of a "multiple-profit plan" become vivid. We are quite certain that every week of the year offers on opportunity to enter into a quick-gain trade in some stock or commodity. You need only "set your traps" in many stocks and commodities. Occasionally (two times in ten) you will lose your "bait," but most of the time (eight times in ten) you should trap your game.

TRADING TACTICS

How to act on repeat signals

Experience teaches that when a commodity or stock gives a Repeat Signal it "means business." The market will usually continue in the direction of the signal so that a profit will soon be available for the taking.

In the fast-moving commodity markets, it is best to operate on certain Repeat Signals at the closing price of the day in which one of those Signals is given. These Repeat Signals are CPR, IR after TOB, and IR after TOT. When one of these Patterns is set up, for purpose of a Repeat Signal, it is wise to act immediately at or near the closing price of that day rather than to wait for the opening the following day. On a Repeat Buy Signal there is considerable likelihood that the market will open higher than the previous close. Similarly, when a Repeat Sell Signal comes at the close, the market will likely open lower the next day.

If you are near a telephone you can easily operate at the closing price whenever a Repeat Signal dictates such an operation. Let us say that you are looking for a Repeat Buy Signal in September Wheat which we shall assume is now in a Downswing. The procedure would be to telephone your broker about one-half hour before the close and ask for the low and present price of September Wheat. If you are told that the low was equal to or below yesterday's low, you would know that one part of the "CPR Rule" was already fulfilled and all that is now needed is for September Wheat to close above yesterday's close. If at the time of your telephone call the price is near or above yesterday's close, you could then give an order to *buy September wheat at the close if it closes above 2.00 bid* (assuming that yesterday's close was 2.00).

We have found that not all customer's men ("Accounts Executives") are acquainted with this type of order. But, stand your ground – the order *can* be given. We have personally used the order and have had executions made at the exact closing price which, incidentally, was invariably better than the opening price the following morning.

Let us carry the illustration further and assume that September Wheat closed at 2.00¼. Your broker should then telephone and notify you of the execution at 2.00¼. If this was for Fund S, you could then consult the S/R Table and place an open order to "sell at 1.96 stop" in order to limit the loss to 4¼ cents and at the same time you could place an open order to "sell at 2.04½," and this would gross you 4¼ cents in case September Wheat later sold at 2.04½ before it sold at 1.96. On execution of one order, you would then cancel the other order.

Judging from past records, trades of the above type will prove profitable eight times out of ten. If you would be satisfied with 3½¢ gross profit (see "Break-Even" column) rather than 4¼¢, past records say that you will profit about nine times out of ten.

How to use stop orders

Stop Orders are most commonly thought of as "Stop-Loss Orders," a tool to limit your losses. In commodities they are especially effective for this purpose because you very often get execution at the exact price named in the Stop-Loss Order. In the stock market the Stop-Loss Order has an important function too, although here the executions may not be as favorable as in commodities.

Tables are included in the Thrust Methods and these facilitate the placing of Stop-Loss Order at various price levels for stocks and grains. Using these Tables you can see at a glance just where to place an order to limit your loss.

Stop Orders may also be used to protect profits, or at least to break even, after prices have moved in your favor. If you buy wheat at $2.00, you first place a Stop-Loss order at 1.95¾, and this limits your loss to 4¼¢ plus commission if the trade is closed out at exactly 1.95¾. In the event that this doesn't happen, but instead wheat rises to 2.03½, you then cancel the stop at 1.95¾ and enter a new stop at the purchase price, $2.00. From then on you have a free ride, without risk or worry. If the price rises to 2.07, you change the stop to 2.03½, thus assuring yourself 3½¢ gross profit in the event of a decline back to 2.03½ or lower. If the price goes to 2.14, you change the stop to 2.07, and so forth, in accordance with the schedule for Fund L in which we seek a large profit.

But Stop Orders serve another important function. They can and should be used an aggressive tool for getting into a position at or near the price indicated by a Buy or Sell Signal. With our methods there is always prior action which enables you to calculate in advance, right to-the-eighth, the price at which a Signal will be given, and you can enter your order in advance with your broker for a "Stop Buy" (or "Stop Sell") at that price.

Stop Orders can and should be used for getting into a position near the Buy or Sell Signal

With the order entered in advance, you do not need to be near the tape. You are better off if you make your decisions in the quiet of your own home and leave it to the Stop Order to place your calculated decision into effect. You need not give up your job and go to the broker's office every day. It is better if you do not, because the man who gives all his thought to the market and the news and gossip surrounding it tends to disregard his precise methods and instead takes into account many things which ordinarily prove harmful. Let your Stop Order sit there and work for you.

Under our commodity method, each day after the market closes you can determine the exact price which will be a "Buy" or "Sell" if reached the following day, and you can enter the appropriate "Stop Order" to place you in the market if that price is reached the following day. In case of stocks, you need to compute the stop prices only once a week. After the market closes on Friday, you make your calculations for the following week, and before the opening Monday morning you place a Stop Order to buy or sell if your calculated price is reached anytime during the week This is simpler and more effective than being in close touch with the market during trading hours.

The "Market if traded (MIT)" order

From R.M.R., New York

"Further pursual of the charts in your recent mailing have given me some ideas which coupled with my experience as a past member of the Chicago Board of Trade, may be of some benefit to you.

"First, it seems to me that reliance upon signals given by one option limits the chances of a signal occurring at an advantageous spot. Therefore, I believe all options should be watched (the current option to be discontinued, because of growing thinness of volume, 30 days before expiration and the most recently traded option to be started only after it has been on the board for 60 days).

"Problem: If we use all options and have funds for only one, how do we operate? My answer lies in the form of a type of order which your broker will accept if he is apprised of its existence. Let's assume you are long May wheat and will receive a sell signal in the July if it thrusts down to 2.03⅛ the following day.

"An order may be placed reading: 'Sell 5,000 May wheat at the market if July wheat sells at 2.03⅛.'

"There is another type of order which many traders do not know of and it may be useful to you some day in your personal trading.

"This is the MIT order. Let's assume you're long May wheat at 2.00 and wish to sell it at 2.04. There are times when it will sell at 2.04 exactly – and that's the top. And, because the pit trader has the edge, you're still long when it goes back to 2.00. This problem may be mitigated by entering an order reading: 'Sell 5,000 May wheat @ 2.04 MIT (market if traded).' Then, if May wheat *touches*

2.04, your wheat is sold 'at the market.' You'll probably get 2.03⅞ – but surely an eighth is small insurance for this kind of protection. Naturally, this may be used to take short-side profits as well.

"Here is another: Back in the old days when I made 'day trades' – assuming I was long at 2.09 and wanted to get our either at the close or on a stop, order would read: 'Sell 5,000 May wheat @ 2.08 day stop or market on close.' If I was not stopped out at 2.08, then my 5,000 was sold on the bid price on the close. (If you were short at 2.09 and wanted to limit your loss to 1¢, the order would read: 'Buy 5,000 May Wheat @ 2.10 day stop or market on close.')

"As for your problem: 'Buy May Wheat on close if it closes above 2.04, you should say '. . . above 2.04 bid.' If the market closed at 2.03⅞ to 2.04⅛ your broker would be in a quandary. (Incidentally, this question of spreads on closings can some day make you miss a good move based on a CPR. If a fellow uses a newspaper which gives the offering price, he may get a CPR and another fellow using another paper may not get one. Best plan I think is to get the bid price from broker and consistently use that.)

"In connection with your signals in stocks, it occurs to me that Puts and Calls might be used in volatile stocks, instead of buying them outright or selling short outright. Capital required for a position of 100 shares in 20 different issues would approximate $3,000 and a fabulous return may eventuate."

When to use "market if touched (MIT) order" and when to use "stop order"

Assume that July Wheat is 2.00 and we want to *buy* if it declines to 1.98: "Buy 5,000 July Wheat at 1.98 MIT." (This means that in the event of a decline to 1.98, July Wheat would be bought at the market.)

Assume July Wheat is 2.00 and we want to *buy* if it *rises* to 2.01: "Buy 5,000 July Wheat at 2.01 Stop." (This means that in the event of a rise to 2.01, July Wheat would be bought at the market.)

From the above let's make the general rule: "If you want your execution made at a *worse* price than today's price use STOP ORDER. If you want the execution made at a *better* price, use MIT ORDER. Both types of orders become market orders when the stipulated price is reached. If this stipulated price is more favorable than today's price, use MIT ORDER; if it is less favorable, use STOP ORDER. Let's see if this general rule applies to the following:

Assume that July Wheat is 2.00 and we want to *sell* if it *declines* to 1.98: "Sell 5,000 July Wheat at 1.98 Stop." (1.98 is less favorable than the price at which we could sell today. Therefore, use STOP ORDER.)

Assume July Wheat is 2.00 and we want to *sell* if it rises to 2.01: "Sell 5,000 July Wheat at 2.01 MIT." (We want to sell at a better price than today's price; therefore, use MIT.)

Each order as worded above would be a one-day order. If we want to leave the order stand for more than one day, the word "open" should appear in each order.

Should you trade in stocks or commodities?

When wheat sells at $2.00 a bushel, you can buy and sell $10,000 worth of wheat (5,000 bushels) and the commission is only $18 for the entire buying and selling transaction. A total overhead of $18 amounts to about one fifth of 1% on the $10,000 deal.

If you buy $10,000 worth of a $25 stock (400 shares), the broker will charge you $110 to make the purchase. If later you sell the same stock at, say, $25, the overhead is another $110 plus the Federal and NY State taxes on sale and transfer of stocks. The total round trip overhead on the $10,000 transaction will be around $250 or 2½%. Forty of such deals, with neither gain nor loss, will mean that the broker and government will pocket all of your $10,000.

You can buy $10,000 worth of wheat with $1000 (or less!) capital – or about 10% margin. To handle $10,000 worth of stock you must possess $7000 capital when the minimum margin is set at 70%.

In other words, the capital requirements are relatively small in commodities and the "grind of the wheel" ("percentage take") is quite insignificant in commodities as compared with stocks.

But, that isn't all! In a few weeks' time commodities often make movements which offer profit potentials that may take months, or even years, for the average stock to offer. A 20 per cent movement in wheat, from $2.00 to $2.40, will give more profit than a 100 per cent gain in a stock which you bought at $25 and later sold at $50. Wheat often offers 20 per cent profit-potentials in a few months' time. It usually takes years for a stock to double in value.

Stock		Wheat	
Buy 400 shares @ $25	$10,000	Buy 5,000 bushels at 2.00	$10,000
Sell 400 shares @ $50	20,000	Sell 5,000 bushels at 2.40	12,000
Gross Gain	10,000	Gross Gain	2,000
Less Overhead	250	Less Overhead	18
NET GAIN	9,750	NET GAIN	1,982
139% Profit on $7000 capital		199% Profit on $1000 capital	
(May take *years*)		(May take only *months!*)	

Now all of this makes a convincing case in favor of commodities, but, of course, there is another side to the picture; namely, just how good are your Signals and Operating Plan? If you can be right most of the time, the odds are much more favorable in commodity trading. But, beware if you are going to be wrong most of the time! The small margins and fast movements can prove to be your downfall. If you make too many mistakes in stocks, it usually means a "slow, lingering death." But too many mistakes in commodities, with a thin margin, certainly means "fast suicide."

These "odds and ends" in the fascinating business of commodity trading could go on and on without end. The *Robert Moody Grain Analysis* has often presented sidelights which are of unusual interest to students of commodity markets. In addition, the clearcut daily grain charts, published each week by this service, are a boon to those traders who are not inclined to make their own charts.

"GAINS IN GRAINS"

The three charts on the following pages are among the current contracts at the time this is written (late June, 1954).

These charts illustrate the actual applications of Rules 1, 2, and 3, and the various Repeat Signals are also shown on these charts.

No Operating Plan is represented on these charts. A precise Operating Plan is just as important as the Signals. The choice of an Operating Plan is, however, a matter which each trader must necessarily decide for himself.

December 1954 Oats shows a Rule #2 Buy Signal at 71. This is based on the two Buy Patterns, TOB and IR, followed the day after the second Pattern by the minimum upside Thrust of ½¢. A Repeat Buy Signal came on the low day of the next Downswing when a CPR appeared. This came at a lower price (70⅝) than the original Reversal Signal. This is not at all uncommon, although more times than not the first Repeat Buy Signal will come at a higher price than the original Reversal Signal.

July 1954 Corn shows a Rule #3 Buy Signal at 1.48⅞. This is based on a PT followed by an upside Thrust equal to the range of the PT day. Here is a case where a Rule #3 Signal was desirable for effecting a Buy Signal at an attractive price. In following several commodities, the trader might well prefer to operate on #1 or #2 Signals which ordinarily come at better prices than the #3 Signals. (For example, July 1954 Wheat gave a #1 Buy Signal at a lower level than this

Fig 4.39 Chicago Grain Futures – daily prices (a) December 1954 Oats, (b) July 1954 Corn

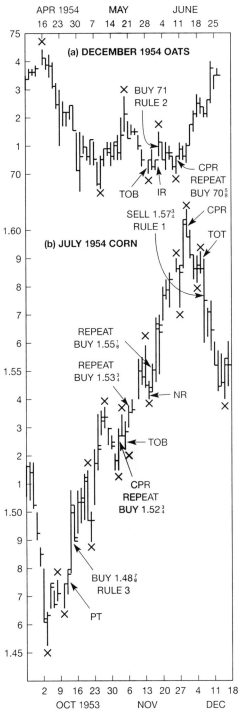

#3 Buy Signal in July 1954 Corn.) Notice the Repeat Buy Signals on the way up in July Corn and finally the #1 Sell Signal at 1.57¾ – based on CPR and TOT, followed by a downside Thrust equal to the range of the TOT day.

LOSSES ARE INSURANCE

In July 1954 Wheat we have an instance where an excellent signal was whip-sawed and then the good signal was reinstated.

On the very first day of the major decline a Rule #1 Signal came to sell at 2.18⅞. Unfortunately, this signal was repudiated when the #1 Buy Signal came a few days later at 2.20¼. But, the main trend was again recognized two days later with the Sell Signal at 2.17. This signal held fast, and, in fact, was reaffirmed by Repeat Sell Signals, throughout the subsequent decline to below 1.90.

From this we can learn the lesson that small losses are the insurance premium we must pay in order to be right during the main swings.

Neither the September nor the December contracts in wheat gave the whipsaw shown in the July option at this point – and both September and December gave a Reversal Sell Signal on the *first day* of decline after a long run skyward. I have chosen to show the July contract because I think it is well to remind the reader of losses, as well as profits in these illustrations.

REPEATED OPPORTUNITIES

The record shows that we can avoid some of the losses inherent in the Reversal Signals by waiting for the first Repeat Signal before acting. This procedure gives a smaller gain *in the long run* (because of the more attractive prices when the Reversal Signals are right) but it avoids many of the irritating small losses.

Here in September 1954 Corn we have a good example of how Repeat Signals may soon follow a correct Reversal Signal. Often when the Reversal Signal is *not* correct, no Repeat Signal will follow it, and consequently at those times a loss is avoided by waiting for the possible appearance of a Repeat Signal before taking action.

SOYBEANS

This chart illustrates an adjustment – which you may care to make for volatile, high-priced soybeans.

Fig 4.40 Chicago Grain Futures – daily prices (a) July 1954 Wheat, (b) September 1954 Corn

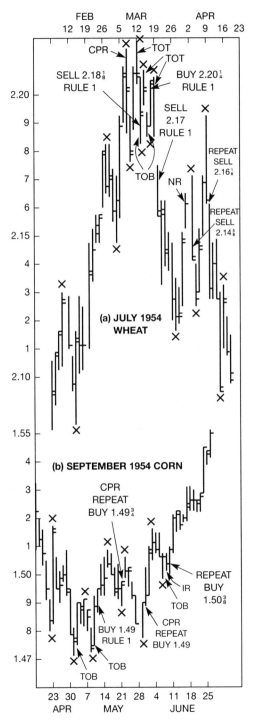

Fig 4.41 Chicago Grain Futures – daily prices July 1954 Soybeans

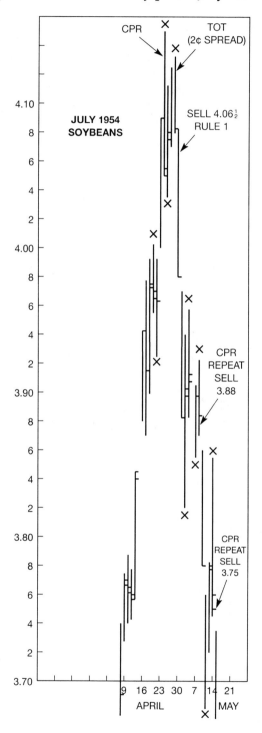

The text mentions that if 1¢ is a measurement for a TOT in the case of wheat and corn, then some figure larger than 1¢ should be appropriate for soybeans. If we make this figure 2¢, a TOT occurred in July 1954 Soybeans on the high day of the Upswing at the end of April.

This TOT was accompanied by a CPR at the Top of the preceding Upswing. Hence, two Sell Patterns were set up, and this was followed the next day by the maximum 1½¢ downside Thrust to give a Reversal Sell Signal at 4.06½. (Incidentally, this signal closed out the previous Buy Signal – not shown on this chart – for 31½¢ profit.)

I hasten to mention that this "adjustment" is not hindsight. The coaching service, "Market Forum," which was being published early this year gave *ahead of time* the Sell Signal at 4.06½. The issue which was mailed Saturday, May 1, stated:

> " 'Gains in Grains' mentions that adjustment of the mechanical rules seems appropriate in the case of volitile soybeans. If we allow 2¢ as the spread between Tops, two Sell Patterns are now present in July Soybeans. Sell Monday on decline to 4.06½ – Rule 1."

At this time I am not publishing a "Coaching Service," but possibly will engage in that work from time to time in the future. Starting in July, 1954, and for several months thereafter, I expect to be fully occupied with the development of ONE-WAY FORMULA.

Supplement

INTRODUCTION TO ONE-WAY FORMULA

*A Universal Method for Trading
in All Stocks and Commodities*

Progress Report #1

July 20, 1954

(Reprinted December 1955)

ONE WAY

INTRODUCTION TO ONE-WAY FORMULA

Life is sweet but also short – too sweet and short to live in a colossal incinerator. So, with regrets to the L. A. Chamber of Commerce which won't miss me anyway, I shall soon make my departure from sunny, smudgy, smoky, smelly, smoggy Southern California to good old foggy, windy, air-conditioned San Francisco. Come around and see us some time!

These reports are going to be very informal as in them I expect to do a lot of thinking out loud in order to give you thoughts and findings as we go along with the research on "One-Way Formula."

Edison made a few hundred experiments (or perhaps it was a few thousand) before he brought forth the electric light – which goes to show that all research involves a considerable amount of trial-and-error. I am sure that in the development of One-Way Formula we are going to make many trials and many errors, but if you will have patience I am certain that in the end we too will have light – at least we are going to have much more guiding light than that which we possess today.

I intend to investigate various matters in the order of what appears to be their relative importance rather than in the order of a preconceived, systematic plan. For instance, I think one of the most important matters before us now is to improve on our present methods for buying near Bottoms and selling near Tops, so I intend to take up that problem first, even though logically in the development of One-Way Formula other considerations should come before it. Therefore, many discussions in these early reports will appear to be unrelated to the main problem of producing a One-Way Formula and it may be difficult to see how these things are going to fit eventually into our overall plan.

Furthermore, in these early issues. I fully expect to make many tentative statements which later, in the light of further research, will be revised or even denied. So, do not expect too much organization or continuity in these early reports. You are going to witness many "trials and errors," but you are also going to learn new things which you can use in a practical way. In order to get started immediately on producing new tools which we can use *soon*, it is fitting that we first seek further methods for signalling Tops and Bottoms. Later it will be soon enough to determine how we are going to assemble these tools into a workable apparatus – "One-Way Formula" – for trading in *all* stocks and commodities.

This first "Progress Report" is merely introductory to give you some background information about my plans, 'ambitions,' etc. , so I'll continue here to comment at random on introductory matters. At the end of the comments, I'll outline, in question form, some of the things which I am now starting to investigate. You will likely find in this short outline some new ideas which you too may want to investigate in your own chart studies.

The "prerequisite for this course" is that the subscriber be a reader of "Gains in Grains" or "The Thrust Method in Stocks" (without that background a reader of these reports would not know what we are talking about). Since the latter papers are not on the current list of best-selling literature, it is unlikely that "One-Way Formula" will ever become a board-room expression. Maybe that is just as well, as I wouldn't care to join Dow in turning over too often in the grave. Frankly, I've about decided that during my remaining years on earth I'd rather trade in the market "leisurely" and "with peace of mind" (if such a thing can be done) than to continue in the advertising-and-publishing business. So, I hope to make this my last and best effort. I own an active trading account and, of course, it would be the realization of years of work to see it pyramid profit-wise. And, sincerely, I'd like to see the same thing happen in your account.

I have no idea now how many of these reports will be issued or how long the complete job will take. In our eagerness to discover things we sometimes neglect to *count* the actual number of times a certain thing works and the number of times *it doesn't work*. In testing new and old ideas, I intend to do a lot of *counting* – tabulating. Whenever I have something new and important to say, whether it be positive or negative ("what to do" or "what not to do"), I'll issue a report. I expect that reports will be mailed to you at irregular intervals for at least a year. All of us should learn things as we go along – things which we can use currently in actual operations.

Perhaps I shouldn't mention this matter here as I don't want any present subscriber to feel that I am directing these remarks to him personally. All of you have been very kind and considerate, and I appreciate your thoughtfulness. But, occasionally I get one or a few readers who are geniuses in figuring out new ways of putting me to work. For their understanding, in case they should become subscribers to these reports, let me say this: Although I do get some very constructive help from outside sources, in most ways I'm a "one-man organization." Please don't expect me to drop current work in order to spend considerable time on matters which may be of more interest to you personally. "First things first," and maybe eventually I can get to most of the other things. But, I do like to get mail; I like to get your ideas, suggestions and criticism; and I certainly want to answer your questions if I can. But, kindly do not pile new tasks on me. I assure you that I already have an inventory of unfinished work on hand.

Another introductory matter comes under the question, "Why a One-Way Formula?" Well, I think the answer to that is clear to all of us who have tried to cope with many different rules in many different formulae. In "Gains in Grains" we have a set of rules for the grains and actually we should have different rules for some of the grains (the rules for oats and soybeans, for example, should not be the same under our present procedure). We have an entirely different set of rules for cotton and in the case of stocks we have to change the rules for every price level. A subscriber recently sent me a method in lard which looks very good (he has kindly given me permission to pass it on to you, which I shall do later), and here again we have a new set of rules. I would like to have a method for cocoa, eggs, etc., but if we are to continue with our present procedure we would have to develop a separate set of rules for each of these. And so on – there is no end to the research we could do and the rules we would have to concoct in order to take care of particular stocks or commodities. It would, of course, be much easier if we could apply the same rules to *any* stock, *any* grain, cotton, wool, eggs, lard, cocoa, etc. And, why can't we?

> *Human nature is the same whether expressed in the soybean market or in the stock market*

Human nature is the same whether it is expressed in the soybean market or in the stock market. If there are "natural laws" which govern human actions, then we must believe that the same natural laws are being expressed in all active, competitive markets. Our mechanical rules are simply means of trying to describe these natural laws. But, we know our descriptions (mechanical rules) of how the mass mind operates are far from perfect. We certainly will never be able to describe perfectly and invariably the exact time at which human sentiment changes – the time at which prices will change their trend.

Mechanical rules can only measure roughly an *average situation*; they cannot proclaim a rigid law which will be obeyed in a particular situation. Human behavior, the maker of price movements, is seemingly an erratic phenomenon. The natural laws ("evolution or growth," "probability or law of average," "compensation or law of action and reaction," "momentum or law of inertia," etc.) which are expressed in human behavior are seen only over a *period of time*. Our mechanical rules measure imperfectly the unfoldment of these natural laws over a *period of time*. They try to state what will happen in the *average situation*, not what will happen in any particular situation. A *single* formula, if based on sound principles, should serve us in the *long* run just as effectively as the net result from several separate formula. Principles must be right *all the time*; rules must be right *over a period of time*. We are dealing with the *law of averages*, and why should we go to all the bother of making up scores of rules when a single set of "one-way rules" will serve profitably in the long run? Why should we continue to try to hold in mind a certain set of rules for cotton, another set for wheat, another for lard, one for low-priced stocks, one for high-priced stocks, etc. when a single set of rules will give us gains in the "average situation?' Today we certainly cannot depend upon gains in the *single trade*; we must rely upon the "law of averages" and get our net gains over a *series of trades*. I feel positive that this can and will be done through our forthcoming "One-Way Formula."

How? Cotton moves in units of $\frac{1}{100}$ of 1¢; lard moves in units of $2\frac{1}{2}/100$ of 1¢; wheat moves in units of ⅛¢, stocks moves in units of $⅛, etc. Some of these things are volatile and move over wide areas while others are more sluggish and move in relatively narrow limits. How are we going to get all these widely diversified things down to the basis of a common denominator so that we can turn to any chart and read it intelligently and profitably with a single formula in mind?

Well, my thought is to make use of price *ranges* and price *swings*. Here are a few examples of what I have in mind:

1. For a TOB we are now obliged to change our definitions for various commodities and stocks. A low-priced stock has a different rule for a TOB than a medium-priced stock, and this in turn is different than the rule for a higher-priced stock. A TOB in oats is one thing, and this should be something different for wheat which, in turn, should be different than soybeans. When we come to cotton a TOB is expressed in new units which doesn't resemble our many TOBs in stocks or our present TOB in grains. Lard, potatoes, rubber, must each have its own TOB the way things are now. Wouldn't this single definition serve in the *long-run* just as effectively as the many separate definitions we must now use?:

   "A TOB is present if the low price or the closing price on the lowest day (or week, if we are using weekly data) of the current Downswing is inside the range of any of the last three Bottoms."

Now, I don't know at this time whether this definition is a good one or not, but I am sure that some definition similar to this will serve just as effectively in the long run as the many definitions we are now using. And, *much more simply*.

2. The matter of "Trust" is related to price ranges, as already pointed out in the texts. Somehow we must measure our Thrusts in the same way for everything. I think that further study of price ranges and the impetus necessary to effect a valid signal will bring to light a good definition.

3. For limiting losses, protecting profits, taking quick profits, etc., we can certainly learn much by studying *price swings*. Shouldn't the actual behavior of the stock or commodity over past swings have something to do with our present plan for limiting losses and taking profits? We certainly want more profit per bushel in wheat than in oats, and since wheat swings over a larger area than oats, can't we find out what profit to take in wheat, and what profit in oats, through a simple method of tabulating on our charts the profits which were available during recent price swings? Incidentally, this should tell us too whether to follow certain signals – perhaps a buy signal should not be followed when it comes so far from the Bottom that "the average past profit available" does not warrant the risk.

At any rate, those are thoughts, and not answers, regarding the work to be done on One-Way Formula. Right now though, as already stated, we are going to concern ourselves with improving our present techniques for buying near Bottoms and selling near Tops. Here are some typical questions which I want definitely answered (perhaps these questions will give you ideas too in looking over past or current charts):

(If weekly data is being used, change "days" to "weeks" in all of the following. Later, in giving answers, I'll illustrate these points with charts. Right now I'm merely asking questions.

1. **PB and CPR.** A PB occurs and on the same day, or within a "few" days, prices make a Bottom Reversal (CPR). Is this a "selling climax" – an indication that the downward drive has been spent? Should we buy immediately on the appearance of the CPR or should we wait for an upside Thrust to follow the CPR?

2. **PT and CPR.** Prices rise above the last Top (PT) and on the same day, or within a few days, they make a Top Reversal (CPR). Is this a "buying climax" – an indication that a Top has been reached? Should we sell immediately on the appearance of the CPR or should we sell if and when a downside Thrust appears?

3. **PB and IR (or NR).** If the last Bottom is penetrated downward (PB) and this is followed the next day, or within a "few" days, by an IR or an NR, does this mean that that the downside movement has lost momentum and a reversal is at hand? Should we buy immediately on the appearance of the IR (or NR) or should we wait for an upside Thrust?

4. **PT and IR (or NR).** Prices make a PT and this is followed shortly by an IR or an NR. Does this mean that the upward movement has lost its drive? Should we sell immediately when the IR (or NR) appears or should we wait for the possible appearance of the downside Thrust?

5. **PB and UPDAY.** A PB comes and this is followed immediately by an upday (higher low and higher high). Does this mean an important reversal to the upside? Should we wait for signs of further strength (upside Thrust) before buying.

6. **PT and DOWNDAY.** A penetration of the last Top (PT) is followed immediately by a Downday (lower high and lower low). Does this indicate a climax reversal to the downside, and should we sell immediately on the appearance of the Downday or wait for downside Thrust?

7. **PB and NR on same day.** If a PB is also an NR, does this not mean that the downside momentum has dried up? Shouldn't we consider this a favorable indication for buying in the event of upside Thrust?

8. **PT and NR on same day.** If a single day is both a PT and an NR, doesn't this mean that there is little enthusiasm left for carrying prices higher? Shouldn't we sell if a downside Thrust follows such a day?

9. **TOB and CPR on same day.** In stocks we use this combination as fulfilling requirements of two Buy Patterns. Cannot we do the same in commodities in order to get a Buy Signal on the day following the low of a Downswing?

10. **TOT and CPR in single day.** This is considered as two Sell Patterns in stocks. Shouldn't the same consideration be used in commodities in order to sometimes get more favorable sale executions?

11. **Rule 1 at Bottoms.** Assume that the last Bottom has a Buy Pattern. If the present low price is below that Bottom and it is a TOB in respect to the Bottom, shouldn't we consider this as two Buy Patterns for a possible Buy Signal on Thrust the next day?

If the current low price is a TOB in respect to any one of the last two (or three?) Bottoms, and if that Bottom had a Buy Pattern, shouldn't we consider this as two Buy Patterns with Buy Signal on Thrust following the current low day?

If there was an IR, or an NR, on the day following the last Bottom shouldn't we consider this a Buy Pattern just the same as we now consider a TOB at the last Bottom as a Buy Pattern? If so, this at times will give an early Buy Signal after the low of a current Downswing.

12. **Rule 1 at Tops.** The same general reasoning applies to Rule 1 at Tops. Can't we often get early and profitable signals near tops if we consider it two Sell Patterns when (1) the current high is above the last Top and is a TOT in respect to that Top, provided, of course, that this Top is also a Sell Pattern, (2) when the current high is a TOT in respect to a Top other than the last Top – provided this Top was also a Sell Pattern, and (3) there was either an IR or an NR on the day following the last Top – provided the current high is also a Sell Pattern?

13. **Closing Reversal after IR.** My friend, George R, gave me this one: Prices are in a Downswing and an IR appears. The next day prices go below the close of the IR day but close higher than the *close* of the IR day. Should we buy immediately, or wait for upside Thrust?

For a Sell Signal, prices are in an Upswing and then an IR appears. The next day prices rise above the close of the IR day but close lower than the close of the IR day. Should we sell immediately or wait for downside Thrust?

(This "IR Reversal" Pattern doesn't happen often, but from what I've seen so far it looks very good when it does occur.)

14. **Thrust.** For Thrust, can't we get better results if we use ½-range Thrust if it occurs in a single day or full-range Thrust if it occurs in two days? Perhaps this, or something similar, can be done which will lead to executions closer to Bottoms and Tops (due to ½-range Thrust rather than full range) and will also give us favorable executions where we are now missing them (if we use full-range Thrust in two days rather than in a single day). Of course, we must not make our Thrust so sensitive that it causes an unduly high number of whipsawing signals. Also, for Thrust perhaps we can devise a simple way of using the "average range for several days" rather than using the range of the Pattern Day. It seems that it should eliminate the present necessity of establishing maximum and minimum limits.

Well, perhaps, this is enough to keep me going for a while. If you would like to join me in thinking and testing of some of these things, please let me know your thoughts and/or findings. However, please do *not* send me anything "confidential, for my own use exclusively." I do not want to be restricted in what I can tell in these reports; I want to feel entirely free to publish all ideas that come my way, and shall be glad to give you full credit for any findings you send me.

WILLIAM DUNNIGAN

1955, when the above Progress Report No. 1 was reprinted in *New Blueprints for Gains in Stocks and Grains*, the author stated:

> "the investigation on ONE-WAY formula is nearly completed and subscribers will soon possess the discoveries made in about 20 months of continuous research".

However, Mr. Dunnigan found the task more difficult than he then anticipated. It was only after an additional 18 months of work or a total of over three years of research on this one project that his final paper on ONE-WAY FORMULA was published. This was in August of 1957, only two months before he died.

Students of market action are indeed fortunate that he concluded this work – a refinement of the principles he used in "The Thrust Method in Stocks" and "Gains in Grains." ONE-WAY FORMULA was his pride, the best method he had ever produced and it proved to be the final one. It provides an effective, positive plan for capitalizing on the market swings.

EDWIN S. ANDERSON

ONE-WAY FORMULA FOR TRADING IN STOCKS AND COMMODITIES

by

William Dunnigan

FOREWORD

The development of One-Way Formula has occupied over three years of my time. I've learned many new things – both "what to do" and "what not to do," and I'll tell you of these things in this paper. There is much more to be learned – undoubtedly, there always will be. But eventually each of us must settle down to some *single* method. Just as "too many cooks spoil the broth," so do too many methods spoil any chance of success. I, for one, am willing to settle down to One-Way Formula.

I am sure that the past record of One-Way Formula is better than anything I have heretofore seen. I fully realize that in the days ahead there will be some difficult periods, but when they come I think I'll be willing to take my losses and go back into the market for the overall profits which I think are certain. I feel too that you, the reader, can profit in stocks and commodities if you will follow One-Way Formula faithfully.

The purpose of this research has been to design a *single method* which can be used in "everything" – all stocks, wheat, corn, oats, rye, soybeans, lard, cotton, coffee, eggs, onions, etc. We sought a "universal method" which would enable us to apply the *same rules* to *any stock* or *any commodity* which is traded actively and listed on an organized exchange. We desired a method which could be followed readily on our price charts without time-consuming calculations, such as moving averages. We insisted that the method be 100% mechanical and that there be no string of long, drawn-out rules to confuse us. We even asked that there be no tables to consult for purpose of guiding us through the completion of trades. In other words, we wanted *any* chart to tell us *everything* – when to enter into a trade and the complete plan of action until the trade was closed out.

Now, all of this was a big order but we have been nearly 100% successful in filling it. It is true that there are small differences between stocks and commodities, and it is helpful to consult two simple tables – one for stocks and one for commodities – for guidance in our Operating Plan. But, I think we can bear that "burden" in view of the excellent results which appear to be in store for us in actual operations.

In presenting this study I am assuming that the reader has already read "Gains in Grains" and *The Thrust Method in Stocks*. These papers are given in my text, *New Blueprints for Gains in Stocks and Grains*. It will be helpful to read "New Blueprints" as it includes material and discussions which will not be repeated here. The present paper is, however, complete in that it gives the step-by-step procedure by which One-Way Formula can be used in stocks and commodities.

Part I

ONE-WAY FORMULA FOR TRADING IN STOCKS

HOW TO SELECT STOCKS AND CHART PRICES

In the commodity markets we use daily data. In the stock market we save time and work by using weekly data – the weekly high, low and closing prices. These prices are charted in the ordinary manner of a bar chart except the graph paper is graduated to show clearly the exact prices to the $⅛. A large stationery store, or a supply house for engineers, can likely provide you with suitable chart paper. The weekly high, low and closing prices of stocks can be found in the Sunday edition of several metropolitan newspapers (*New York Times*, *Los Angeles Times*, etc.) *Barron's* gives comprehensive weekly data on stocks and is available on Monday morning almost anywhere in the United States by air mail.

I believe that One-Way Formula would work well if daily prices were used. In some stocks (Chrysler, for example) the Formula would probably work better on a daily basis. But I have made no tests using daily data because there appears to be no source where one can purchase suitable daily charts. We must be able to read the exact prices from our charts because the Formula is strictly mechanical and every little movement, even the last $⅛, may have a meaning of its own. It is a laborious task to prepare a daily chart for a few years back in even a single stock, and any real test should cover at least 25 stocks over a period of a few years at least. I do not have the time for such an undertaking.

In fact, in most stocks it appears unnecessary to fret over whether the stock might perform better on a daily basis. The weekly figures do very well in a good majority of stocks. I believe you will agree with this when the charts are presented later in this paper and in the Coaching Reports. Stocks are less volatile than commodi-

> *We must read the exact prices from our charts because the Formula is strictly mechanical*

ties. Stocks take longer to prepare for their major movements and they spend more time in their main-trend performances. A bull or bear market in a stock may last for years while a commodity often runs through a complete major cycle, up and down, in less than 12 months. Weekly data in stocks will serve us nicely in most cases while daily data appears to be imperative in commodities.

What stocks should we chart? If one is building a set of permanent charts, it would be wise, I think, to include a diversified list of the highly volatile stocks. Selections can be made from my list of "Fast-Moving Stocks" published in *New Blueprints for Gains in Stocks and Grains*. These fast-movers are ordinarily sensitive to trend changes and they usually surpass the average stock in their trend movements.

Also, I think it would be a good idea to watch "The Week's 20 Most Active Stocks" and the "Group Stock Averages" (both in *Barron's*). These may give leads worth following at a particular time.

Finally, I would suggest that if you subscribe to a service which shows the "relative price action" of individual stocks you use that information in conjunction with One-Way Formula. A stock which starts performing in a manner which is "better-than-the-average" may prove to be a very good purchase if One-Way Formula agrees that the Main Trend is pointing up. Similarly, if the relative performance is "worst-than-the-average", and One-Way Formula confirms the bearish indication, a short sale might be the right course of action or, at least, it would appear improper to own the stock.

In back-testing One-Way Formula I used stocks "selected at random." Mr. Roy Eagle kindly mailed me a duplicate set of his stock charts and I applied One-Way Formula to these charts (about 90 of them). I had no voice in the selection of the stocks so, as far as I was concerned, their names could have been drawn from a hat – blind selection. This paper will show pictures of several of these stocks. I have a feeling that since One-Way Formula works very well in many blind selections it might do even better if we put forth the effort to discover other stocks in which it has worked "almost perfectly." I may later get around to this search and publish the findings in the Coaching Reports.

HOW TO RECOGNIZE BAROMETRIC MOVEMENTS:
Upswings, Downswings, Tops and Bottoms

We need first a background, or setting, so that we can get our bearings in the present market. Recent Upswings and Downswings and their Tops and Bottoms provide this setting. These are the Swings from which we get our barometric signals and we lead up to their identification by first defining certain types of price action as seen on our weekly charts.

All other weeks not included in the foregoing definitions might be regarded as "Neutral Weeks" – such as a week with a high equal to the high of the previous week but with the low below the low price of the previous week, or a week with a low equal to the low of the previous week but with a high above the high price of the previous week.

It is important that we recognize the various types of weeks in order to establish a uniform method of setting up Swings with their Tops and Bottoms.

Fig 1.1 Types of weeks

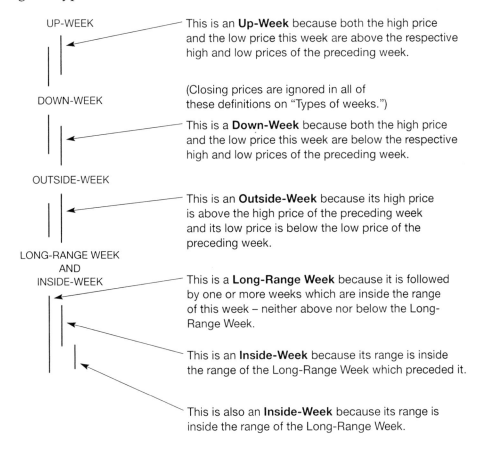

UP-WEEK — This is an **Up-Week** because both the high price and the low price this week are above the respective high and low prices of the preceding week.

(Closing prices are ignored in all of these definitions on "Types of weeks.")

DOWN-WEEK — This is a **Down-Week** because both the high price and the low price this week are below the respective high and low prices of the preceding week.

OUTSIDE-WEEK — This is an **Outside-Week** because its high price is above the high price of the preceding week and its low price is below the low price of the preceding week.

LONG-RANGE WEEK AND INSIDE-WEEK — This is a **Long-Range Week** because it is followed by one or more weeks which are inside the range of this week – neither above nor below the Long-Range Week.

This is an **Inside-Week** because its range is inside the range of the Long-Range Week which preceded it.

This is also an **Inside-Week** because its range is inside the range of the Long-Range Week.

In setting up Swings we look *only for Up-Weeks and Down-Weeks*. Therefore, we are only concerned with the other foregoing definitions in that they distinguish Up-Weeks and Down-Weeks from other types of weeks. Some students persist in using an Outside-Week, or an Inside-Week, as an Up-Week (or Down-Week). Such practices must be avoided if one chooses to use the plan I have adopted. Now, it is not required that everyone adopts my exact procedure. Throughout this paper you will be given mechanical rules. If you wish to make alterations in these rules, it is certainly your privilege to do so. My mechanical rules do not represent hard-fast laws which govern price action. If you prefer to deviate from my rules, and if your deviations are within reason, and if you adhere to them consistently, I am sure that your results over a period of time will be just as good as mine. We must cling steadfastly to *right principles*. The particular mechanical rules which we use to express these principles can take on an almost infinite variety of forms. Indeed, in previous writings on One-Way Formula we learned many rules which will not be even mentioned in this paper. Those rules are still good, but these in this paper should be just as good – and much simpler.

How to set up swings and their tops and bottoms

An UPSWING can be defined as a "run of one or more Up-Weeks." The highest price in an Upswing is called a TOP. Once an Upswing gets under way it can be terminated only by the appearance of a Down-Week. In other words, if prices are in an Upswing there can be Outside-Weeks, Long-Range-Weeks, Inside-Weeks and Neutral-Weeks, and these have no effect on the termination of the Upswing. The Upswing ends only on the appearance of a Down-Week and this appearance automatically puts prices in a Downswing.

A DOWNSWING can be defined as a "run of one or more Down-Weeks." The lowest price in a Downswing is called a BOTTOM. Outside-Weeks, Inside-Weeks, etc., can intermingle with the Down-Weeks without affecting the status of the Downswing. The Downswing ends only on the appearance of an Up-Week.

Fig 1.2 Swings, tops and bottoms

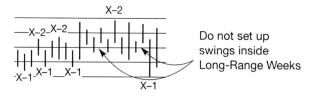

X-1 to X-2 is an Upswing in each of the above movements. The X-2s are Tops.

X-2 to X-1 is a Downswing in each of the above movements. The X-1s are Bottoms.

(In actual charts, both Tops and Bottoms are simply marked "X".)

We do not under any circumstances set up Swings Inside a Long-Range Week. Formerly we did set up Swings if the Long-Range Week had an equal high (or low) after it. But, as illustrated in Figure 1.3, this is now changed. X-1 to X-2 is NOT an Upswing in the lower section of this drawing and X-2 to X-1 is NOT a Downswing in the upper part of the drawing.

I know there are many cases where it is desirable to set up Swings inside a Long-Range Week. But, I am sure that there are more cases where this practice is undesirable. Since we cannot tell ahead of time whether or not it would be advantageous to set up Swings inside a Long-Range Week, it is fitting that we adopt the "majority rule" and do not set up such Swings at any time.

Fig 1.3 Swings inside a long-range week

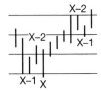

The matter of setting up Swings is really simple and I hope no reader will try to make a big problem out of it. Sometimes "unusual situations" appear and these may cause trouble. The charts in this paper will likely illustrate my answers to such "unusual situations." If my answers do not satisfy a reader, he can adopt in his own procedure and I am sure no long-term harm will be done. In nearly all cases the Upswings and Downswings are "normal" – a Down-Week sets up a Downswing and an Up-Week sets up an Upswing. Hundreds of these normal Swings are illustrated in the actual stock charts in this paper so further illustrations are not needed here. But, Figures 1.4 and 1.5 are two examples of "special cases" which appear from time to time.

Fig 1.4 Special case for setting up Swings

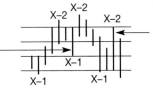

This week is not a Down-Week with respect to the week preceding it because the highs of the two weeks are equal. But, it is a Down-Week in respect to the high week of the Upswing. In such cases, we set up a Downswing.

This week is not an Up-Week in respect to the week preceding it because the lows of the two weeks are equal. But, it is an Up-Week with respect to the low week of the Downswing. When such a week appears we set up an Upswing.

In view of the above we can now state: A Downswing should be set up (by marking the Top with an "X") if there is a Down-Week with respect to either the preceding week or the high week of the Upswing. And, we can also now state: An Upswing should be set up (by marking the Bottom with an "X") if there is an Up-Week with respect to either the preceding week or the low week of the Downswing.

Fig 1.5 Special cases for not setting up Swings

This week is an Up-Week with respect to week X-1. But, because there is no Down-week after this week, it cannot be considered as a Top. X-1 may be considered as a "Tentative Bottom" pending further market action. The "Actual Bottom" comes later at X-2.

This week is a Down-Week in respect to X-1 week. But, there is no Up-Week after this week. Since there is no Up-Week after it, this week cannot be a Bottom. X-1 can be thought of as a "Tentative Top." The "Actual Top" proves later to be X-2.

These "special cases" do not appear frequently. The large majority of Swings can be easily recognized by the simple rules: "A Downswing is a run of one or more Down-Weeks" and "An Upswing is a run of one or more Up-Weeks."

Mention should be made here that quite often *equal low weeks* of a Downswing may cause some confusion in deciding whether to set up an Upswing. We solve this problem by using the *longest range* of the equal low weeks. If there is an Up-Week with respect to the longest range of the equal low weeks, we should then set up an Upswing. In the same manner, if there are equal high weeks we set up a Downswing if there is a Down-Week with respect to the week with the *longest range* of the equal high weeks.

New readers shouldn't worry here about such technicalities. The problems will be readily solved when we come to them in the actual charts.

A BIRD'S-EYE VIEW OF ONE-WAY FORMULA

Let us now look at a few charts on actual stocks in order to gain a broad view of how One-Way Formula gives its signals. We will leave the details, "little technicalities," and Operating Plan for later sections of this paper.

In accordance with the foregoing instructions we first set up the Upswings and Downswings with their Tops and Bottoms marked with "Xs" and we are then ready to look for signals to buy or sell. I am selecting here a few stocks which start with the letter "A" in order to demonstrate the method in what might be considered the "average stock." (I could have moved along farther in the alphabet and selected other stocks which perform better than the average stock – and, of course, I could have selected other stocks which do poorer!)

The Maintrend is down at the start of this chart so we are looking for a Reversal Buy Signal to direct us to cover shorts and go long. X-1 is the lowest week in the Main Downtrend. X-2 is an "Ascending Bottom (ASC)" in respect to X-1 because its range is entirely above X-1. This ASC establishes a "Preliminary Buy Signal" when the Upswing X-2 to X-3 is completed. One other pattern will also establish a Preliminary Buy Signal; namely, "Penetration of Two Tops (P2T)." This occurs when the high week of an Upswing closes above the two preceding Tops. Notice that the high week of the Upswing X-2 to X-3 closed above the two Tops preceding it. So, in Anaconda we have both a P2T and an ASC to affirm a Preliminary Buy Signal, although a single pattern (either a P2T or an ASC) is all that is required. We take no action on this Preliminary Signal but instead we wait for the Downswing X-3 to X-4 to be completed. When that is done we then cover shorts and buy at the closing price of the first Up-Week following X-4, provided said closing price is not below the

Fig 1.6 Signals to buy, Anaconda Co

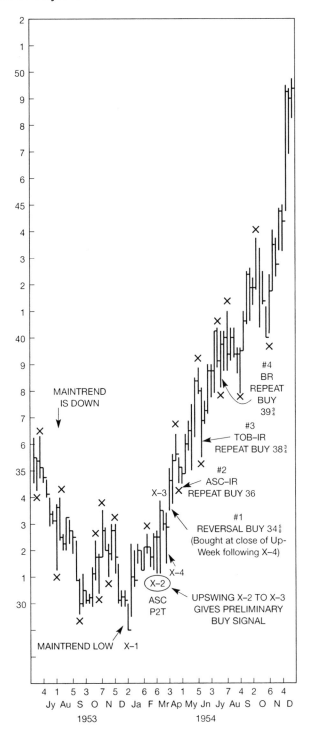

closing price of week preceding it. (If the close of the first Up-Week following X-4 had been below the preceding close, we would have then waited for another Downswing and again would have tried to buy at the close of the first Up-Week following that Downswing.)

Our trading capital for a single stock is divided into four equal parts. On Reversal Signal following X-4 we use only ¼ of the capital so if the Signal should be wrong our loss will be relatively small. Another ¼ is used in each of the following Repeat Signals. However, there must be a paper profit in each preceding trade before a new trade is made. This ordinarily assures us that we are in tune with the Maintrend and that profits are forthcoming.

More about ASC

An ASC is always related to the Bottom which has the *largest range* starting with the Bottom at the Maintrend Low.

If the Bottom following X-1 had a larger range than X-1, then in this chart X-2 would not have been an ASC. For a Bottom to be an ASC its range must be entirely above the *largest range* Bottom starting with the Bottom at the Maintrend Low.

(The Maintrend Low is the lowest point reached since the last Reversal Sell Signal.)

Nullification

A Preliminary Buy Signal is nullified if before a Reversal Buy Signal is given the range of the low week of any Downswing is entirely below the Bottom which gave the ASC or P2T. This simply means, in the case of American Smelting, X-2 would have been nullified if the entire range of the lowest week of some Downswing after X-2 had been below X-2. This didn't occur so we bought on the first Up-Week after X-4.

REPEAT SIGNALS

Repeat Buy Signals, explained in full later, must occur at progressively higher prices. This assures us that all prior trades have a paper profit when a new trade is entered into. We are willing to hold four "lines" at one time, two of them for Fund L (the larger, long-term profits) and two of them for Fund S (the smaller, quick profits). The original Reversal Signal and first Repeat Signal are

Fig 1.7 Signals to buy, American Smelting

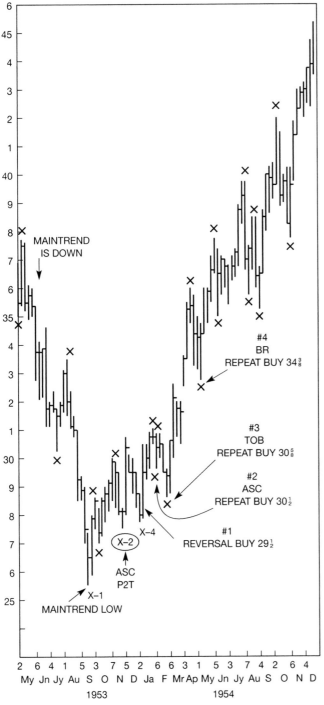

MAINTREND
IS DOWN

#4
BR
REPEAT BUY $34\frac{3}{8}$

#3
TOB
REPEAT BUY $30\frac{5}{8}$

#2
ASC
REPEAT BUY $30\frac{1}{2}$

X–4

X–2

#1
REVERSAL BUY $29\frac{1}{2}$

ASC
P2T

X–1
MAINTREND LOW

2 6 4 1 5 3 7 5 2 6 6 3 1 5 3 7 4 2 6 4
My Jn Jy Au S O N D Ja F Mr Ap My Jn Jy Au S O N D
        1953   1954

A considerable majority of stocks gave excellent buy signals in 1953–1954 when the Big Bull Market took off under full steam.

American Smelting, like Anaconda (preceding), gave a "double" Preliminary Buy Signal – an ASC and a P2T, although only one of these patterns is required to announce a possible early reversal in the Main Downtrend. This reversal was confirmed in American Smelting at the closing price of the first Up-Week following the Bottom at X-4. At that time ($29-\frac{1}{2}$) we covered shorts and bought with $\frac{1}{4}$ of our trading capital for this stock. The remaining $\frac{3}{4}$ was used in the Repeat Signals which followed. This conservative practice of starting off slowly ordinarily assures us that the profits will exceed losses by a wide margin.

for Fund L and the next two Repeat Signals are for Fund S. Whenever closed out of a Fund S trade with a profit we enter into another Fund S trade on the next Repeat Signal – provided the price is above the last purchase price ("trade with the trend" always). We always try to keep two Fund L positions working for us, so if stopped out of a Fund L position we would enter into another Fund L trade on a Repeat Signal before taking on another Fund S trade.

Repeat Buy Patterns are TOB, ASC, and BR. We buy at the closing price of the first Up-week after TOB or after ASC. When BR (Bottom Reversal) appears in a Downswing we buy immediately at the closing price of that week.

SELL SIGNALS

Sell Signals are identical to Buy Signals except we are now looking down the hill instead of up. A Preliminary Sell Pattern comes from two types of patterns:

1. A "Descending Top (DES)" where the highest range in an Upswing is entirely below the range of the Maintrend High; or if another Upswing followed the Maintrend High and it has a larger range (on its high week) then the range of the Maintrend High, the DES must then be entirely below that larger-high range. (The Maintrend High is the highest point reached since the last Reversal Buy Signal.)
2. A "Penetration of Two Bottoms (P2B)" where the low week in a Downswing closes below the preceding two Bottoms.

Nullification of a DES or a P2B takes place when the range of the high week of an Upswing is entirely above the high point of the DES or the P2B. (When a Downswing produces a DES or a P2B we immediately circle the high point of that Downswing in order to identify easily the point of nullification.) A Reversal Sell Signal must come before a DES or a P2B is nullified.

We do not act on a Preliminary Sell Signal. Rather, we wait for an Upswing and then sell longs and go short at the closing price of the first Down-Week following that Upswing, provided that closing price is not above the closing price of the week preceding it. If it is, we must wait for another Upswing and again try for a Reversal Sell Signal by selling at the close of the first Down-Week following that Upswing.

Repeat Sell Signals (for further short selling) must each come at a lower price than the selling price of the preceding trade. The patterns for Repeat Sell Signals are "Test of Top (TOT)." "Descending Top (DES)" and "Top Reversal (TR)," all of which are explained later in the text.

Fig 1.8 Signals to sell, Ame...

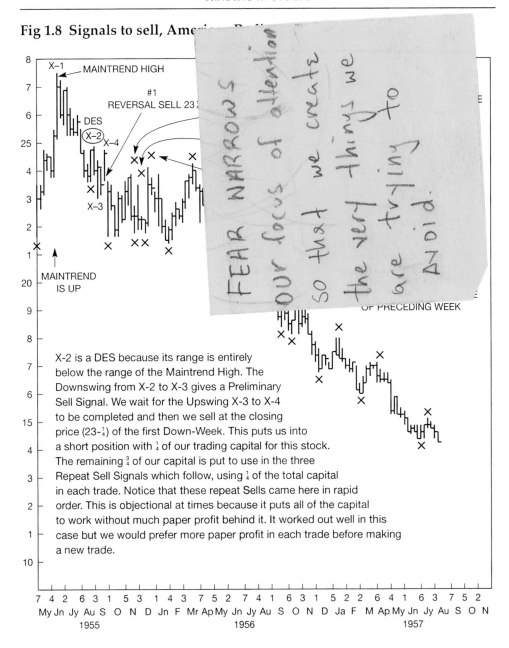

X-2 is a DES because its range is entirely
below the range of the Maintrend High. The
Downswing from X-2 to X-3 gives a Preliminary
Sell Signal. We wait for the Upswing X-3 to X-4
to be completed and then we sell at the closing
price (23-⅛) of the first Down-Week. This puts us into
a short position with ¼ of our trading capital for this stock.
The remaining ¾ of our capital is put to use in the three
Repeat Sell Signals which follow, using ¼ of the total capital
in each trade. Notice that these repeat Sells came here in rapid
order. This is objectional at times because it puts all of the capital
to work without much paper profit behind it. It worked out well in this
case but we would prefer more paper profit in each trade before making
a new trade.

We now start looking for Repeat Sell Signals. The first Down-Week after X-7
closed at 67½ (it was a Down-Week in relation to the high week). We did nothing at that time because this price was above the previous selling price at 66½.
X-8 is a TR so we sell immediately at the close 64. Our next short sale must be
below 64 and this comes on the TR at 61¼, X-13. Finally, we get short again

Fig 1.9 Signals to sell, ACF Industries

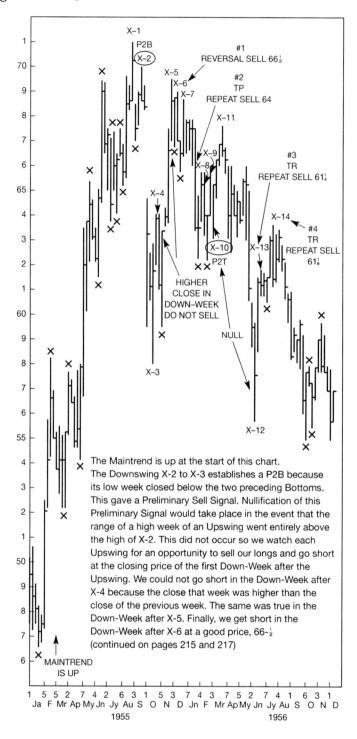

The Maintrend is up at the start of this chart.
The Downswing X-2 to X-3 establishes a P2B because
its low week closed below the two preceding Bottoms.
This gave a Preliminary Sell Signal. Nullification of this
Preliminary Signal would take place in the event that the
range of a high week of an Upswing went entirely above
the high of X-2. This did not occur so we watch each
Upswing for an opportunity to sell our longs and go short
at the closing price of the first Down-Week after the
Upswing. We could not go short in the Down-Week after
X-4 because the close that week was higher than the
close of the previous week. The same was true in the
Down-Week after X-5. Finally, we get short in the
Down-Week after X-6 at a good price, 66-$\frac{1}{2}$
(continued on pages 215 and 217)

after X-14, on the first Down-Week which closed at 61⅛. (The TR here had a higher close than the last sale; hence, wait for Down-Week.)

The Upswing X-10 to X-11 set up a Preliminary Buy Signal when its high week closed above the preceding two Tops. But, before a confirmed Buy Signal could come, this Preliminary Buy was nullified when the range of the low week of the Downswing X-11 to X-12 was entirely below X-10.

The preceding pages give information on One-Way Formula which will not be repeated in the following pages. Therefore it is important that you take time to understand the contents of the preceding pages before going on. If you have any questions, relax as they may be answered in the pages to come.

[If not, write me and I'll answer them in forthcoming Coaching Reports.]

RECOGNIZING THE MAINTREND

Our first concern is to be right in recognizing the direction of the Maintrend. This is very important as we wish to keep our trades in line with the main-trend direction. We hope to confine our activities to the long side only in bull markets and to the short side only in bear markets.

Yes, there are sharp declines in bull markets and sharp rallies in bear markets and we could design a method which would produce profits in these counter-trend movements. In fact, in "Gains in Grains" and "The Thrust Method in Stocks" we have methods which are qualified to make profits in any sharp movement whether it be with or counter to the Maintrend.

> *Our first concern is to be right in recognizing the direction of the Maintrend*

But, we have found that such methods are often too sensitive. They not only give us the signals we want near tops and bottoms but they also give us signals we don't want! They don't distinguish, for example, whether a decline in a bull market will be only a trivial movement or whether it will endure to the point where it is of real profit-making importance. Going short near the top of a small decline means not only that we must disturb our profitable main-trend position but also that we will likely take a loss on the short sale. We must try to avoid such disheartening "whipsaws" which are so commonplace in nearly all market trading.

Indeed, in the early pages of "The Thrust Method in Stocks" we learned a method whereby we can buy at almost the very bottom of a bear market and sell very close to the peak of a bull market. But, we learned too that such a sensitive method is constantly in-and-out, long-and-short, hot-and-cold. Experience proves that we can't *long follow* such a method even if a net profit in the long run is almost a certainty. The trader is completely winded long before he reaches the finishing tape of such long runs.

In entering into new trades it is much better that we seek only buying opportunities in bull markets and only selling opportunities in bear markets. This is true for both stocks and commodities.

So, let us take things easier. Let us "desensitize" our Formula so it will not become jumpy every time the market declines in a bull market and every time it rallies in a bear market. More often than not a decline in a bull market should be a happy occasion. Very often it is an opportunity for more purchasing through our Repeat Signals. A decline in a bull market should seldom be frowned upon as an ominous sign of trouble ahead.

Let us give the market (a stock or a commodity) a good chance to tell its own story before concluding that the Maintrend has actually turned down, or up, as the case may be. Let us insist first upon a "Preliminary Signal" – a *possible* change in the Maintrend. And then, before taking any action let us insist that this Preliminary Signal be confirmed by an actual "Reversal Signal." When the Reversal Signal is given it will be soon enough to start working on the probabilities that an actual turn has taken place in the Maintrend.

Readers who followed my "Progress Reports" during the years 1954, 1955, 1956 and early 1957, are well aware of *some* of the difficult plans I devised for coping with the problems of (1) how to recognize the direction of the Maintrend and (2) how to avoid a run of losses. I did not publish all of the schemes I pondered over, as many of them were so complicated that I thought it best not to burden the reader with them. Of course, nobody will ever find the perfect solution to these problems, but it is almost embarrassing to tell you now that a quite satisfactory solution is found in a simple procedure. Evidently, I was making a mountain out of a molehill.

HOW TO RECOGNIZE A POSSIBLE CHANGE IN THE MAINTREND – Preliminary Signals

Let us assume that a Reversal Sell Signal has just been given. We are short and are watching our stock chart for a signal to cover the short and go back into a buy position. First we need a Preliminary Buy Signal to give us a clue that the Maintrend may possibly be changing back to the upside. This can be done through either an Ascending Bottom (ASC) or a Penetration of Two Tops (P2T).

In order to get an ASC we must first locate the low point to date of the Main Downtrend. The Maintrend Low is simply the lowest point reached to date since the appearance of the last Reversal Sell Signal. We can't go back into history any farther than the last Reversal Sell Signal in order to locate the present Maintrend Low.

An ASC appears whenever the range of the low week of a Downswing is entirely above the range of the week which is the Maintrend Low. Or, if later a low week of a Downswing has a longer range than the range of the Maintrend Low, then the ASC must be related to that longer-range week – that is, to be an ASC the low price of a Downswing must be above the high price of the longer-range week, which is simply another way of stating that the ASC range must be entirely above the range with which it is compared. When this condition prevails the ASC is established just as soon as an Upswing gets under way.

For a P2T we are not concerned with the Maintrend Low. A P2T appears whenever the high week of an Upswing closes above the preceding two Tops. Of course, we can't determine the high week of an Upswing until there is a Down-Week. Therefore, if some week in an Upswing closes above the last two Tops, it does not necessarily follow that a P2T will be set up. Sometimes this happens and then the high week has a large decline at the close to put the close under one or both of the last two Tops.

A P2T can be set up immediately after a Reversal Sell Signal if the following Upswing closes above the two Tops preceding the Reversal Sell Signal. For an ASC we start fresh from the point of the Reversal Sell Signal and all prior price action is ignored. But, for a P2T we can use the two Tops preceding the Reversal Sell Signal for purposes of setting up a P2T on the very first Upswing after the Reversal Sell.

When a Preliminary Buy Signal is given the Bottom identifying that signal is circled, $\bigcirc\!\!\!\!X$. I tried to think of a good name for this kind of a Bottom and in one paper came out with the term "Power Bottom." But, I think now it is unnecessary to adopt a new term. If we simply call such a Bottom a "Preliminary Bottom" I'm sure that all of us will have a common understanding that the Preliminary Bottom represent a point of potential strength. We put a circle around the Preliminary Bottom to emphasize that it is a crucial point in our calculations for a Reversal Buy Signal.

The Preliminary Bottom is nullified if, before a Reversal Buy Signal comes, a Downswing declines to the point where the high price of its low week is below the low price of the Preliminary Bottom. In other words, the range of the low week of the Downswing is entirely below the range of the Preliminary Bottom.

If a Preliminary Bottom is nullified another Preliminary Bottom can be set up on the basis of ASC using the old Maintrend Low (or larger range, if any).

Or, on the basis of P2T, a new Preliminary Bottom occurs any time the high week of an Upswing closes above the preceding two Tops. Of course, if a new Maintrend Low appears we must use the new Maintrend Low to get us established toward a new Preliminary Buy through an ASC.

If we get a Reversal Buy Signal and afterwards the Preliminary Buy is nullified, we simply ride the purchase out for better or worse. If worse, our Operating Plan will stop us out without too large a loss, and sometimes even after the Preliminary Bottom is nullified the market turns back up and the trade works out profitably.

Preliminary Sell Signals follow the same procedure in reverse. In view of Figures 1.6–1.9 and explanations, it appears unnecessary to comment further here on Preliminary Signals.

HOW TO RECOGNIZE A "REAL" CHANGE IN THE MAINTREND – Reversal Signals

The quotes around the word "real" in the above heading denote that there is nothing "sure" in the stock and commodity markets – except commissions

The odds for success become more favorable when a Reversal Signal follows a Preliminary Signal

always and income taxes when we profit. At any particular time we are dealing in probabilities, not certainties. The odds for success become more favorable when a Reversal Signal follows a Preliminary Signal, but that doesn't mean that a risk no longer exists.

We have stated that we take no action to reverse our position on the appearance of a Preliminary Buy Signal. We do not close out our shorts; in fact, we continue to act on Repeat Sell Signals even in the face of a Preliminary Buy. But, while doing this we become increasing alert to the possibility that an early Reversal Buy Signal will appear. If such a signal comes, we then immediately close out all shorts and go long.

After a Preliminary Buy Signal we wait for a Downswing. If this Downswing does not nullify the Preliminary Bottom, we buy at the closing price of the first Upweek if the closing price is equal to or higher than the closing price of the preceding week. If the closing price is lower, we must then wait for a new Downswing and again try to buy at the close of the first

Upweek. If the Maintrend is really up, the closing price requirement will not long delay us in getting into a long position.

Patterns (TOB, ASC, BR) do not enter into the consideration of Reversal Signals. The requirements for a Reversal Buy Signal are simply (1) we have a preceding Preliminary Buy Signal which has not been nullified and (2) this is followed by a "Thrust." This Thrust is simply the first Up-Week after a Downswing, provided the Up-Week has an equal or higher close.

Thus, all stocks and commodities are placed on an equitable, "one-way" or "universal" basis. The procedure for setting up Swings with their Tops and Bottoms, the derivation of Preliminary and Reversal Signals, and the calculation for Thrust – everything – is identical for all things.

Equal highs of Upswings and equal lows of Downswings

This is a good place to add that problems sometimes arise because of equal high weeks of an Upswing and because of equal low weeks of a Downswing. We solve the problem, whatever it is, by using the *longest range*. Thus, if equal highs of an Upswing bring up the problem of whether a Downswing has occurred, use the longest range of the equal high weeks in determining the answer. Where equal highs, or lows, create a problem as to whether an ASC, DES, P2T or P2B is present, find the solution by using the longest range of the equal high, or low, weeks. If equal low weeks cause confusion in determining whether a nullification of a Preliminary Bottom has taken place, avoid that confusion by using the longest range. And, for Repeat Signals, use the longest range of equal low weeks in deciding whether a BR is present, as well as the longest range of equal high weeks in deciding whether a TR is present.

If the rare case should arise where, say, there are two equal low weeks and both have equal ranges one of which gives one solution and the other another solution, all I can say in such a case is to "take your choice," or perhaps better yet, give an affirmative answer to your question. For example, an Upswing might have two equal high weeks with ranges of equal length. One of these high weeks closes above the last two Tops and the other doesn't. Question: Is a P2T present? Answer: Yes.

Remember it is not too important how such little technicalities are handled. It is only important that we set up some consistent procedure for handling them at all times.

HOW TO RECOGNIZE A CONTINUATION OF THE MAINTREND – Repeat Signals

Repeat Signals can be used for:

1. Pyramiding for long-term gains on top of profitable long-term positions already established.
2. Entering into initial long-term positions (Fund L) for traders who failed to follow the original Reversal Signal.
3. Trading for small but fast short-term gains (Fund S).

When we use the words "long-term" and "short-term" we do not necessarily refer to "capital gains" from an income tax viewpoint – although we do prefer to hold "long-term investments" longer than six months. "Long-term" here refers to Fund L for the larger profits, and "short-term" refers to Fund S for the smaller, faster profits.

Whether or not we use Repeat Signals in actual trading will depend upon the Operating Plan we individually choose to use. In this research on One-Way Formula we considered several Operating Plans. Others are given in "Gains in Grains." Still another, and I think it is the best from a conservative viewpoint, is given in the next section of this paper. At any rate, we shall assume that each of us will want to use Repeat Signals at various times and, therefore, we should have a clear understanding of them.

A Repeat Signal, of course, follows the original Reversal Signal. If our initial position is long and we desire to make an additional purchase on a Repeat Signal, we first wait for a Signal Pattern on the low week of a Downswing. Then we buy at the closing price of the first Up-Week following that Signal Pattern – except for "BR" in which case we buy immediately on the appearance of the BR. Let us go into detail.

The Repeat Buy Patterns are:

1. Ascending Bottom (ASC)
2. Test-of-Bottom (TOB)
3. Bottom Reversal (BR)

A Repeat Buy Pattern might be followed by one or more Inside-Weeks (designated on our charts as "IR" or Inside Range). These have no bearing on the basic patterns, ASC, TOB and BR. We must remember, however, never to interpret an IR as an UP-Week even if it is "up" in respect to an IR preceding it. The Up-Week for purposes of getting a Repeat Buy Signal must be in relation to the low week of the Downswing. Here are the definitions:

Ascending Bottom (ASC)
An ASC is present when the entire range of the low week of a Downswing is above the range of the *last Bottom.*

Buy at closing price of first Up-Week following ASC, provided said closing price is not below closing price of preceding week.

Test-of-Bottom (TOB)
A TOB is present when any part of the range of the low week of a Downswing touches any part of the range of *either of the last two Bottoms.*

Buy at closing price of first Up-Week following TOB, provided said closing price is not below closing price of preceding week.

Bottom Reversal (BR)
A BR is present when the closing price on the low week of a Downswing is above the closing price of the preceding week.

Buy immediately at closing price of BR week.

The Repeat Sell Patterns are:

1. Descending Top (DES)
2. Test-of-Top (TOT)
3. Top Reversal (TR)

The definitions for these patterns are:

Descending Top (DES)
A DES is present when the entire range of the high week of an Upswing is below the range of the *last Top.*

Sell at closing price of first Down-Week following DES, provided said closing price is not above closing price of preceding week.

Test-of-Top (TOT)
A TOT is present when any part of the range of the high week of an Upswing touches any part of the range of *either of the last two Tops.*

Sell at closing price of first Down-Week following TOT, provided said closing price is not above closing price of preceding week.

Top Reversal (TR)
A TR is present when the closing price of the high week of an Upswing is below the closing price of the preceding week.

Sell immediately at closing price of TR week.

Why do we make it so difficult to get Reversal Signals and so relatively easy to get Repeat Signals?

Well, I think the question has already been answered. Through our Reversal signals we are trying to get strong evidence that the Maintrend has actually turned. In our quest to avoid losses, particularly a run of losses, we have found that it is best to avoid changing a Maintrend position very early in a new movement. We have found that too often the new movement proves to be only a temporary, minor reaction which is soon followed by a resumption of the main, major movement. Early in this research I sought diligently for some "climax patterns" which would sometimes point out the approximate low week of a Main Downtrend and the approximate high week of a Main Uptrend. I didn't find any such patterns which worked out profitably better than half of the time. After that experiment, and many others, I am convinced that a real change in trend can be recognized with a reasonable degree of accuracy only after prices have gone through a pretty thorough period of preparation – as recognized by our ASC, DES, P2T and P2B – and then make a Thrust, such as recognized by our Up-Week and Down-Week. Once this is done and we find that we are actually riding a new Maintrend with profits, we can then relax in our rules and make it comparatively easy to trade with the Maintrend for more profits through Repeat Signals.

HOW TO ENGAGE IN PRACTICAL OPERATIONS –
Operating Plan

The preceding pages have told how to derive Signals by One-Way Formula. The rules seem very simple to me, and I hope I have made the explanation clear. Like anything new, it will take some study and practice on your charts before you can expect to spot the signals at a glance. And that goes for me too – in fact I know from experience that apparent simplicity sometimes leads to carelessness and mistakes. But, I think that with some effort each of us can become quite proficient before too long in handling the method according to the rules. I'll try to help you through Coaching Reports and actual charts.

We come now to the matter of the all-important Operating Plan. What are we going to do with the Signals? It is not good practice to buy and then sit back and do nothing until a sell signal appears. We need a plan for limiting losses, protecting profits, and taking profits.

First, each of us must decide individually whether or not to use "multiple funds." By "multiple funds" I mean that the total capital for a stock or commodity is divided into two or more parts and only part of it is used when the Reversal Signal is given and the remaining part or parts are used in the Repeat Signals which ordinarily follow a profitable Reversal Signal.

In doing this we have the comfort of taking a loss on only part of our capital when the Reversal Signal is proved immediately wrong. (If Repeat Signals follow the Reversal Signal in rapid order we can still take a loss on all of our capital, but this does not happen often.) In the event that we are trading during one of those occasional, inevitable periods where everything goes wrong, it becomes really important that we confine our run of bad luck to only part of the total trading capital. However, in way of compensation, the larger profits in the long run are to be made in following the original Reversal Signals with all of the capital set aside for trading in a particular stock or commodity. So, it is up to the individual. Do you want to risk more in order to gain more? Or, do you want to risk less and gain less?

Another thing which each of us must decide individually (assuming the decision has been made to use "multiple funds") is whether to use the Repeat Signals for pyramiding for long-term profits or for short-term gains. That is, on a Repeat Signal should we buy and hold for a long-term gain or should we try only for a small but quick profit?

The plan I am presenting here appeals to my personal taste. All or parts of it may not appeal to you. If so, I am sure you can work out a satisfactory plan for yourself. The most important thing is to *trade with a PLAN!* My plan is simply this:

- Assume I am watching a stock which has had a long decline and it starts "acting better." I plan on buying 100 shares of the stock in the event of a Reversal Buy Signal. Rather than to buy 100 shares on the original Reversal Signal my thought is to buy only 25 shares at that time and "see what happens." The signal may be a "false one," and if it is my loss will be taken in only 25 shares rather than 100 shares (assuming I get no Repeat Signals before the loss comes.) This original 25 shares will be Fund L (long-term holding for the larger gains).

- If the stock moves up, I'll buy another 25 shares (again for Fund L) on a Repeat Signal which gives a higher purchase price than my original purchase. I don't want to "average up" my cost by buying lower. I want to be sure that I'm right so far – that I have a paper profit in my original trade. Only then will I take on an additional lot.

- I now have 50 shares for long-term holding and it leaves me with 50 shares more to buy for quick-profit trading (Fund S). Again I want to swim with the tide so I'll not buy another 25 shares unless I have a paper profit in each of the two 25-share lots already bought. In other words, my third purchase must be made at a higher price than that paid for the second lot. And the same goes for the fourth lot; it must be bought at a higher price than the third lot. If all goes well, I will now have purchased my 100 shares and I'll be a dignified "investor" with 50 of the shares and with the other 50 shares I'll stay young and have fun grabbing quick profits here and there as the stock dips and rallies during its Maintrend movement!

- If during the course of the Maintrend movement I should get stopped out of a Fund L position, I'll make another Fund L trade before engaging in further Fund S trades. No telling where the stock may go and I want two Fund L lots working for me at all times. I suppose I'll have to take a loss now and then, but if the stock is really "ready," I'm right in there riding a winning horse most of the time.

Now, all through this plan I'm hoping that I'll be real sorry I didn't buy 100 shares right at the start. I'm hoping the stock will go sky-high and make me feel bad because I didn't shoot the works when the original Reversal Signal came. If I had done that, I probably could have made 50% more profit. But, since I can't see the future ahead of time, and since the boys who know keep telling me to never, never overtrade, I'll try to content myself with less profit for the sake of less risk.

Well, anyway, I like the idea and I think it will work out profitably much more often than not. Now to get down to brass tacks and figure out a definite, mathematical formula to go along with it:

After a considerable amount of work with other plans, I have turned back to the Square Root Theory as the basis of an Operating Plan in stocks. We need some plan whereby all stocks, regardless of their price level, can be put on an equitable or one-way basis. If we buy one stock at $10 and at the same time buy another stock at $50, we should plan to limit our losses and accept profits in the two stocks according to some basic common denominator which recognizes how the two stocks tend to fluctuate in respect to each other. From the Square Root Theory we can formulate a plan whereby the price movements in all stocks are "equalized" or put on a one-way basis.

I am not so sure that we should call it the "Square Root *Theory*." It appears to be an accepted *fact* among a number of first-rated statisticians. Homer Fahrner was one of the few early pioneers who tested and developed the Theory, and his work today continues to show considerable respect for square roots. I see favorable recognition to the Theory in publications such as *Journal of the American Statistical Association, The Analysts Journal, Econometrica, Investor's Future,* and *Barron's.* And, I see that at least one University has conducted research into the Square Root Theory and found it valid. So, let's accept the word of the authorities and make something out of square roots for our own use. Fortunately, to turn the Theory into a practical plan we don't have to be very smart. Even if we can't extract the square root of a number, we can still use the Theory. (Anyone interested in background might, as a starter, read my paper, "Trend Trading with Square Root Methods," published in *New Blueprints for Gains in Stocks and Grains.*)

I am using square roots here only as a means to get started on a "one-way" basis for all stocks at any price level. I could use square roots throughout in the Operating Plan, but I believe some readers would find it boresome to become acquainted with a Table I compiled for that purpose. Besides, I now want all commodities to follow the same Operating Plan which is used in stocks and I don't think it would be practical to put many commodities on a square root basis.

The most important thing is to get *started* on a common-denominator, equitable basis and this is done in stocks by the Square Root Theory. After once getting started, we can then let the price action of each stock take care of itself in complying with the remaining procedure of our Operating Plan.

At the very start of any trade the most important thing to do is to limit the loss. If we can keep our errors down within reasonable limits, the hits we make will assure us of a winning score when the game is over. We turn to square roots for the amount of loss we are willing to take at any price. And, to carry on, we can use the same limit-loss figure for calculating how we are going to protect and accept profits. In fact, we can think of this figure as the "Profit Factor (PF)" because each item in the Operating Plan is related to this basic figure.

If we buy a stock at $14, the PF is $4 and each figure in the Operating Plan for that stock is a multiple of $4. If we buy another stock at $33, the PF is $6 and each figure in the Operating Plan for that stock is a multiple of $6. (For the benefit of those who are "technically minded," the figure for PF represents a rise of ½ square root. A slightly smaller figure should be used for a decline of ½ square root but I am ignoring this to avoid complications.)

The Operating Plan for stocks selling from $1.50 to $150.00 is given below. It was derived from these schedules:

FUND L
(For the Larger, Long-Term Profits)

Example: When PF is $4

1. Limit loss to PF.

2. After 50% PF paper profit limit the loss to 50% PF.

3. After 80% PF paper profit limit the loss to 20% PF.

4. After 100% PF paper profit place stop to break even.

5. After 120% PF paper profit protect 20% PF profit.

6.*After 200% PF paper profit protect 40% of maximum profit.

1. Limit loss to $4.

2. After $2 paper profit limit the loss to $2.

3. After $3¼ paper profit limit the loss to $¾.

4. After $4 paper profit place stop to break even.

5. After $4¾ paper profit protect $¾ profit.

6.*After $8 paper profit, protect $3¼ profit and thereafter protect 40% of the largest paper profit shown at any time.

FUND S
(For the Smaller, Short-term Profits)

Example: When PF is $4

1. Limit loss to PF

2. After 50% PF paper profit limit loss to 50% PF.

3. After 80% PF paper profit limit loss to 20% PF.

4. Take 100% PF profit.

1. Limit loss to $4.

2. After $2 paper profit limit loss to $2.

3. After $3¼ paper profit limit loss to $¾.

4. Take $4 profit.

All figures in the above schedules are gross, without regard to commissions.

In forthcoming mailings I'll send you actual stock charts showing how all of this works out in actual practice.

---

*In Fund L we purposely keep our stop a sizeable distance away from the maximum profit attained in order to try to avoid being stopped out by a secondary reaction. We hope to let Fund L ride for a large gain and finally get closed out by a Reversal Signal.

Table 1.1 Operating Plan in Stocks

When price is nearest* $	Profit factor PF	1. Limit loss	2. After 0.50PF paper profit	2. Limit loss to 0.50PF	3. After 0.80PF paper profit	3. Limit loss to 0.20PF	4. Break Even** after 1PF paper profit	5. After 1.20PF paper profit	5. Protect profit of 0.20PF	6. After 2PF paper profit protect 40% of maximum paper profit
1½	1½	1½	¾	¾	1¼	¼	1½	1¾	¼	3
3	2	2	1	1	1⅝	⅜	2	2⅜	⅜	4
5	2½	2½	1¼	1¼	2	½	2½	3	½	5
7½	3	3	1½	1½	2⅜	⅝	3	3⅝	⅝	6
10½	3½	3½	1¾	1¾	2¾	¾	3½	4¼	¾	7
14	4	4	2	2	3¼	¾	4	4¾	¾	8
18	4½	4½	2¼	2¼	3⅝	⅞	4½	5⅜	⅞	9
22½	5	5	2½	2½	4	1	5	6	1	10
27½	5½	5½	2¾	2¾	4⅜	1⅛	5½	6⅝	1⅛	11
33	6	6	3	3	4¾	1¼	6	7¼	1¼	12
39	6½	6½	3¼	3¼	5¼	1¼	6½	7¾	1¼	13
45½	7	7	3½	3½	5⅝	1⅜	7	8⅜	1⅜	14
52½	7½	7½	3¾	3¾	6	1½	7½	9	1½	15
60	8	8	4	4	6⅜	1⅝	8	9⅝	1⅝	16
68	8½	8½	4¼	4¼	6¾	1¾	8½	10¼	1¾	17
76½	9	9	4½	4½	7¼	1¾	9	10¾	1¾	18
85½	9½	9½	4¾	4¾	7⅝	1⅞	9½	11⅜	1⅞	19
95	10	10	5	5	8	2	10	12	2	20
105	10½	10½	5¼	5¼	8⅜	2⅛	10½	12⅝	2⅛	21
115½	11	11	5½	5½	8¾	2¼	11	13¼	2¼	22
126½	11½	11½	5¾	5¾	9¼	2¼	11½	13¾	2¼	23
138	12	12	6	6	9⅝	2⅜	12	14⅜	2⅜	24
150	12½	12½	6¼	6¾	10	2½	12½	15	2½	25

* If price is midway between two figures, use the higher figure. Examples: If purchase price is 16, use 18; if purchase price 64, use 68; etc.

** For Fund L use all Columns, 1 through 6.

For Fund S use Columns 1, 2, 3 and 4, and take profits equal to amounts in Column 4.

SOME PRACTICAL CONSIDERATIONS

Ex-dividend prices

It would entail a considerable amount of extra work to give consideration to ex-dividend dates in back-testing a method. If adjustments were made in prices when a stock became ex-dividend, the results would undoubtedly be changed here and there. Perhaps such changes would work out to one's advantage about as often as disadvantage. In actual practice you can make allowance for ex-dividend prices if you care to do so. Unless the dividend is a couple of dollars or more, I think that ordinarily I will disregard it. Certainly, the effect of an ex-dividend is not long enduring and usually it can be entirely disregarded after a few new Swings have been set up. In the case of stock dividends and splits, where there is a large change in price, we must, at the start, adjust the new prices to correspond with old prices, but this too can soon be forgotten when the new stock starts setting up its own Swings.

Buying and selling at the closing price

When we enter into a new trade the rule is to buy (or sell) at the closing price of the week. It may be difficult to get an execution at the exact closing price in the week in which said closing price is made. Nearly always, though, we can wait until the following week and get an execution at the prior week's closing price. But, such matters are not too important. In actual practice it is not essential, or even possible, to follow every rule in a rigid manner which is 100% mechanical. The market itself will force on us little deviations from strict mechanics, and these deviations will likely balance out about even in the long run. Some will prove to our advantage and some to our disadvantage.

Some of us may even be tempted from time to time to "fudge" on the rules. If I am looking for a Reversal Buy Signal in a certain stock and early in the week I see the stock rallying strongly, I very likely would jump the gun and buy before the close of the week. But, such matters come under the subject of "Trading Tactics," and each of us will have to work out the problems in "Tactics" according to our personal feelings and experience in such matters.

Another word on mechanical rules

In back-testing a method we *must* set up strict mechanical rules and then follow these rules in the manner of a robot. We must do everything according to rigid Formulae; we cannot deviate by as much as $\frac{1}{8}$. If we didn't do this we would likely invent new rules, or proclaim great reasons, to handle properly every situation which arose. You may have read the popular book in which the author gives page after page of market history and has a good rule for taking the right course of action at every turning point. Yes, if you have enough rules on hand (I once listed 115 of them), or if you can argue loud enough, you can really beat the market in *past* years. To do market research honestly we must use a procedure which controls the frailties of the mind – the procedure must be mechanical.

But, for the purpose of actual trading we should realize that mechanical rules, at their best, can only express "average tendencies" which prevailed in the past. Obviously, a single market movement is likely to deviate from the "average movement" in at least some of its respects.

If through intensive research we found the average figures which in the long run gave the best results for the amount of Thrust to use, the point at which to place a stop-loss order, and the points at which to protect paper profits for each and every one of the commodities and stocks, such figures could only be what they really are – the best average figures for a long stretch of *past* market action. In the very next trade some other set of figures would almost certainly do better than the hard-won average figures.

If the average height of the men in the US Army is 5 feet, 9 inches, we are not surprised when the next soldier who happens along turns out to be over 6 feet, or perhaps only 5½ feet. If on the average it is best to protect a paper profit in a stock after it has risen $5 above the purchase price, we should be neither surprised nor sour if in the next trade the stock rises only $4 and then turns against us to wind up the trade with a loss.

In other words, whatever set of figures we use in mechanical trading we cannot depend upon the single trade to perform according to average expectations. We must look ahead to a considerable number of trades and even then we are not likely to realize "average results." We may do better or worse because future markets will certainly not be exact duplications of past markets from which the "best average figures" were derived. Since that is the case, I see no point in searching forever for something which could very well prove to be no better than that which we already have. Our present mechanical rules border somewhere near "average conditions." We need not, for all practical purposes, try to become more exacting.

It was emphasized in "Gains in Grains" that *principles* are more important than mechanical rules. Our principles must be absolutely right in each and every trade. TOB, BR, ASC, Thrust, etc., embody sound principles and we should see that these principles are respected in each trade. On the other hand, our mechanical guides can only be rough approximations as to how any single trade should be handled. But, notwithstanding the imperfections of mechanical rules, if we stay with sound principles in every trade our mechanical approximations will carry us through safely and profitably in the long run.

In brief, don't judge One-Way Formula harshly when it doesn't perform "rightly." A little, lone ⅛ movement will at times be the cause of a loss. Give the mechanical rules a chance to "average out" over a series of trades. Then, I believe, they will not fail you.

Part II

TRADING IN COMMODITIES WITH ONE-WAY FORMULA

- Some special considerations in commodities
- Operating plan in commodities

One-Way Formula in commodities is identical to the procedure in stocks except:

1. Daily data is used instead of weekly.
2. The Profit Factor (PF) is based on "average margin requirements" instead of square roots.

If I were to write here the complete explanation of One-Way Formula in commodities it would be largely a word-by-word repetition of the stock section of this paper except instead of "stocks" I would substitute "commodities" and instead of "weeks" I would write "days." Obviously, that would be a waste of time and an unnecessary expense.

The purpose of this research was to provide a universal or one-way method which would be applicable to both stocks and commodities. The goal has been reached. Therefore, if you are interested in commodity trading simply read

1. the stock section of this treatise, keeping in mind that daily statistics are used in commodities and
2. the following pages which deal specifically with commodities.

SOME SPECIAL CONSIDERATIONS IN COMMODITIES

If we buy a share of stock we can ordinarily hold it for a lifetime and then pass it on to a survivor who likewise can hold it indefinitely. But, if we buy 5,000 bushels of May 1958 Wheat we must dispose of it by some time in May 1958 or else take actual delivery of the wheat (if we sell short May Wheat, we must cover our short or deliver the actual wheat before the future expires in May 1958.) This has caused many stock traders to avoid the commodity markets – they don't want to wake up with a "carload of wheat on their front porch." Actually, if they didn't sell their wheat, but instead took delivery, they likely would never see the physical wheat. But, there would be storage and insurance to pay, and capital would be needed to pay for the wheat in full. In all, it would be an expensive nuisance, and the thing to do is to sell the wheat before you are required to take delivery (unless, of course, you are in the grain business and have use for the actual wheat).

The purpose of this research was to provide a universal method applicable to both stocks and commodities

This "limited life" of a commodity brings up certain trading problems which must be met in some manner. Usually it is not of great importance how we handle these "special considerations" other than whatever decisions we make we should adhere to them consistently – particularly, in backtesting. Here is how I am taking care of these problems in my testing of past commodity futures.

1. In starting a new option we get our bearings on the Maintrend from the preceding option. If trading has just started in May Wheat, we assume that the Maintrend is the same in May Wheat as it is in the March option. (Actually in my research I sometimes used the prior December option to get my Maintrend bearings in the new May option because I had no past charts for the March option.) If we are just starting to chart the July option, we should use the May option to determine the direction of the Maintrend in the new July option, etc. Also, in the early days of a new option we may have to use the prior option to determine whether a Signal Pattern is present. However, as early as possible we put the new option "on its own" and use it exclusively for its own Signals.

   A variation of this plan would be to use in the new option the Maintrend which prevails in the majority of the prior options. But, this might not be so satisfactory as the new option may be concerned with a different "crop year" and its price action might reflect fundamental influences which are not present in the older options. During the month of March, the March future may be more concerned with the "cash position" of wheat while the December future may be discounting future crop expectations – therefore, March might be strong while December is relatively weak.

2. We enter into a new option on the first appearance of a Signal Pattern and, if necessary, Thrust. As already stated, whether a Signal Pattern exists in the new option may be determined in the early days of the new option by the price action of the prior option.

   For example, if the prior option has already given a Preliminary Buy Signal we require only a Thrust for a Reversal Buy Signal in the new option. (After a Downswing we buy at the closing price of the first Upday if said Upday does not have a lower close.)

   But, if the prior option has already given a Reversal Buy Signal, we require only the "Repeat Signal Thrust" to get us started with a Repeat Buy Signal in the new option. In other words, we can enter into a trade immediately on the appearance of BR but must wait for close of first Upday on appearance of either TOB or ASC at Bottom of Downswing.

3. We do not enter into any new trade after the 20th of the month preceding the Delivery Month.

4. We close out any open trade at the closing price of the day before the Delivery Month.

The above stipulations deal with the "limited life" of a commodity. Another oddity of commodity prices is that they often open and close at two figures. If a close has two figures it is known as a "split close." We use both figures in determining whether a BR, or a TR, is present. A BR is present if the low price in today's split close is above the high price in yesterday's split close (assuming, of course, that the Maintrend is up and today is the lowest price so far recorded in a Downswing.) A TR is present if the high price in today's split close is below the low price in yesterday's split close (assuming, of course,) that the Maintrend is down and today is the highest price so far recorded in an Upswing). In other words, both figures in a split close must confirm to give a BR or a TR Pattern.

We also require "confirmation of split closes" in determining whether to buy at the close of the first Upday (or sell at the close of the first Downday). We do not buy if *both* closes are lower than the low split of the day before. If one is lower and the other is equal (or above) the low split of yesterday, we will buy. Similarly with sales: we do not sell if *both* splits today are above the high split of yesterday. If only one of the splits today is above the high split of yesterday we will sell.

The foregoing "special considerations" are not "musts." You can change them to suit your own inclinations and I am sure it will make little difference in the long run. For example, you may not care to buy a commodity in the very early days of its life when the trading is relatively light and the executions may be bad. Use your own experience and judgment in such matters, or consult your broker for his views.

Of more importance is the Operating Plan, the subject to be taken up now.

OPERATING PLAN IN COMMODITIES

The Operating Plan in various commodities is summarized in Table 2.1. This Table and the current price charts are all that will be needed once the Formula is well in mind.

In my research I turned to many plans in trying to determine the best way to limit losses and to take profits. I was particularly anxious to use the size of swing as the guiding light to an Operating Plan in various commodities. The swings in soybeans are larger than the swings in oats; therefore we should expect more profit in soybeans than in oats. Perhaps an equitable basis for determining a scale for limiting losses and protecting profits in each commodity could be worked out by further intensive study of the behavior of each commodity as evidenced particularly by the size of its typical swings. But, that job is for someone else to consider. After wrestling with swings for some months I've decided to follow an easy-does-it procedure which was suggested to me over a year ago by Mr. C. H. Burns. He wrote:

"If we were to test 20 different wheat options using a 3, 4, and 5-cent stop on each option, I have an idea that the average results for the 20 options would be much the same whether we use a 3, 4 or 5-cent stop. We would, of course, have smaller individual losses with the 3-cent stop but we would have more of them.

"If this is so, then the exact amount of the stop over a period of time is not too important, and there may even be room for individual preferences. This suggests a simple way of determining stops for a One-Way Formula:

"*Fix your stop at one-quarter of your broker's minimum margin requirement.*

"At a certain time it might work out something like this:

Table 2.1

Commodity	Minimum margin	¼ of minimum margin
Wheat	20 cents	5 cents
Corn	15 cents	3¾ cents
Oats	8 cents	2 cents
Rye	20 cents	5 cents
Soybeans	30 cents	7½ cents
Lard	2 cents	½ cent

"This is, of course, a rough way of arriving a stop but it is simple and after all do we have any evidence that a more complicated method would produce better results? It goes without saying that the individual trader can raise or lower an individual figure if he thinks conditions require it."

I have carried on with Mr. Burns' original suggestion and have used the "margin requirements" as the basis for not only limiting losses but also for protecting profits. The "powers-that-be" who set the margin requirements are shrewd gentlemen. They keep close score on the fluctuations in each commodity and set the margin requirements at figures which ordinarily eliminate any risk on their part. We may do well to fall in line with their figures for purposes of arriving at an equitable, common-denominator Operating Plan for all commodities.

Our Operating Plan uses, for each commodity, a rough average of the margin requirements since 1952. I call this the "basic margin." (Odd figures are sometimes used for convenience in calculating gains and losses – eg $960 in lard.) Of course, brokers raise and lower their margin requirements from time to time in order to keep in line with the price level and volatility of a commodity. Also, at a given time the margin requirements may vary among different brokers.

In wheat, for example, I have set the basic margin at 16½ cents and have used this figure throughout in my backtesting regardless of what the actual margin requirement was at a particular time. Today (September 1957) some brokers require only 12 cents per bushel in wheat, but our Operating Plan continues to use 16½ cents as the "basic margin." If sometime later the margin in wheat rises to 18 cents we will naturally have to deposit at least 18 cents per bushel with the broker, but the "basic margin" will remain the same at 16½ cents. I would see no reason to change the operating formula in wheat unless the margin requirements went above 20 cents or below 10 cents.

The Profit Factor is simply 30% of the basic margin. Thus, in wheat the Profit Factor is 30% of 16½ cents or approximately 5 cents. In soybeans the basic margin is set at 24 cents; the Profit Factor is therefore 30% of 24 cents or about 7¼ cents. In lard the basic margin is set at 240 point which gives us a PF of 30% of 240 or 72 points, and for convenience we make this an even 70 points. In wheat we limit the loss to 5 cents, in soybeans to 7¼ cents, and in lard to 70 points. And so on for all the other commodities as shown in Table 2.1.

The Profit Factor is used not only to limit losses, but it is the guiding figure in telling us how to protect and accept profits. The calculations are made exactly as they were in stocks. In wheat the plan-of-action is this:

FUND L
(For the Larger, Long-Term Profits)

Wheat (PF is 5¢)

1. Limit loss to PF.

1. Limit loss to 5¢.

2. After 50% PF paper profit limit the loss to 50% PF.

2. After 2½¢ paper profit limit the loss to 2½¢.

3. After 80% PF paper profit limit the loss to 20% PF.

3. After 4¢ paper profit limit the loss to 1¢.

4. After 100% PF paper profit place stop to break even.

4. After 5¢ paper profit place stop to break even.

5. After 120% PF paper profit protect 20% PF profit.

5. After 6¢ paper profit protect 1¢ profit.

6.*After 200% PF paper profit protect 40% of maximum profit.

6.*After 10¢ paper profit, protect 4¢ profit and thereafter protect 40% the largest paper profit shown at any time.

FUND S
(For the Smaller, Short-term Profits)

Wheat (PF is 5¢)

1. Limit loss to PF

2. After 50% PF paper profit limit loss to 50% PF.

3. After 80% PF paper profit limit loss to 20% PF.

4. Take 100% PF profit.

1. Limit loss to 5¢.

2. After 2½¢ paper profit limit loss to 2½¢.

3. After 4¢ paper profit limit loss to 1¢.

4. Take 5¢ profit.

All figures in the above schedules are gross, without regard to commissions.

All other commodities follow the same operating procedure. Hence, using margin requirements as a common denominator, all the important trading commodities are placed on an equitable, "one-way" basis, and the trader is provided with a plan of systematic guidance in whatever commodities he may choose for actual commitments.

We operate the L and S Funds in commodities in the same manner as is done in stocks. The total trading capital for a specific commodity is divided into four equal parts. On a Reversal Signal we use only ¼ of the total margin at our disposal. That is, if we have sufficient capital to margin 20,000 bushels, we would buy only 5,000 bushels on a Reversal Buy Signal. This would be for Fund L. The remaining ¾ of the capital would remain inactive until such time that prices started trending upward when we would purchase another 5,000 on the first Repeat Signal which gave a higher purchase price than the original commitment. This also would be for Fund L. Then, if the trend continued upward we would become active with the remaining ½ of the capital, employing it ¼ at a time for Fund S, always buying higher than the preceding purchase price. Thus, in pronounced Maintrend movements our goal is to follow the trend with all of the capital at our disposal.

In the event that prices did not move up after the initial purchase, a loss would be taken in only 5,000 bushels. If prices went up slightly and then reacted, a loss might be taken in 10,000 bushels. Only rarely, I think, will a loss be taken in more than 10,000 bushels at one time. The usual loss will be in the minimum 5,000 bushels involving ¼ of the total trading capital. This, in effect, makes the ¾ inactive capital a protective cushion – something to fall back on in the event of a run of losses.

I am convinced that a string of losses from time to time is inevitable by *any method* whether the method be known as "One-Way Formula" or whatever its name or procedure may be. Since at least the days of Charles Dow at the turn of this century many thousands of persons have diligently sought for the "golden key" to market success. I am sure that the "key" has long been in our possession but I am also sure that no one has yet whipped the whipsaws. At this time I don't know any method that I would rather follow than the present One-Way Formula. But, I also know that it will put me out of the running if I overtrade.

One-Way Formula is designed to avoid overtrading. It seeks to be lightly committed when the signals are wrong and to be heavily committed when the signals are right. Ordinarily we will have a reserve behind us when the market goes against us and we will have the opportunity to use that reserve when the market goes in our favor. Furthermore, when prices go in our favor *temporarily* and then turn against us, our plan calls for a *reduction* in the amount of loss which may be taken. In other words, the entire plan is designed *for small losses and large profits*. Various mechanical procedures could be set up for the purpose of (1) avoiding overtrading and (2) cutting the losses short and letting the profits run. Of the many plans I have experimented with, the one in this paper is best.

From time to time I will mail past charts on various commodities to subscribers. These charts will illustrate past performances which were "excellent," "average" and "poor." This entire work is represented as *research*. I don't have any axe to grind or hidden motives. I have no present ambitions to expand into a "big service" nor to take on the responsibility of handling large sums of money for other people. Maybe I've "reformed." At any rate, I think that you can trust that during the coming months I'll tell and

> *One-Way Formula is designed for small losses and large profits*

show you the worst about One-Way Formula as well as the best. You will receive some chart pictures which are sad sights. More often you will receive pictures which are highly pleasing or at least average, for the latter groups are far in the majority.

With this mailing I am enclosing two charts on soybeans. I have added the One-Way notations to these excellent, original charts which were prepared by Mr William R. Kern, 171 West Quincy Street, Chicago 4, Ill. Mr Kern is now making up past charts on wheat, corn, rye, oats and soybeans. These will soon be available to commodity traders and students at a very nominal cost. Questions about these charts should be addressed to Mr Kern rather than to my office.

Table 2.1 Operating Plan in Commodities

Commodity	Contract	Minimum fluctuation: In price	Minimum fluctuation: Equals per contract	1 cent movement equals per contract	Basic margin: per unit "BM"	Basic margin: Equals per contract	1. Profit factor "PF" 30% of "BM" limit loss	2. After Q- PF paper profit	2. Limit loss to Q- PF	3. After 0.8PF paper profit	3. Limit loss to 0.2 PF	4. Break even after 1 PF paper profit	5. After 1.2 PF paper profit	5. Protect 0.2PF profit	6. After 2PF paper profit protect 40% of maximum paper profit	Round trip commission per contract*
Wheat	5,000 bu.	⅛¢ per bu.	$6.25	$50.00	16½¢ per bu.	$825	5¢	2½¢	2½¢	4¢	1¢	5¢	6¢	1¢	10¢	$18.00
Corn	5,000 bu.	⅛¢ per bu.	6.25	50.00	12¢ per bu.	600	3⅝¢	1⅞¢	1⅞¢	2⅞¢	¾¢	3⅝¢	4⅜¢	¾¢	7¼¢	18.00
Oats	5,000 bu.	⅛¢ per bu.	6.25	50.00	8¢ per bu.	400	2⅜¢	1¼¢	1¼¢	1⅞¢	½¢	2⅜¢	2⅞¢	½¢	4¾¢	15.00
Rye	5,000 bu.	⅛¢ per bu.	6.25	50.00	16½¢ per bu.	825	5¢	2½¢	2½¢	4¢	1¢	5¢	6¢	1¢	10¢	18.00
Soybeans	5,000 bu.	⅛¢ per bu.	6.25	50.00	24¢ per bu.	1200	7¼¢	3⅝¢	3⅝¢	5¾¢	1½¢	7¼¢	8¾¢	1½¢	14½¢	18.00
Lard	40,000 lbs.	2½/100 ¢ per lb. (2½ points)	10.00	400.00	2.4¢ per lb. (240 points)	960	70 points	35 points	35 points	55 points	15 points	70 points	85 points	15 points	140 points	20.00
Cotton	50,000 lbs.	1/100¢per lb (1 point)	5.00	500.00	2¢ per lb. (200 points)	1000	60 points	30 points	30 points	50 points	10 points	60 points	70 points	10 points	120 points	40.00
Soybean oil Cottonseed oil	60,000 lbs.	1/100¢per lb (1 point)	6.00	600.00	1.6¢ per lb. (160 points)	960	50 points	25 points	25 points	40 points	10 points	50 points	60 points	10 points	100 points	30.00
Soybean meal Cottonseed meal	100 tons	5¢ per ton	5.00	($1=$100)	$8.00 per ton	800	$2.40	$1.20	$1.20	$1.90	50¢	$2.40	¢2.90	50¢	$4.80	30.00
Cocoa	30,000 lbs.	1/100¢per lb (1 point)	3.00	300.00	4¢ per lb. (400 points)	1200	120 points	60 points	60 points	95 points	25 points	120 points	145 points	25 points	240 points	60.00
Coffee	32,500 lbs.	1/100¢per lb (1 point)	3.25	325.00	8¢ per lb. (800 points)	2600	240 points	120 points	120 points	190 points	50 points	240 points	290 points	50 points	480 points	60.00
Copper	50,000 lbs.	1/100¢per lb (1 point)	5.00	500.00	3¢ per lb. (300 points)	1500	90 points	45 points	45 points	70 points	20 points	90 points	110 points	20 points	180 points	50.00
Eggs	15,000 doz.	5/100¢ per doz. (5 points)	7.50	150.00	6¢ per doz. (600 points)	900	180 points	90 points	90 points	145 points	35 points	180 points	215 points	35 points	360 points	36.00
Hides	40,000 lbs.	1/100¢per lb (1 point)	4.00	400.00	2¢ per lb. (200 points)	800	60 points	30 points	30 points	50 points	10 points	60 points	70 points	10 points	120 points	40.00
Onions	600 sacks (30,000 lbs.)	1¢ per sack or 1¢ per 50 lbs.	6.00	($1=$600)	65¢ per sack.	390	20¢	10¢	10¢	16¢	4¢	20¢	24¢	4¢	40¢	22.00
Potatoes (New York)	450 sacks (45,000 lbs.)	1¢ per sack or 1¢ per 100 lbs.	4.50	($1=$450)	$1.00 per sack	450	30¢	15¢	15¢	24¢	6¢	30¢	36¢	6¢	60¢	20.00
Rubber	22,400 lbs.	1/100¢per lb (1 point)	2.24	224.00	4¢ per lb. (400 points)	896	120 points	60 points	60 points	95 points	25 points	120 points	145 points	25 points	240 points	40.00
Sugar	112,000 lbs.	1/100¢per lb (1 point)	11.20	1120.00	0.8¢ per lb. (80 points)	896	24 points	12 points	12 points	19 points	5 points	24 points	29 points	5 points	48 points	30.00
Wool tops	5,000 lbs.	1/10¢per lb	5.00	50.00	20¢ per lb.	1000	6¢	3¢	3¢	4.8¢	1.2¢	6¢	7.2¢	1.2¢	12¢	40.00

* Commissions vary in some commodities according to price level.

** For Fund L use all columns, 1 through 6.
For Fund S use columns 1, 2, 3, and 4, and take profits equal to amounts in column 4.

DUNNIGAN'S
COACHING REPORTS

ONE-WAY FORMULA

DUNNIGAN'S COACHING REPORT No. 1
August 29, 1957

This is the start of a new series of COACHING REPORTS pertaining to a *new* method. To avoid confusion do not hereafter refer to Coaching Reports or text preceding this issue.

Fig i Watch for a buy signal

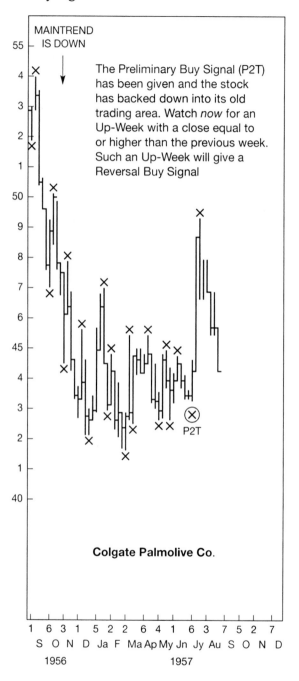

The Preliminary Buy Signal (P2T) has been given and the stock has backed down into its old trading area. Watch *now* for an Up-Week with a close equal to or higher than the previous week. Such an Up-Week will give a Reversal Buy Signal

Colgate Palmolive Co.

Fig ii Acting strong

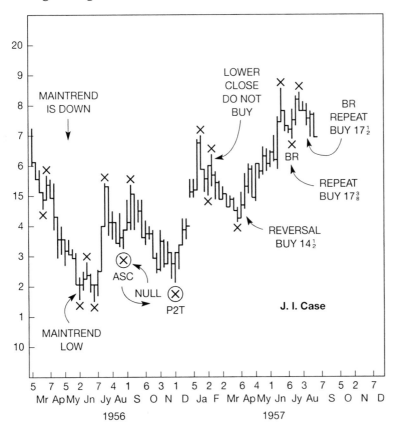

This chart illustrates a number of things explained in the text – ASC, NULLIFI-CATION, P2T, REVERSAL BUY and REPEAT BUY. The stock has held very well so far during a sharp general market decline.

DUNNIGAN'S COACHING REPORT No. 2
August 29, 1957

Good performance, early repeat buy in sight

A double Preliminary Signal (both ASC and P2T) announced last September the possibility of a change in trend to the upside. This was confirmed by a Reversal Buy Signal at 16⅝. Two Repeat Buys followed and another one may come very soon. On a BR we buy immediately at the close of the BR week. On ASC or TOB we wait for the first Up-Week and then buy at the close. Remember, the next Repeat Buy must be above 21⅛.

Fig iii Early repeat buy

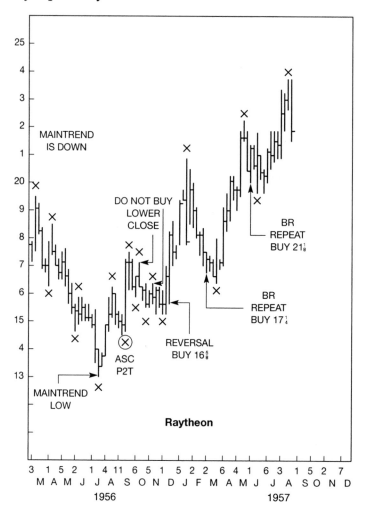

A reversal buy soon?

The Preliminary Buy Signal has been given and the likelihood exists that a Reversal Buy Signal will be given soon. Watch for Up-Week with a close equal to or higher than the previous week.

Fig iv A reversal buy soon?

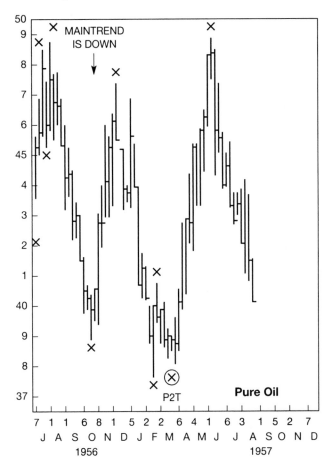

DUNNIGAN'S COACHING REPORT No. 3
August 29, 1957

Will it say "buy"?

An Up-Week from the current level would give a Reversal Buy Signal around the low price to date. Notice too that the Preliminary Buy (P2T) might soon be nullified.

Fig v Will it say "buy"?

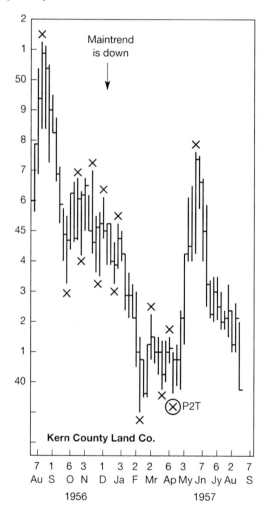

A repeat buy soon?

The current decline has placed many stocks in a position to give a Repeat Buy Signal. Sperry Rand is a typical example. You will find others on your own charts. Up-Week in Sperry Rand must close above 23⅝ to give effective Repeat Signal (also it must not close lower than preceding week).

Fig vi A repeat buy soon?

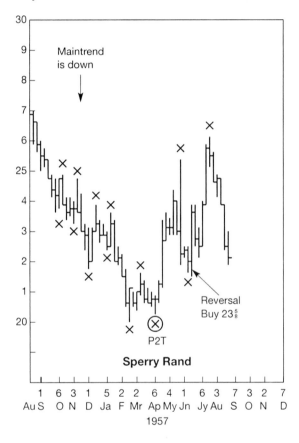

Sperry Rand

DUNNIGAN'S COACHING REPORT No. 4
August 29, 1957

Another profitable signal soon?

Air Reduction shows nothing but profits since 1954. There is now a good possibility of an early Repeat Buy Signal.

The last two weeks set up an ASC with an IR after it. Watch now for an Up-Week with a close equal to or higher than the previous week.

If a Repeat Signal is given, a quick profit of $7 to $8 might soon be realized (profit depends upon the purchase price – see Table).

No Preliminary Sell Signal yet, but there exists in possibility of a P2B in the event of further weakness in the current Downswing. So, watch low week of this Downswing for possibility of a P2B.

If a BR should appear on the low week, the signal is to buy immediately – don't wait for close of first Up-Week.

Fig vii Another profitable signal soon?

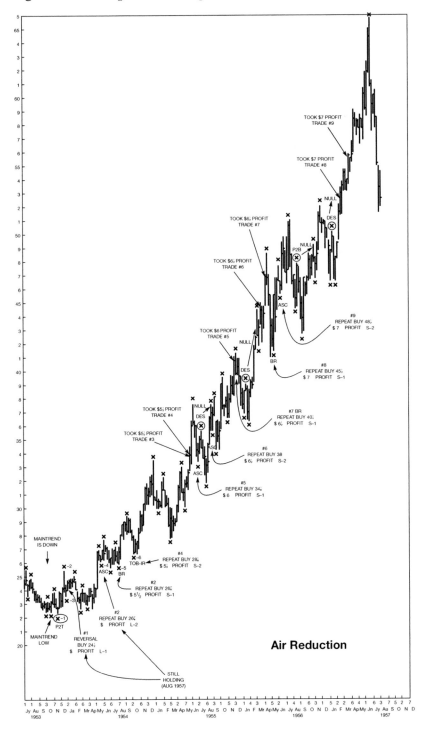

Air Reduction

Still holding for long-term gains in Air Reduction

After a P2T on Upswing X-1 to X-2, we bought at close (24½) of first Up-Week after X-3. A Repeat Buy then came at 26⅞ at the close of week after X-4. Both of these purchases were for long-term holding, L-1 and L-2. Our Operating Plan has not yet closed out these purchases. A Stop at 41 in L-1 and at 42⅜ in L-2 now protects 40 per cent of the maximum paper profit attained when price reached 65¾. We will likely sell higher than these figures through a Reversal Sell Signal later on.

DUNNIGAN'S COACHING REPORT No. 5
September 21, 1957

Repeat buy may come soon

To keep us in line with the direction of the Maintrend each purchase must be made at a higher price than the preceding purchase. This means that the next Repeat Buy in Flintkote must be above 40⅛. If this purchase is made it will be for Fund L-1 in order to reinstate the position which was stopped out after 1.2 PF paper profit.

Fig viii Repeat buy may come soon

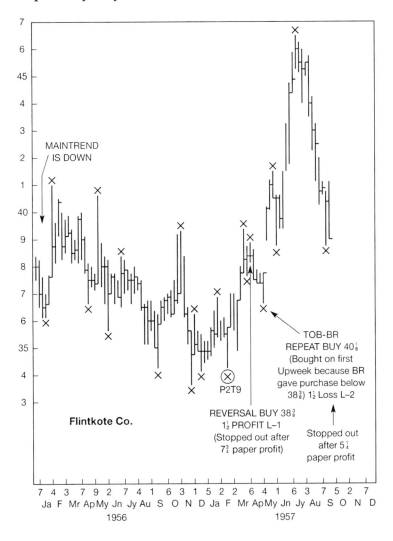

Most stocks are in downtrend

A substantial majority of stocks are at present in a Main Downtrend. Republic Steel has resisted the general decline quite well to date. A TR this week gives a Repeat Sell in it.

Fig ix Most stocks are in downtrend

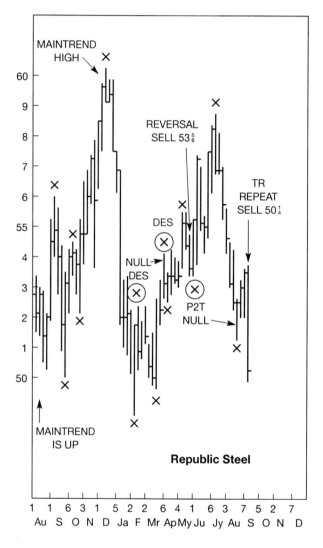

Another prospect for repeat buy

This range is longer than range at Maintrend low. Therefore, any new ASC must be related to this range, or to a still longer range if one should follow this range at the Bottom of a Downswing.

Fig x Another prospect for repeat buy

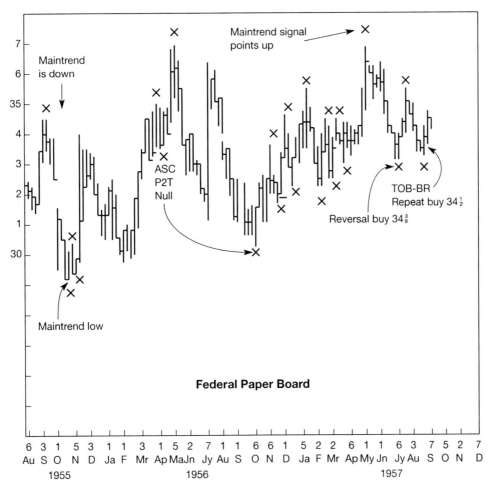

Federal Paper Board

In position for a reversal buy

General Motors can be watched now for a possible Reversal Buy Signal. An Upweek, with a higher or equal close, will give the Signal. But, be sure and watch too for a possible nullification of the Preliminary Bottom in some early week.

Fig xi In position for a reversal buy

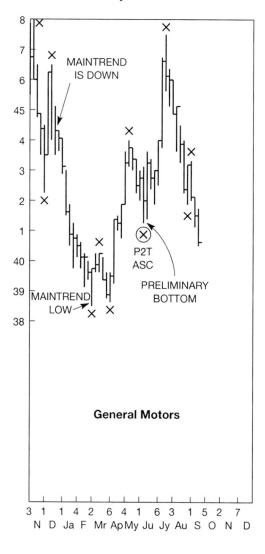

General Motors

Possible purchase

The next purchase, if any, in Heyden Chemical must be above 14⅞. Wait for Downswing and then buy immediately on BR above 14⅞. Or, if Bottom of Downswing is TOB or ASC, buy on first Upweek if close is above 14⅞, provided the close is equal to or higher than close of preceding week.

Fig xii Possible purchase

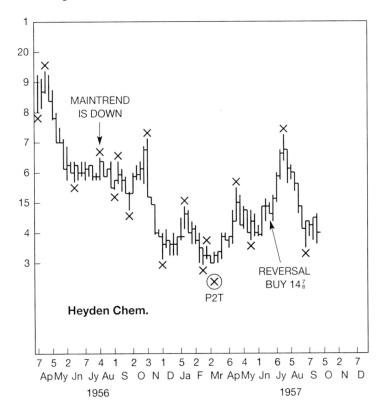

COMMODITIES

Soybeans, corn and lard gave Reversal Sell Signals at prices above today's. May Rye gave a Reversal Sell this week. Wheat is in Preliminary Sell position. Next Report will give current charts in commodities.

DUNNIGAN'S COACHING REPORT No. 6
October 15, 1957

A practical test of One-Way Formula

In these Coaching Reports on commodities I shall use the July 1958 contracts in wheat, corn, rye and soybeans. This will permit you to view a fair test of One-Way Formula as prices unfold in the future. By the end of next June all the points in the formula should be amply demonstrated. Also, from an actual test in price movements yet to come, you will gain a good idea as to what to expect from the formula in the way of profits.

From the point of view of my "business," a better way to illustrate One-Way Formula would be to select only those situations which have worked out admirably – a temptation which all market services find hard to resist. But, I'll do it the hard way and, come what may, I'll use the July 1958 options throughout in the forthcoming Coaching Reports.

Current signals – commodities

As shown on the next few pages, we are short in the July contracts in wheat, corn, rye and soybeans. Reversal Buy Signals came yesterday in December, March and May Wheat and in January Soybeans. March, May and July Soybeans are now in a Preliminary Buy position. Also, January Lard has given a Pre-Buy and the same is true for May and July Rye. So, at the moment it appears that we may soon have some activity on the upside.

Current signals – stocks

This observation was made in the last Coaching Report (Sept. 21): "A substantial majority of stocks are at present in a Main Downtrend." The past three weeks has witnessed a continuation of the general decline with the result that today nearly all of the 86 stocks which I chart are either in a Main Downtrend or a Preliminary Sell position.

The Operating Plan has already closed out long positions in many of the Pre-Sell stocks. Other long stocks can be closed out by Reversal Sell Signals which may likely come after an Upswing. A few of the 86 stocks are still in a Main Uptrend, with no Pre-Sell Signal yet; namely, Air Reduction, Bristol Myers, Colgate, Deere, General Electric, Merck Chemical and Reynolds Tobacco "B." Only one Downtrend stock is now shaping into a Pre-Buy (P2T), Liggett & Myers.

Fig xiii July 1958 Corn

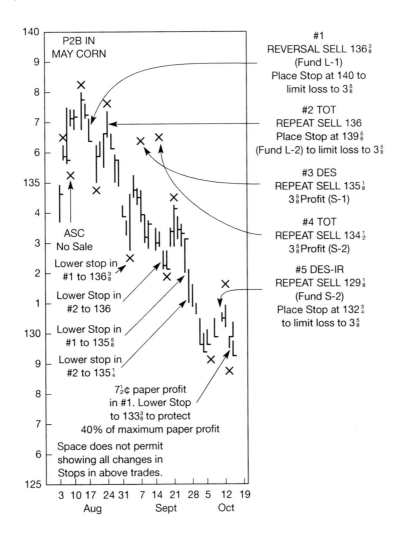

Fig xiv July 1958 Wheat

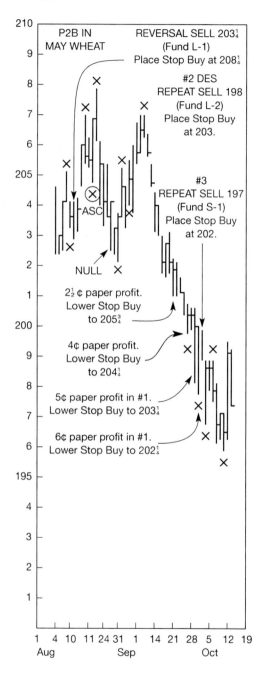

Fig xv July 1958 Rye

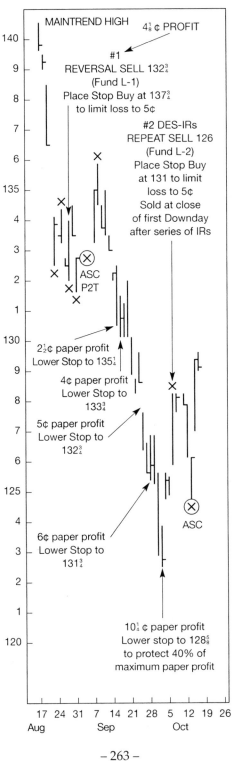

Fig xvi July 1958 Soybeans

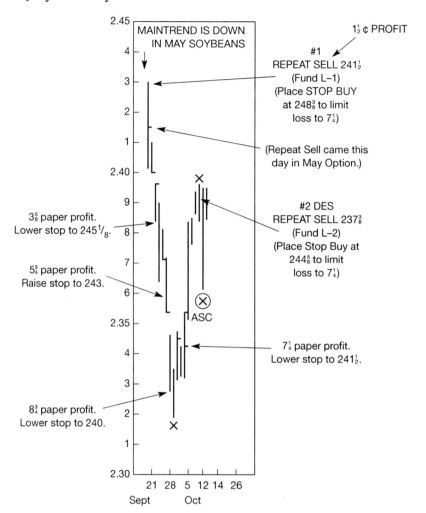

MAINTREND IS DOWN
IN MAY SOYBEANS

$1\frac{1}{2}$ ¢ PROFIT

#1
REPEAT SELL $241\frac{1}{2}$
(Fund L–1)
(Place STOP BUY
at $248\frac{3}{8}$ to limit
loss to $7\frac{1}{4}$)

(Repeat Sell came this
day in May Option.)

$3\frac{5}{8}$ paper profit.
Lower stop to $245\frac{1}{8}$.

#2 DES
REPEAT SELL $237\frac{3}{8}$
(Fund L–2)
(Place Stop Buy at
$244\frac{5}{8}$ to limit
loss to $7\frac{1}{4}$)

$5\frac{3}{4}$ paper profit.
Raise stop to 243.

ASC

$7\frac{1}{4}$ paper profit.
Lower stop to $241\frac{1}{2}$.

$8\frac{3}{4}$ paper profit.
Lower stop to 240.

21 28   5 12 14 26
Sept   Oct

– 264 –

Fig xvii September 1957 Soybeans

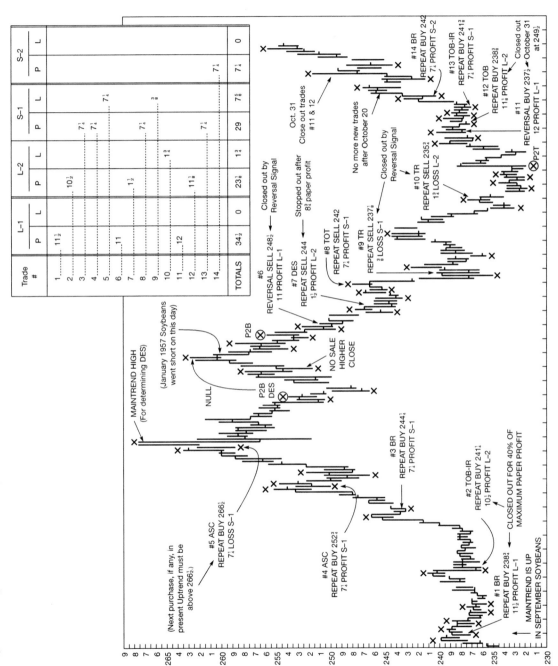

Fig xviii January 1957 Soybeans

Daily High, Low, & Close Chicago Board of Trade JANUARY SOYBEANS 1957 Cents per Bushel

INDEX

Printed in the United States
129177LV00007B/4/A